Business Process Outsourcing

Business Process Outsourcing

Growth and Country Experiences

Edited by

T P Rajmanohar
P Sivarajadhanavel

2010

Icfai Books
The Icfai University Press

Business Process Outsourcing – Growth and Country Experiences

Editors: T P Rajmanohar and P Sivarajadhanavel

First Edition: 2010
Printed in India

Published by

The Icfai University Press
52, Nagarjuna Hills, Punjagutta
Hyderabad, India – 500 082
Phone: (+91) (040) 23430–368, 369, 370, 372, 373, 374
Fax: (+91) (040) 23352521, 23435386
E-mail: info@icfaibooks.com, icfaibooks@icfai.org, ssd@icfai.org

ISBN: 9788131408148

Editorial Team: P Krishnaveni and A Neelima
Quality Support: V Sandhya Srikanth and S Sirisha

CONTENTS

SECTION II

COUNTRY EXPERIENCES

Overview

Outsourcing dates back to the 1960s from where it has grown to different levels from the time-sharing data process model to business process outsourcing (BPO) and then to knowledge process outsourcing (KPO). Recently, companies follow the business strategy of outsourcing entire business activities, such as technology operations, customer relationship, logistics, finance and document processing. The history of outsourcing started in the United States, when it was struck with economic stagnation and rising inflation rates. This forced Federal Reserve to increase the interest rate to around 20 percent to control the inflation. It reacted well in controlling the price but it increased the dollar value and attracted heavy investments in US government bonds. But the US industries faced problems. The costs of industrial production went up and many industries were closed down due to heavy losses, so that the US economy faced heavy job loss. This became a huge cost advantage to the industries in other countries. American car companies started closing their factories in the US and started their operations in Mexico during the 1970s. Auto industry jobs from the US were continuously outsourced to reduce cost. Capital industries outsourced their service related jobs to other locations to regain their profitability. Since, then US companies started outsourcing to cheaper locations.

This trend continued in the US, and later in the 1990s the process of outsourcing accelerated. After the North American Free Trade Agreement (NAFTA) among the United States, Mexico and Canada, American firms started looking towards Mexico and Canada markets for export and new factory locations. More industrial plants were started along the Canadian border as the low cost wage there proved to be a significant advantage over America. Canada was best suited to low cost labor with good English speaking people, whose culture was similar to the American culture. Automakers in America received benefits of cost reduction in the manufacturing of their supply parts with their low labor and overhead rates through outsourcing to Canada and Mexico. Canada has a greater export advantage as they had exported 11 percent of their parts manufacturing only to United Sates in the first eleven months of 2002. Not only is their production of auto parts outsourced, but also back office services have started moving to other cheap cost locations in Europe and Asia. For the back office services, Asian locations have proved to be profitable with quality services at cheaper costs. High end jobs like research and development, product innovations, and design outsourcing have started moving to other locations mainly in Asia.

In the 1970s and the 1980s, the Japanese and American firms Toshiba, Motorola and Texas Instruments moved their production facilities to the low cost locations of Taiwan and Singapore. In the early years, only the manufacturing activities were being outsourced to the low cost locations but, in the 1990s, liberalization and globalization of the world economy brought the various markets in the world closer. Later, US companies started outsourcing information technology (IT) activities to low cost locations in India. Some of the companies have also started their offshore facilities in India and Philippines. Most importantly, manufacturing companies outsource research and designing activities also to low cost locations.

Initially, the cost reduction was considered to be the motivating factor for the US and Japanese to outsource their activities to low cost locations, as the cost of hiring one engineer in US cost $70,000, but for the same cost it can hire 10 persons in the developing countries. Through the outsourcing process, US companies have benefited most by reducing their cost occurrences and improving their profit ratio.

After the flourishing of information technology (IT) in the late 1990s and 2000s, outsourcing has spread to all the IT nations. The internet business boom is the main drive for this success. Especially two Asians giants China and India are the leaders in providing outsourcing services to the American industries. China has proved handy with low cost labor for the original equipment manufacturers (OEM) in Europe and America. Later, it became the market leader in information technology outsourcing to the US industries. The boom in information outsourcing happened only after the globalization of the economy. The financial outsourcing and business modeling was done on a large scale only after the economic boom. Mainly top US and European investment banks have opened their offshore outsourcing facilities in low cost locations like Ireland, Philippines, China, India, Mexico, Australia, and Singapore. India and China lead the market with the opening of their economy to the world.

According to Gartner Inc, outsourcing has got more revenue opportunities for the developing countries. It is a big business generating global revenue of $298.5 billion in 2003. The global business process outsourcing is valued around US $400 billion and is growing by well around 11 percent. It is estimated to double soon. Forester's research estimates that by 2015, 3.3 million US jobs and $136 billion worth wages will be moved to countries like India, China, Russia, Pakistan, Vietnam and South Africa. In the last ten years, developing countries have attracted more foreign investment and revenues mainly due to outsourcing. The outsourcing industry has also moved into high jobs of knowledge process outsourcing (KPO). India is considered to be a dominant player in outsourcing along with the Philippines, Canada, Australia, China and Ireland. India has the huge advantage of a large pool of skilled human resources with good education, suited to the US clients' business needs. Spanish speaking countries like Mexico, Brazil and Spain are the dominant players in BPO. Other developing countries entering the BPO industry are Sri Lanka, Pakistan, Malaysia, South Africa and Kenya. As other developed countries move towards high end outsourcing services, new entrants are building their space through low end outsourcing jobs.

Innovation of information and technology has made business process outsourcing grow to a large scale as many call centers have started their operations early through direct operations from the original manufacturers. But, now, most of the captive BPOs are being operated by third party service providers, who provide service to the original equipment manufacturers at lower costs. Call centers are set up to handle incoming calls from the customers mainly to answer their queries and solve their problems. Later BPOs started to handle outgoing calls too. In the course of business outsourcing the non-voice BPOs entered into accounting and banking transactions. The next development was that companies started outsourcing HR related activities like calculation of salary, leave and wage administration. BPO companies have also advanced to design outsourcing and research and development (R&D). Now BPOs have also started high end consulting jobs.

Over a decade, the industry has grown to a great level and will continue to grow in all the locations. India is considered to be among the most preferred destinations in the world. Reasons for the preference of India are its skilled human resources with best infrastructure and climatic conditions that are suited to the clients' business activities. India has more than 2 million graduates and 3, 00,000 post graduates coming out of colleges every year. These human resources have the best English speaking skills. Outsourcing to India is cheaper than outsourcing to other locations in the world and this is the main reason for companies outsourcing to BPOs in India.

This book on business process outsourcing covers major areas like evolution of outsourcing from the manufacturing industry to the service industry, growth of outsourcing at different levels of industrial development and the country's experiences. It also discusses the experience of the BPO industry in creating worldwide opportunities in terms of revenue, product innovation and economic growth of the service sector. The various developments in outsourcing and business models have been discussed. In outsourcing there are three models - transactional, niche and comprehensive models, which give more flexibility to the clients in choosing the business models which will be closely related to their business. Captive BPOs are started by the parent companies to work for their processing jobs. Later many captive BPOs moved towards offshore locations in order to gain cost benefits. BPOs are classified as onshore, offshore and nearshore BPOs based on their functions and locations.

The book is divided into two sections. The first section discusses the evolution and growth of Business Process outsourcing (BPO). It deals with the evolution of outsourcing services from the manufacturing industry in the US to other industries in other outsourcing destinations. The second section covers the country experiences of the outsourcing business. The US experiences of outsourcing and its benefits and the loss of jobs are elaborately discussed along with the experiences of other countries like Europe, France, Italy, Japan, Philippines, China, India, Sri Lanka and South Africa.

The first article of the book "**Outsourcing from Manufacturing to BPO and Beyond**" written by *T P Rajmanohar,* traces the evolution of outsourcing from the manufacturing industry. Actual outsourcing by corporates started around 30 years back in the manufacturing industry. It soon spread to the services. Major outsourcing of manufacturing took place in the US around 20 years back due to the strong dollar and competition. The business process outsourcing industry began in the 1990s and soon spread leading to offshore outsourcing. The knowledge process outsourcing industry started around five years back and is growing very fast. Outsourcing is now spreading to business processes and is called Business Process Transformation. But the primary focus of outsourcing by the manufacturers is on their core business. The second benefit of outsourcing is the cost benefit they receive in the outsourcing of their process to the low cost locations.

The second article "**Global ITO and BPO Trends in 2006**" by *neoIT analyzes* the trends in business process outsourcing in 2006. Since the growth of Information Technology Outsourcing (ITO) and global Business Process Outsourcing (BPO) industries are driven by globalization and an explosion of outsourcing services in 2006. The outsourcing service industry would see a large increase in vendors, spread in wide geographies, and a rapid acceleration of tactical execution by the industry's leading suppliers with a growth of 40% from year to year. The success of outsourcing depends on the commitment of top managers and their risk management. The top buyer and supplier market predicts that India will strengthen its position as a leading offshore destination for US firms, though the country faces competition from developing economies. China will remain the preferred sourcing location for Japanese firms as the Czech Republic, Poland, and Hungary will remain favorite destinations for Western European firms.

The third article "**Business Transformation Outsourcing: Just Another Alphabet Game**" by *Tapati Bandopadhyay*, explores the various forms of BPO such as business process outsourcing, business process offshoring, business application outsourcing, multi-sourcing, and shares services or insourcing. The delivery models of BPO, onshoring, which is outsourcing within the same country, nearshoring outsourcing to a country nearby and offshoring outsourcing to another country are discussed in the article. The non-voices BPOs are becoming a serious business model for BPOs. This is likely to lead to the growth of the KPO industry. Business transformation outsourcing (BTO) involves the transfer of all back office functions as well as a comprehensive business change management process to an external vendor. It is bound to transform the business process.

The fourth article "**Multi-Sourcing: Managing a Portfolio of Deals**" by *Peter Munro,* studies why companies go for multisourcing. Multisourcing means companies signing smaller deals with multiple outsource service providers for their requirements rather than signing mega long-term contract deals with big service providers. Companies around the world are currently interested in going for multisourcing, as long-term deals in the past had not delivered to the expectations of the companies which had outsourced. It has been found that 80 percent of outsourcing deals did not meet the company's expected return on investment. Currently, the average length of a BPO contract period declines from 5.5 years to 4.8 years. Multi-sourcing companies break up their requirements to different service providers with the best capabilities for performing their outsourcing activities. The value of outsourcing can be maximized by adopting a multi-sourcing strategy in building partners on the following basic outsourcing strategies – sourcing services, focused partnerships, collaborative transformations, and strategic alliances. In multi-sourcing, the outsourcing strategy must be tightly aligned with the overall business strategy and the service provider has to use different tactics for different service requirements in supplier selection, procurement approach, and contract terms. In the coming years, companies would plan for multisourcing their service to different service providers based on skills rather than big deals with single service providers.

The fifth article "**Captive Business Process Outsourcing Units: Workflow Models**" by *Dipesh Kumar Dipu,* discusses the growth of the captive business process outsourcing industry. The BPO industry has brought in more competition in the industry with more captive BPO companies being established in the market by the original manufacturers. These captive BPO models were established on the operational parameters of cost efficiency and quality concern by the parent company. Earlier, the captive BPOs operated nearshore and later offshore due to cost concerns. This article deals with the captive BPO model lifecycle growth based on the cost structures, operational efficiencies, nature of work to be outsourced, human resources etc.

The various models discussed are *(i) Software Offshore-Onsite Model* which is followed by the software vendors working with clients offshore outsourcing, *(ii) Third Party BPO Model* where outsource service providers work on the billing hour based/ number of work-items delivered to the clients. *(iii) Dedicated Teams Model* is followed in the offshore site where the teams are formed on the basis of skill sets to work for onsite requirements and *(iv) Offshore Home Office Model* is followed by the parent company as a representative office offshore which coordinates all the workflow from the home offices to offshore and vice versa working in the foreign country. Finally, the article discusses the success of all these models depending upon research on the applicability of each offshore business unit.

The sixth article "**BPO/IT Bundling: Position Paper**" by *Technology Partners International* explains that the emergence of business process outsourcing (BPO) has not only brought smaller outsourcing contract values, but also a trend of "bundling" ITO and BPO in outsourcing relationships. Bundling is a combination of one or more companies from traditional IT spheres with one tower or more from BPO in one outsourcing contract. This paper explores the characteristics of the trend, reasons for its emergence, benefits and drawbacks of bundling, and potential developments in bundling. Bundling is increasing in outsourcing as more companies focus on adding business value, rather than merely updating technology for cost savings. ITO/BPO bundling is happening because major service providers are now able and willing to offer and promote it, having prepared themselves through evolution, acquisition or partnering. Of 46 bundled deals industry wide from 2001-2003, 14 were won by EDS; 6 by IBM; 5 by Accenture, 5 by ACS and 1 by HP. Other non-Big-Six firms account for the remainder.

The seventh article "**IT Outsourcing Rediscovered: Getting Your Share this Time Around**" by *Ralf Dreischmeier, Peter Balnaves* and *Anthony Datel* explains how information technology has helped outsourcing. Although IT outsourcing has been around for many years, some companies have mastered its planning and execution and many companies are making decisions that needlessly reduce the business value through BPOs. The companies have to find and follow the value, manage outsourcing service as a lifecycle, not as a transaction, make the bidding more collaborative and competitive, build a partnership, not a contract, pressure-test the economics, manage the organizational change effectively, maintain checks and balances on the outsourcer's access and influence, and start working on renegotiation and renewal to capture greater value from their IT-outsourcing efforts. Maximizing the value of business process outsourcing (BPO) efforts requires deep economic and organization-specific business analysis so as to capture a more promised value without putting the rest of the business at risk. Successful outsourcing demands skilful implementation of all the strategies adopted and it is very important to follow these levers to succeed.

The eighth article "**Global Outsourcing: BPO to KPO – The Way Ahead**" by *Priya Angle* explains the outsourcing and offshoring models and the shift of the industry from BPO to KPO industry. BPO primarily constitutes outsourcing of non-core, non-value-adding tasks to destinations with distinct cost advantages in terms of cheap labor. KPO, on the other hand, would encompass outsourcing some of the core activities of an organization to locations where qualified manpower exists—the objective being highest quality at the best possible price. This article attempts to understand the BPO model as it exists today and explores initiatives that are required to be taken up proactively in order to maintain the country's competitive advantage in the years to come. It also deals with how the Indian BPO/KPO industry can specialize in the emerging areas of the industry, such as engineering services or remote education, and develop a distinct advantage over others in the context of increasing competition. In many outsourcing locations like Bangalore, problems such as rising wages and high attrition rates amongst BPO/KPO and IT professionals are constraints on supply of talent. Such a shortfall is going to increase in future. If these issues are tackled, no doubt, India will be a global KPO hub.

The ninth article "**Business Process Outsourcing: Innovation and Growth Strategies**" by *P Sivarajadhanavel,* discusses the innovation and growth strategies of the BPO industry. Global competition is the most important issue facing top decision makers in some of the world's largest companies today and companies today are focusing their resources on their core competencies as business strategies to compete profitably in a global market. There are three different BPO business models – transactional, niche and comprehensive models, as strategies of business success. Now the companies have started concentrating on product innovation, which helps their clients to reduce their product introduction cost by 30 to 50 percent. It also facilitates flexibility product pricing and designing the product to fully exploit the market capabilities and technology innovation. Today outsourcing industry is moving towards a high level of specialization with great competition from low end process to high end process jobs like knowledge process and analytical process outsourcing jobs. The outsourcing industry is focusing on creating high revenue growth opportunities through its services in research and development (R&D) and other areas like legal process, research, product innovation, equity research, consulting and market research.

The last article of this section "**Emerging Outsourcing Destinations**" by *Sandeep Varma,* highlights the emergence of outsourcing destinations in various countries. Today many new, expanding outsourcing destinations take root outside India as a result of the rise in labor costs and employee turnover rates in India. Companies have started transferring outsourcing assignments to other parts of the globe like Mexico, Vietnam and Chile, though India remains the most preferred IT outsourcing destination, with $17.7 billion in software and IT services exports in 2005, compared with $3.6 billion for China and $1 billion for Russia. The Indian outsourcing industry is still growing at a faster pace than other outsourcing destinations. Many new outsourcing destinations have started outside India as a result of rise in the labor costs and employee turnover rates in India. Companies have started sending outsourcing assignments to other parts of the globe. The article also discusses other major emerging destinations in the world like China, Vietnam, Mexico, Philippines, Brazil, and Chile and their entry into the BPO business with fast growing developments in infrastructure and improved human resources. But moving of outsourcing into developing countries like Vietnam or China can also pose big risks, such as insurmountable language and cultural differences, geopolitical instability, and the risk of stolen intellectual property.

The first article in second section of the book "**Beyond the Outsourcing Angst: Making America More Productive**" by *Thomas F Siems,* throws light on the experience of America in outsourcing its services to other, low cost locations. For years, American companies have focused on their core competencies and contracted out the other activities which could be accomplished better, faster and cheaper by specialized external providers. The best companies keep costs low and boost productivity by doing what they do best and outsourcing the rest to outsource service providers at low cost locations. The article also explores the reasons for opposition to overseas outsourcing in the US. The wider offshore outsourcing of white collar jobs and the recent increase in offshore of high-end knowledge work has been followed by a surge in anti-outsourcing legislation by US State Governments. The protectionist policies devised by US also entail significant economic costs. As a technological powerhouse, with skilled workers and adept managers, the US should strive for the most complex and rewarding tasks, while other countries specialize in the routine, labor-intensive tasks. The key to the US economy's future lies in maintaining a flexible labor market, where resources can flow from declining sectors to emerging ones. The outsourcing of jobs by US companies to poor countries is inevitable. It had saved $11 billion in 2004 by outsourcing to India alone. A portion of that money combined with enormous industry profits would go a long way toward prolonged unemployment and health benefits as well as job creation for outsourcing victims.

The article "**BPO Fuels European Outsourcing**" by *Technology Partners International (TPI)* examines the growth of BPO and observes the processes that lead to BPO growth in Europe. It also explores some unique factors that have inhibited or encouraged BPO in Europe. There has been a significant growth in Business Process Outsourcing (BPO) due to the boom in the manufacturing industry. The recent pace of commercial growth in Europe has fuelled the region's total outsourcing growth. TPI measures show that by the third quarter of 2004, Europe accounted for slightly more (22) BPO deals in the broader market than America did (21) in transactions valued at greater than US$50 million. Financial Services organizations have spearheaded BPO in America and Europe, partially because companies in this sector have more readily perceived the potential for a substantial return on investment through outsourcing. Major global service providers are aggressively targeting Europe. Thirteen service providers competed for and won BPO transactions in Europe in the first three quarters of 2004.

The third article "**Outsourcing and Information Management: A Comparative Analysis of France, Italy and Japan in both Small and Large firms**" by *Alessandro Innocenti* and *Sandrine Labory*, compares outsourcing processes in France, Italy and Japan in two types of firms, large firms and small firms. It is shown that outsourcing has increased over the last two decades in both small and large firms in all three countries and that, mainly in the last decade, the tendency has been to increasingly involve some of the suppliers in product development going for low cost outsourcing. This is evident from a cognitive framework related to the activity of information management. Specifically, it is shown that the more the relationships among suppliers and users are characterized by two-way communication, decentralized information processing, and accordingly balanced contractual power, the more the incentives to create knowledge and to innovate autonomously are guaranteed. Although large firm disintegration has been a major factor contributing to the growth of the occupational share of small firms, the process of outsourcing among small firms has also been significant in France, Italy and Japan, where vertical disintegration has concerned an increasing number of firms since the 1970s.

The fourth article "**Getting Ready for the Deluge: Outsourcing in Philippines**" by *Richard Mills,* discusses the development of outsourcing in Philippines. The outsourcing sector in Philippines has been steadily picking up momentum over the past few years. The analyst estimates the growth rates for BPO at 40% to 50% annually, while many of the contact center organizations are growing ahead at rates approaching 100%. Sykes is a large US-based contact center and IT support organization with operations in both India and Philippines shifting much of its Indian capacity to the Philippines. Dell increased the number of jobs in Philippines by over 1000 because of the "strong language and communication skills of its high-quality workforce. Convergys, another large BPO organization, was to employ 8000 people in Philippines by the second quarter of 2006. Philippines is a superior choice overall for the best reason that quality people are more available in Philippines. Filipinos are also said to speak better English with a better customer service mind-set. But, some of the worldwide industry trends affecting the BPO growth in Philippines are discussed in this paper.

The fifth article "**The Changing Face of China: China as an Offshore Destination for IT and Business Process Outsourcing**" by *AT Kearney* deals with the growing popularity of China in the space of the business process outsourcing (BPO) in recent years. China's popularity as an information technology outsourcing (ITO) and BPO destination is mostly reserved for companies serving their Asia-Pacific markets due to geographic proximity and Chinese language and cultural affinity with nations in Asia-Pacific. This paper highlights the findings of AT Kearney's most recent study of ITO and BPO markets served by China featuring its strengths and weaknesses and also dispelling certain long-held misperceptions. The strength of China is its geographic location, language and cultural affinity to nearby nations, cheap labor costs, and technical education standards. The paper also assesses the weakness in outsourcing to China as—inadequacy in the intellectual property rights, language proficiency and management skills. AT Kearney examines how China is faring in its efforts to become a preferred offshore destination for IT and business process offshoring. Finally, the article concludes on the note that as China continues to improve, dispelling misperceptions and improving on its drawbacks – IP piracy, non-Chinese deficiency and limited management skills – it will undoubtedly host more competitions, at home and abroad.

The next article "**R&D Outsourcing: Indian Scenario**" by *N Janardhan Rao* and *Ravi Babu Adusumilli,* discusses high level outsourcing of research and development (R&D) in India. New trends are emerging in many organizations. Outsourcing the critical value chain activities such as R&D (Research and Development) is gaining ground across geographies especially in India. Outsourcing R&D activities helps companies continue their R&D activities without having to worry too much about the money they will have to spend. Many companies have been ambitious enough to outsource a significant portion of their R&D activities to outside the home country. A recent McKinsey survey of global executives has ranked India as a more attractive destination for R&D investments. Already 150 MNCs such as IBM, Texas Instruments, Google, GE, Electrolux, DaimlerChrysler and Hyundai have opened their R&D laboratories in India. Indian pharma majors such as Ranbaxy, Dr. Reddy's Laboratories and Sun Pharma have been attracting the attention of foreign companies for collaborative and contract manufacturing in drug discovery and clinical research. A recent study by Frost & Sullivan has predicted that the R&D outsourcing market in India is set to grow from $1.3 bn in 2003 to over $8 bn by 2008.

The article "**BPO in Sri Lanka Prospects: Problems and Challenges**" by *T Venkat Ram Raj* traces the growth of Sri Lanka in the field of outsourcing. Sri Lanka known as Ceylon, the land of gems, is attracting the attention of the BPO world. Kris Canekeratne, the father of BPO in Sri Lanka, is working hard to build a strong BPO base in Sri Lanka along with other BPO gurus in India and with the support of the local government. Learning from the success story of India, the policy makers and other stakeholders are aiming at making Sri Lanka a very attractive BPO destination. The article provides insights into the prospects, problems and challenges of the Sri Lankan BPO sector and offers a few suggestions on how to select stakeholders and design a better future for the sunrise sector.

The final article of this book "**Joburg, The African BPO Hub**" highlights the opportunities and facilities to develop the BPO industry in Johannesburg, South Africa. Johannesburg is a compelling destination for call centers and South Africa has a strong business process outsourcing and offshoring (BPO&O) industry. This is due, in no small part, to the country's remarkable history and the quality of its economy, business leaders and, above all, its can-do citizens. South Africa was voted the 24th most competitive country in the world by the Economist Intelligence Unit in 2001. Gauteng and Joburg are moving powerfully into the Call and Contact Center industries, which the government has targeted as a priority. Already, 60% of contact center operations for South Africa are in Joburg. The rents in Joburg are 40% to 70% cheaper than in London, New York or other G7 capital cities in the world. The average cost of electricity in the city is US$0.038 cheaper than in New York ($0.14) or London ($0.20). It has the finest telecommunications network in Africa, which is almost entirely digitalized. A report by international management consultancy McKinsey & Company estimates that between 65,000 and 100,000 new jobs (15,000-25,000 direct, and 45,000-75,000 indirect) could be created in the call center industry by 2008, and $90m-$175m could be attracted in cumulative foreign direct investment, resulting in a GDP contribution of between 0.3-0.5%. It has been found that South Africa has an indigenous call center community of more than 410 sites – which is bigger than that of India, Scotland, Wales, Ireland, the Philippines, Italy or Spain.

Section I

Evolution and Growth

1

Outsourcing from Manufacturing to BPO and Beyond

T P Rajmanohar

The outsourcing by corporates started around 30 years back in the manufacturing industry. It soon spread to the services sector. The major outsourcing of manufacturing took place in US around 20 years back due to the strong dollar and competition. The Business Process Outsourcing industry began in the 1990s and soon spread, leading to offshore outsourcing. The knowledge process outsourcing industry started around five years back and is growing very fast. The outsourcing is now spreading to business processes and is called business process transformation.

Introduction

Outsourcing has become a term widely used in the last ten years. Wikipedia says "Outsourcing" involves transferring or sharing management control and/or decision-making of a business function to an outside supplier, which involves a degree of two-way information exchange, coordination and trust between the outsourcer and its client. Such a relationship between economic entities is qualitatively different from traditional relationships between buyer and seller of services. The involved economic entities in an "outsourcing" relationship dynamically integrate and share management control of the labor process rather than enter in contracting relationships where both entities remain separate in he coordination of the production of goods and services."[1]

There is a school of thought which feels that outsourcing has existed since the stone ages when manufacture of certain weapons was outsourced. However there was no outsourcing industry till the 1990s. The manufacturing industries which existed in the nineteenth century and early part of the twentieth century quite often manufactured everything that went into a product. In the 1980s the US automobile and some sections of the US and Japan electronics industry resorted to outsourcing. This led to an outcry from US trade unions and some automobile manufacturers were forced to stop outsourcing.

The 1990s were very crucial for the outsourcing industry. The manufacturers who started outsourcing in the 1980s saw the benefits in outsourcing in terms of better profits. They decided to outsource in a big way. In this period countries like China and India opted for liberalization. This saw manufacturing outsourcing shift to China. The IT industry also started outsourcing primarily due to the salary difference between US and low cost countries like India. This led to a huge number of IT jobs being shifted from US to India. In the first few years of the twenty-first century China became the outsourcing hub for manufacturing and India became the outsourcing hub for IT and BPO industry.

Reason for Outsourcing

The primary reason for outsourcing is the need to focus on core competence. All companies have some core strengths, which they are not able to concentrate on because their energies and resources are spread over both core and non-core activities. Once an organization decides to concentrate on areas where it has core competence, it outsources the non-core activities and benefits more as it is able to spend more on the areas of its competence.

The rise of manufacturing and services outsourcing was due to the option—to make or buy decision. Companies had to decide whether it was worthwhile manufacturing/undertaking it in house or purchasing/outsourcing it from an

[1] Outsourcing Overview *http://en.wikipedia.org/wiki/Outsourcing*

outside vendor. A number of public sector companies in the UK found it cheaper to outsource services like canteen services, refuse collection etc., than doing it themselves. The decision to outsource manufacturing to Mexico and then to China was due to this make or buy decision.

In order to meet competition, a number of companies have decided to go for total quality management. They realized that very good outsourcing companies were available, which already had a total quality management system in place. Hence the companies only manufactured the very essential items and outsourced the non-critical items to these outsourcing companies.

The outsourcing in manufacturing was due to competition and the need to cut costs and maximize profits. The US companies realized that foreign companies were in a position to manufacture the items at a cheaper rate due to the strong dollar. Hence there was a need to purchase these items at a cheaper rate from foreign sources. The worldwide recessions also saw the industry benefited from outsourcing, as large companies were not willing to invest in plants which would fall idle due to recessions. The outsourcing companies bought the excess machinery from the companies and set up new manufacturing facilities in low-cost countries like China.

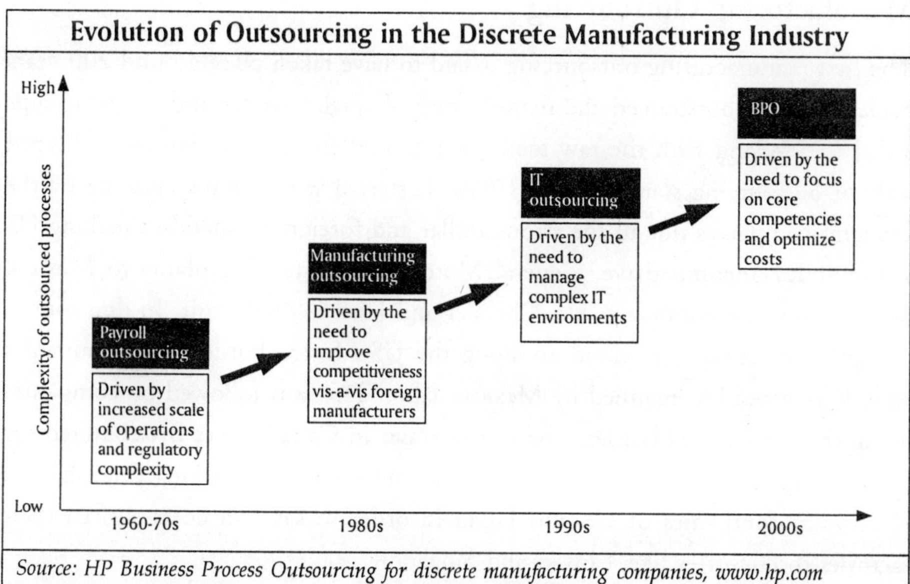

Evolution of Outsourcing in the Discrete Manufacturing Industry

Source: HP Business Process Outsourcing for discrete manufacturing companies, www.hp.com

The next reason is that the outsourcing companies have world-class facilities. This means that the company has access to the latest – in technology and skills and benefits due to the extended skills. Hence he can introduce products, which are of good quality, current design and also low in cost.

In order to save costs a lot of companies are going through a reengineering process. The chances are that as part of the reengineering process all non-core activities will be eliminated. It makes sense for the company to purchase non-core products and services from an outsourcing company.

In terms of cost-benefit, the outsourcer benefits as the outsourcing company is likely to have a lower cost structure. The company also benefits by transferring/selling some of its assets to the outsourcing company.

The other benefits of outsourcing are the improvement in quality of a product. Some low cost countries like India and Thailand have adopted Japanese quality techniques and standards and also become quality certified. Hence outsourcing to companies from these countries, resulted in not only low costs but also the added advantage of very good quality.

Manufacturing Outsourcing

The first manufacturing outsourcing is said to have taken place around 200 years back. The US outsourced the manufacture of wagon covers and clipper ships sailed to Scotland with the raw material imported from India. However the real start of outsourcing started in the 1980s. It started with the outsourcing by the US auto companies due to the strong dollar and foreign competition making US automobiles uncompetitive. General Motors shifted ten US plants to Mexico. Soon, other auto companies like Chrysler and Ford followed suit. In due course, a number of companies came up along the US Mexico border. The companies were US owned but manned by Mexican labor. This was followed by companies along the US Canada border. These companies in Canada were better suited for outsourcing as their employees had an added advantage of speaking English. The electronics companies of US and Japan in order to save on costs shifted their factories to countries like Taiwan and Singapore.

The '90s saw the manufacturing industry being shifted to China. The advantages of China include very low wages, fixed currency, cheap loans coupled with land and factories for new companies. One of the major advantages was huge economies of scale with large mass of workers producing a single product. In addition, the environmental regulations were lax and there were no laws for protecting workers rights.

The companies which outsourced manufacturing were called contract manufacturers. In certain industry segments the contract manufacturers have started to dominate manufacturing. The electronics industry is dominated by contract manufacturers and they are known as Electronic Manufacturing Services (EMS). Some of these EMS providers are very huge and organized. They are about ten of them who produce 50% of the total electronics products outsourced. Similarly in pharmaceuticals we have contract manufacturers who are willing to produce any pharmaceutical product. A recent phenomenon is that contract manufacturing has also entered the manufacture of complete automobiles.

Business Process Outsourcing

The last decade has seen the growth of the BPO industry. In BPO an organization's critical or non critical processes are managed using a technology/specialist vendor. The BPO differs from an Application Service Provider (ASP) as some amount of risk is transferred to the service provider. The software, the people and the process management constitutes the BPO. The BPO depends upon Information Technology and hence it is also called Information Technology Enabled Services or ITES. The global BPO industry is worth more than US$150 billion dollars and of this the offshore BPO is worth around US$12 billion. The industry is growing at around 25% and is expected to grow at this rate till 2010.

The BPO industry started with call centers in the 1980s but came of age in the 1990s with the introduction of new technologies like LAN based switches, internet based transaction processing, client/server software systems, advanced call handling and custom management system. SearchCRM.com defines a call center as "a physical place where customer and other telephone calls are handled by an organization, usually with some amount of computer automation. Typically, a call center has the ability to handle a considerable volume of calls at the same

BPO Opportunities Across the Discrete Manufacturing Value Chain

Product development → Sourcing and procurement → Supply-chain planning and execution → Manufacturing execution → Marketing → Sales and service

Product development

- Product concept and strategy
- Design and engineering
- Product prototyping
- Product data management
- Product lifecycle management

Sourcing and procurement

- Sourcing
  - Make vs. buy
  - Vendor selection
  - Negotiation
- Spend management
  - Monitoring/ Analysis
  - Allocation across categories
- Procurement support (3)
  - Supplier administration
  - Order management
  - Requisition creation
  - PO processing
  - Payment processing
  - Query handling

Supply-chain planning and execution

- Supply-chain planning
- Inventory management
- Warehousing
- Supplier collaboration
- Delivery
- Inbound and outbound logistics
- Reverse logistics*
- Supply chain analytics (5)

Manufacturing execution

- Long-term capacity planning
- Plant build-out
- Demand planning and forecasting
- Production planning and scheduling
- Plant operations
- Quality management
- Plant maintenance
- Contract manufacturing

Marketing

- Marketing strategy development
  - Market research
  - Competitor analysis
  - Customer segmentation
- Promotion planning
- Campaign management*
- Analytics (5)
  - Customer
  - Profitability
  - POS data
- Call center for
  - Claims*
  - Complaints and returns*
  - Product info*

Sales and service

- Sales planning and forecasting
- Retail channel management
- Account management
- Bid response management#
- Alternate channel management*
  - Telesales*
  - Catalog sales*
  - Direct sales*
  - Internet sales*
- Sales force management
  - Field force support
  - Commissions and incentive management
- After-sales service
  - Spares planning
  - Warranty management
- Order fulfillment (4)
  - Order processing
  - Credit analysis and approval
  - Pricing, billing and invoicing
  - Supply chain processing
  - Collections
  - Dispute resolution
  - Claims/Returns handling

☐ = BPO opportunities

* Relevant for B2C companies—auto, high-tech sub-segments

\# Relevant for B2B companies—aerospace, industrial, engineering sub-segments

1 Finance and accounting—AP, AR, FA, GL, T&E, Financial Reporting, Tax ac., Treasury ac.

2 HR—Payroll, Benefits, Personnel Administration, Recruitment, Compensation and Benefits, Learning

Source: *HP Business Process Outsourcing for discrete manufacturing companies, www.hp.com*

time, to screen calls and forward those to someone qualified to handle them, and to log calls."[2] In due course of time the BPO industry has moved from voice based BPO to non-voice based BPO.

Evolution of the BPO Industry

The BPO industry has evolved over the past twenty years from a company owned centre to an offshore unit. The different phases of the BPO industry are as follows:

In the first phase the company started a division in the physical premises of the company in order to cater to its own BPO needs. The BPO employees were invariably their own employees. The companies did not get the service expected from the division and some companies disbanded the division.

In the second phase the companies instead of having the BPO activity in the physical presence normally kept the BPO unit away from the company. The companies were able to get better results in this phase though there were not much cost reduction in this phase.

In the third phase the companies went for BPO units in their own country but not owned by them. In this phase there were not much cost reduction but the service level was high.

The fourth phase consisted of company owned units in low cost countries called captive BPO units. Several banks, insurance companies, airlines and manufacturing companies have set up back office service centers in India.

The fifth phase consisted start-up operations in India and other low cost countries by experienced professionals funded by venture capital funds. These companies offered better services and were also more cost competitive than captive BPOs.

The sixth phase witnessed leading IT Services Companies entering BPO. These companies saw the magnitude of such an opportunity and their synergies with the software services business. These companies were able to provide better service due to their high-end physical infrastructure and software. Most large IT services companies

---

[2] SearchCRM.COM

have ventured into ITES. This led to consolidation of the market with the smaller players merging with each other/larger companies for economies of scale.

The seventh phase consisted of domain/industry specialized BPOs. These players have had good experience in the domestic market and have now entered the offshore BPO services. Generalized large BPO players are now focusing on "verticalizing" their competencies and structures.

A majority of the key players in the BPO industry in low cost countries are captive units of MNCs and international BPO companies desiring to take advantage of the low costs in such countries. The risks are limited as their business is assured as they are captive units. These BPO ventures of MNCs are now trying to offer their services to other companies and these are then called shared services. Several ventures have been hived off into independent companies to attract other customers and to become profit centers. The examples include eServe International, World Network Services (British Airways) and GECIS.

KPO

"Knowledge process can be defined as high added value processing chain where the achievement of objectives is highly dependent on the skills, domain knowledge and experience of the people carrying out the activity. And when this activity gets outsourced a new business activity emerges, which is generally known as Knowledge Process Outsourcing."[3] The KPO demands specialized, domain pertinent, knowledge. The KPO depends upon the depth of knowledge, experience and judgment factor.

The future of KPO has a high potential in areas like Legal Processes, Intellectual Property and Patent related services, Engineering Services, Web Development application, CAD/CAM Applications, Business Research and Analytics, Legal Research, Clinical Research, Publishing, Market Research etc.

The National Association of Software and Services Companies (NASSCOM) estimates that Knowledge Process Outsourcing industry (KPO) is expected to reach US$17 billion by 2010. Evalueserve estimates that the global KPO market

---

3 What is KPO *http://www.kpoexperts.com/kpo-india/what-is-kpo.htm*

is likely to grow at a Cumulative Annual Growth Rate (CAGR) of 46 percent, from $1.2 billion in 2003 to $17 billion in 2010. The billing rates for KPO are likely to be around US$40 per hour against the BPO rate of US$12 per hour.

Some BPO companies are also doing KPO high end services like credit rating and customer analytics. The expectation is that traditional BPO services like time voice and data processing services will be overtaken by KPO services like Order Booking and Research and Analytics. The attrition rate in higher end services is low. Hence some BPO companies are likely to move to KPO from BPO.

However the main issue with KPO is doubts in the minds of the clients. Some of the issues are political and regulatory climate, professionalism, and quality and data security. These issues are likely to be solved based on successful experience with the outsourcers. The potential in the KPO space is huge. However only companies with good domain expertise, clear focus and a proactive solution style are likely to succeed.

The Future

The evolution of outsourcing is not yet over. A new term called Business Transformation Outsourcing (BTO) has emerged. The advantage of the BTO is that it is likely to transform the businesses of companies. This involves the transfer of all back office functions to an external vendor. In addition, it also involves hading over a comprehensive business change management process to an external vendor. The theory is that big improvements in performance can only be achieved through business transformation. A number of vendors who are in the BPO or KPO business have started offering BTO services. In BTO, the business processes are being reshaped. A number of companies like IBM, Wipro have entered this field which involves the transformation of the client business. In this, experts in the field, of process, study a company and transform the business processes of the company. They then provide outsourcing help in transforming the business process of the company to international standard. This is at a very early stage and may emerge as the next promising phase, of outsourcing.

Conclusion

The outsourcing industry has its origins nearly a hundred years ago. It has moved from outsourcing of components to outsourcing of services. The industry then moved to outsourcing of non-core services and then to strategic outsourcing. It has now moved to outsourcing of knowledge and is moving towards redesigning of business processes.

(T P Rajmanohar is a Consulting Editor at Icfai Business School Research Centre, Chennai. He can be reached at t_p_rajmanohar@yahoo.co.in)

References

1. A brief history of outsourcing, *www.sudhian.com*
2. Successful Contact Center Outsourcing, *http://multichannelmerchant.com/mag/successful_contact_center_01012006/*
3. Growth Strategies in Outsourcing by John Parker, *http://www.a1technology.com/blog/2004/03/outsourcing-staying-afloat-in.htm*
4. Manufacturing the Future by Katherine Swartz, *http://www.outsourcing-manufacturing.com/future2003.html*
5. A Brief History of Outsourcing by Terri Kelly, Source Global Envision.
6. E-Business and Outsourcing – How this happened and Growth Period Logicaster, *www.logicaster.com*
7. Outsourcing History Source, *http://www.bizbrim.com/outsourcing/outsourcing-history.htm*
8. History of Outsourcing , *http://www.cyfuture.com/history-of-outsourcing.htm*
9. The Evolution of the Call Center to Customer Contact Center, White Paper by Lisa Hawkins, Tim Meier, W Scott Nainis and Henry M James, *http://itsc.stste.md.us*
10. The Evolution of the BPO Industry PWC, *http://www.pwc.com/images/tech/BPOinIndia.pdf*
11. Outsourcing Wikipedia, h*ttp://en.wikipedia.org/wiki/Outsourcing*
12. Why Outsourcing, *www.intelebiz.com*
13. Business Transformation Outsourcing by Tapati Bandopadhyay, Icfai Reader, July 2006.
14. What is KPO, *http://www.kpoexperts.com/kpo-india/what-is-kpo.htm*

2

Global ITO and BPO Trends in 2006

Global services sourcing has evolved to become a mature business model that both leading corporations and global service providers look to leverage. The modern-day corporation's strategic growth plans would not be complete without addressing how global sourcing can impact an organization's bottom line. Maturity among buyers has increased significantly and new geographies are beginning to compete for business that was traditionally destined for India. Risk associated with global sourcing is becoming an increasingly important topic as more and more companies find themselves operating a global services delivery footprint.

neoIT understands the need for buyers and suppliers to have a clear view of where the ITO and BPO industries are headed so that they may align their strategic and tactical plans with potential market movements. neoIT's thought leadership in the industry, coupled with our knowledge of buyer and supplier markets, helps us offer that clear view. We examine the major trends that are likely to impact the services globalization market in 2006.

Executive Summary

Last year, neoIT predicted that in 2005 offshore outsourcing would gain significant importance as offshored processes became a corporate "must have" and companies developed more sophisticated global delivery models across IT and other business processes. We also predicted strong growth for emerging supply destinations including China, the Philippines and Central Europe (particularly Poland, the Czech Republic, and Hungary).

Our predictions for 2005 have all been realized to substantial extent. The services globalization industry shifted its game plan, with leading suppliers aggressively tackling their cost structures and reorienting their offerings and organizations around higher-value customer segments and solutions.

In 2006, we predict the consolidation and extension of 2005's trends as well as the emergence of new trends that will necessitate structural changes in the global service sourcing industry. Specifically, neoIT predicts a diffusion of global sourcing among a larger number of vendors and geographies and a rapid acceleration of tactical execution by the industry's leading suppliers. Beneath the surface of an exciting growth rate of about 40% year-over-year, 2006 will be a year of enormous activities impacting both mature and emerging markets, with significant convergence, consolidation, and realignment.

The number of client organizations adopting a services globalization approach – the extension of offshoring to leverage suppliers' unique abilities in sourced IT and back-office services – will grow in 2006. And the move away from simple cost savings toward increased operational efficiency and accelerated growth will force organizations to leverage integrated sourcing options.

The path toward fully realized services globalization is paved with an historical understanding of discrete outsourcing. But while understanding the lessons learned in past years is important, next year's journey will present several new challenges that could damage expectations if they are based solely on past experience. Organizational structures will have to be realigned, the commitment among top managers tested, tactical services sourcing strategies reevaluated, security and compliance norms emphasized, and change management dealt with at a strategic level. If those challenging tasks are accomplished, a much more complex paradigm will emerge and grow as more core functions are sourced to third-party vendors and captive operations located across the globe. That increasing complexity means that risk management will be that much more important in the coming year. In fact, the success of a client's risk management strategies will be a significant determinant in the overall success of that organization's services globalization initiative.

The ripple effect from increasingly complex transactions will be felt in the supply markets, where the springboards for the next wave of industry evolution will include growth in vertical processes and the process maturity of service providers; the emergence of several new competent supply locations; consolidation among service providers to create larger and better organizations; and capital market accession creating several cash-rich, medium-sized service providers.

India will maintain its stronghold as an offshore destination for US firms, though the country will face competition in several areas from the Philippines, Brazil, Mexico, Israel, Russia, China, and other aspiring supply markets. The China phenomenon will loom large, but the extent of its influence on sourcing options for the US market will be smaller than the current market buzz might suggest. China will remain the preferred sourcing location for Japanese firms as the Czech Republic, Poland, and Hungary will remain favorite nearshore destinations for Western European firms.

Top Industry Predictions

1. Offshore IT Outsourcing will Become a Viable Mainstream Alternative to Onshore Outsourcing

Outsourcing has historically been viewed as a strategic decision, with global sourcing as one component. Increasing maturity in offshore provider markets, a strong global presence, and the growth of offshore vendors, as well as an intense brand-building focus will lead client organizations to realize the importance of services globalization as a strategic decision. This trend will allow for the growth of mainstream offshore vendors that can appeal to US mid-market and European clients.

2. Global BPO will Gain Momentum Via Captive Thrust

The credibility of offshore BPO will grow as firms build more captive centers in emerging markets and as more complex services are performed in these centers. The development of full process delivery competency among captive-turned-third-party and third-party BPO providers will support this trend. The validation of offshore vendors' skill sets will be further complemented as several of the larger offshore BPO providers launch IPOs in 2006.

3. Enhanced Market Acceptance of Global Services Sourcing

Opposition to services globalization will become increasingly limited to over zealous TV news hosts, as major corporations accept the need to operate globally in order to compete in the emerging environment. Governments and associations of emerging supply markets will fine tune their messaging to the US client base, further accelerating the acceptance of nearshore and offshore destinations.

4. Data Security and Disaster Recovery will be Key Points of Focus

In 2005 there were several data security breaches in the services sourcing industry. Security breaches at multiple financial and retail service providers left these companies with lost revenue, increased customer dissatisfaction, reduced shareholder value, and increased lawsuits. Those breaches, in part, emphasized the need for more stringent security policies and stronger DR/BCP plans. New and re-negotiated offshore deals in 2006 will consist of strict SLA-based terms to manage this data security risk. Offshore vendors with security certifications, strong security adherence systems, and multi-location footprints will have higher conversion rates than those without.

5. Discrete Outsourcing and Mega-Deals will Emerge

In 2006, client organizations will focus on sourcing to the most qualified vendors in the most cost-effective supply markets. Discrete outsourcing (a process in which a client selects a mix of vendors and supply markets that will each support individual service requirements in order to mitigate the risks associated with sourcing to a single vendor) will emerge despite the fact that it creates unnatural boundaries between perceived strategic and tactical providers. Mega-deals, too, will emerge, as the trend of sending lower value work to offshore providers continues. Despite greater customer acceptance of global sourcing and the huge growth in offshore IT services, the market for strategic outsourcing will largely remain with incumbent onshore vendors in 2006.

6. Prices for Offshore ITO Services will Appreciate Slightly

Offshore service providers have demonstrated the ability to offer more than cost savings to clients – service providers can now offer business transformation opportunities as well. As a result, established providers will be able to command premium pricing, though overall price increases will remain under 3% in 2006.

Top Buyer Market Predictions

1. Global Services Sourcing will Become a C-Level Issue

As many organizations move past the piloting phase of their global sourcing initiatives and begin to look at long term implementation and transformation, those initiatives will become more visible at all levels of the organization and will begin to attract the attention of top managers. The consolidation of offshore ventures across a client organization will enable a more overarching strategic view for the organization's CEO. That visibility, along with top-level buy-in, will determine the future path of services globalization initiatives within a given client organization.

2. Operational Efficiency and Growth will Emerge as Key Objectives

The next phase of offshoring's evolution will address those benefits of global sourcing that extend beyond cost savings. Some organizations already know those benefits, some are in the discovery process, and others have not even begun. 2006 will be about the discovery process for many client organizations, though they must also focus on keeping existing initiatives on track. The year will mark the advent of true services globalization, which represents a shift away from tactical offshoring to a more transformational approach that seeks not only to leverage low-cost labor but also to transform the organization by making it more efficient, more flexible, more productive, and better prepared to handle external market changes and a dynamic competitive landscape. Global services sourcing will ride on the phrase "necessity is the mother of invention" – a phrase that has never been more appropriate than it is today for companies that see globalization as a means to sustain or increase their growth. Whether it's simply a lack of qualified talent in onshore locations or the prospect of entering newly developing markets, global 2000 companies will use offshore IT and BP outsourcing to generate capacity for new service lines and/or establish bases for future sales and marketing to the more than one billion consumers in developing markets.

3. The Global Sourcing of Core Services, Knowledge Services, New Services, and Complete Processes will Gain Momentum

The year 2006, will witness an increase in the number of mission-critical and select core business functions that are performed via a global delivery platform, mainly due to service providers' investments in developing capability to perform complex processes. As more knowledge-driven services are successfully offshored, the availability of talented employees with certain skill sets in supply markets will become more visible. Business processes such as market research, equity research, clinical research, legal research, judgment-based tax processing, back-office consulting operations, and engineering services will increasingly be performed offshore. The process and vertical skill sets gained by offshore BPO service providers will allow those companies to service end-to-end functions, which will in turn attract an even greater number of clients. In the ITO industry, it will be product incubation and development, infrastructure management, and the implementation of core business applications that will be increasingly performed offshore.

4. Multi-Vendor, Multi-Model, and Multi-Country Contracting will Demand a Stronger Emphasis on Governance and Change Management

In 2006, establishing governance structures to manage and coordinate an offshoring relationship through its initial period of contracting as well as the transition toward ongoing program management will be crucial. We expect to see significant investments in Project Management Offices (PMOs), as the PMO will be a key determinant of the success or failure of any offshoring initiative. Managing internal customers and key influencers — and getting them to participate in the transition will be critical. Change management processes including best-fit internal and external communication strategies must also be set in place.

5. Expectations will be Revised as Several Offshoring Failures Come to Light

neoIT predicts that in 2006 several offshoring relationships that never managed to satisfy client expectations will surface. More than 30% of offshore outsourcing relationships will face challenges due to inadequate planning, unrealistic expectations, inaccurate vendor choices, incomplete process and knowledge transitions, and a lack of focus on ongoing program management. While the exposure of failed initiatives will spur companies to invest in better management of operational challenges, expectations of cost savings and productivity gains will also be revised and more realistic frameworks to gauge the success of offshoring initiatives will emerge.

Top Supplier Market Predictions

1. India will Strengthen its Position as a Leading Offshore Destination

In 2006, India will further enhance its positions as an ideal destination for global corporations. The country will build on its success factors including resource availability, the presence of many mature providers, cost advantage, and strong offshoring legacy. Supported by national and state governments, centers of excellence will arise in key locations to offer more extensive choices and opportunities for clients and service providers.

2. New Supply Markets will Emerge as High-Quality Sourcing Destinations

While India will continue its dominance as the leading global services destination, it will certainly begin to feel the pressure of competition from newly emerging, quality sourcing destinations. Countries in both offshore and nearshore locations will develop strategies to project themselves as viable outsourcing alternatives to India. Supported by government initiatives, US-friendly policies, geographical proximity, and cultural compatibility, Latin American countries including Brazil, Argentina, Mexico, and Costa Rica will develop and grow centers of excellence as nearshore sourcing destinations for US clients. A similar trend will emerge in Europe as countries such as Russia, Poland, Romania, the Czech Republic, and Hungary continue to develop as high-quality nearshore destinations for Western European clients. In Asia, countries including Malaysia and Sri Lanka will emerge as alternative low-cost BPO destinations and will develop as locations offering niche services. We'll also see China progress significantly as a preferred offshoring location, though the extent to which volumes flow to China will be limited in 2006 to smaller project-based contracts. Nevertheless, China will be on the radars of many service providers as companies try to determine their China strategy.

3. Inorganic Growth will be an Important Force within the Offshore Outsourcing Industry

In 2006 we'll see strong growth through the acquisition of companies with complementary capabilities or niche strengths. Mid-sized offshore service providers will be likely targets for larger multinational service providers looking to enhance their offshore delivery capability. And small- to mid-sized service providers with unique vertical capabilities and solid client bases in offshore, nearshore and onshore markets will be likely targets for large offshore service providers looking to bring added credibility to the global service delivery paradigm.

4. Captives-Turned-Third-Party Vendors will Drive Growth in Offshore Service Maturity and Competency

When GECIS (Now Genpact) became a third-party vendor, it signaled an important trend in offshore service delivery. This new business model – one of mature captive units with competency in handling end-to-end functions – will enhance perceptions of offshore delivery capability. In 2006 we'll see several other mature captives following GECIS's path, which will provide added credibility and immense opportunity for all companies in the global services arena.

5. Vendors will Face Operational Challenges as Well as New Opportunities

Attrition levels in offshore markets will remain high but will stabilize as the industry matures and consolidates. The closure of several Indian BPO units that were started by fly-by-night operators and the growing perception among employees that BPO is a viable career will contribute most significantly to the stabilization of attrition rates. Another issue that vendors will have to concentrate on in 2006 is profitability. With prices remaining relatively stable, the increased wage costs, re-badging, and absorbed transition costs associated with large deals will cut into the bottom line. Vendors should be able to at least partially offset the effects of increasing costs by enhancing productivity as service maturity increases and by utilizing resources in low-cost secondary cities.

6. Integrated ITO and BPO Offerings will have Mixed Success

Offshore service providers have yet to leverage the benefits of integrated ITO and BPO offerings. We don't expect that to change in 2006; we predict that business transformation deals to offshore vendors involving both ITO and BPO will be limited in the coming year as client organizations have not yet fully realized the competencies of service providers at the operations realignment level.

7. Small and Mid-Sized Suppliers will Launch IPOs

During the next year, numerous ITO and BPO service providers around the world will prepare to go public in US markets. These $100-400 million revenue firms will morph from small players with relatively few financial resources into companies with significant amounts of cash with access to more through the public markets. That change will cause a significant shift in the service provider landscape, likely setting off a spree of acquisitions that will create much larger companies that can then compete with the more established players in the offshore sourcing industry.

Final Thoughts

The year 2006 will be for client organizations and service providers together to realize the full potential of services globalization. Underlying the trends that we've predicted for 2006 is the fact that more companies than ever before are replacing simple offshoring strategies with more complex services globalization strategies. In contrast to simple offshoring, services globalization allows client organizations to leverage not only lower costs in offshore destinations, but also opportunities to realize increased quality, increased operational efficiency, and accelerated growth.

To do their part to realize the potential of services globalization, client organizations must engage in the global sourcing process from the C-level down. Governance and change management will be more critical in 2006 than before as client organizations globalize core services in efforts to improve operational efficiency and realize growth opportunities. At the same time, it will be important for client organizations to maintain – or revise – expectations of the costs and benefits of a global sourcing initiative to realistically reflect the potential that services globalization offers.

For their part, global service providers must start by reorienting their service offerings around higher-value services. And they must be able to accommodate increasingly complex relationships and provide evidence of competency in high-level areas, including data security and disaster recovery. India's continued dominance as a preferred sourcing destination underscores the importance of service maturity and demonstrated competency. At the same time, the emergence of other sourcing destinations highlights a move toward discrete outsourcing, intended to mitigate risk through vendor and location diversification and to reap unique benefits offered by centers of excellence across the globe.

In these ways buyers and suppliers will together guide the wave of expanding services sourcing options toward a full realization of services globalization in 2006.

(neoIT is a consulting firm that is singularly focused on helping leading firms improve operations and grow their business by capitalizing on services globalization. Email: info@neoIT.com)

Life Cycle Management of Business Process Outsourcing

– P Krishnaveni

Today most of the companies around the world are facing intense competition and striving to satisfy the customers according to their rapidly changing desires. The main reason for outsourcing is cost saving and to achieve the optimal performance within the company by focusing on core capabilities. Outsourcing is defined as an operation of shifting a transaction, which is governed internally through a long term contact to an external supplier. Though outsourcing of IT and other specific services has been in practice for about 50 years, outsourcing of the entire business process, i.e., Business Process Outsourcing, was started in 1980. With the rapid IT application growth in BPO and strategic improvement of business process management, the technical support BPO management is becoming more possible and the procurement of process data becomes easier.

Total Life Cycle Management of BPO

The total life cycle framework is projected to shed light on the relationship between BPO and business process performance. The total life cycle of BPO comprises nine phases.

Strategy

Business Process Outsourcing may bring certain opportunities associated with risks to an outsourcing company. So it is very important to take an all-sided analysis before the "make or buy" decision. Outsourcing is a strategic decision which is discussed and developed at senior levels within any business. It is a premier strategy, that moves the company to a leveraged business model with optimal performance and to focus on core competencies. It is very important to take a decision whether to outsource a particular function, operation, program or project. A few businesses will be required to take legal counsel during this stage.

Reassessment

This stage is not always considered important but the organizations are looking for some internal supply or any other methods of supply to assess whether it can be re-engineered to meet the requirements of outsourcing.

Selecting the Service Providers

This stage covers a set of evaluation criteria to select the prospective BPO service provider. These evaluation factors are cost, quality, IT capability and financial stability. After listing out these evaluation criteria in order of hierarchy, a decision method has to be adopted to identify the potential providers. Then a formal Request For a Proposal (RFP), which meets the above mentioned evaluation criteria, initiates the process. Thus the client and the potential service providers are selected based on price, skills, culture and commitment matching.

Contracting and Negotiating

This phase comprises of negotiating the contracts, schedules, associated and final contract agreements. The two main decisions are to be taken at this stage—whether to negotiate with more than one supplier or not and whether to make an agreement on "heads of terms" or a "term sheet" or not.

Implementation

In this phase the planning and the implementation activities of the outsourced agreement, establishing the detailed budget and administrative functions needed for its management, and formal launching of the program are carried out.

Managing Ongoing Supplier

In this phase of outsourcing, the outsourcing company changes its function from operations management to strategic management and forms a team of management. This phase is confronted

Contd...

Contd...

with some disputes since the methods used by the team to monitor the BPO activities are scheduled by the contracts and also due to inadequate technical support and analytical methodology.

Build Completion

This phase consists of all the completion activities such as development programs and acceptance and the launching of new services. Here the legal personnel can help in issues associated with delay in delivery or implementation, service levels and credits, acceptance testing etc.

Change

In this phase all the outsourcing contracts are subject to change. The changes to the outsourcing contract may be either minor or major changes. The idea of change control is to allow the relationship to proceed with a sense of mutual trust. This change control is more specific in public sector and regulated industries where the law does not allow departure from the original advertised procurement.

Exit

It is inevitable that all the outsourcing contracts come to an end. There are three options for the outsourcing company to terminate the outsourcing contract— to renegotiate the contract with the same supplier, to change the supplier, or to in-source the activity again. The first two options highlight the cyclical nature of BPO while the third option relates to its termination.

(P Krishnaveni, Research Associate in Icfai Business School Research Centre, Chennai. She can be reached at krishnaahmba_2002@yahoo.co.in)

References

1. Dafeng Xu, "Total Life Cycle Management of Business Process Outsourcing Based on Process Performance Analysis", *Tsinghua University.*
2. "The Outsourcing Life-Cycle", 2006, *IAOP.*

3

Business Transformation Outsourcing
Just Another Alphabet Game

Tapati Bandopadhyay

There have been various forms, figures, models and propositions like Business Process Outsourcing, Business Process Offshoring, Business Application Outsourcing, Multi-sourcing, etc. This is an industry where change looks like the only constant. Outsourcing has a fairly long history of evolution by now and Business Transformation Outsourcing (BTO) is a natural extension of the more tactical BPO model, which involves the transfer of responsibility for all back-office functions. If BPO and KPO were unable to help transform the businesses of Fortune 500 companies, BTO would be the solution to deliver that.

Quantity does not say it all, and that is probably the reason that, even with the recent glorious past and glittering future predictions — in the warmth of which the Business Process Outsourcing (BPO) industry is presently basking in —they are chanting one mantra together beyond all intra/inter competitions: and that mantra is "value-added services". No matter what the volume may be, it is not just the cost-cutting spree at micro/individual/organizational levels or

Source: Icfai Reader, July 2006.

economies of scale and cheap labor force at macro/national/international levels that are driving the outsourcing wagon any more. While volume has already been gaining enough momentum and promises to add 3.3 million jobs in India, where productive employment is scarce, the quality also is changing its face as all the big names in the BPO industry are trying their level best to "climb up the value chain" and offer their customers or clients some unique, different, value-added service propositions.

Volume-wise, BPOs are already showing great promise to transform India economically, much in the way oil has transformed the economies of the Gulf countries. Forrester research predicts that 3.3 million US jobs to move offshore by 2015. BPO revenue grew by 60% in the year 2002-03 to touch US$2.3 bn and was slated to grow by another 60% in the year 2003-04 as per Nasscom. Assuming these projections are correct, then, in the year 2010, the BPO industry will directly support the livelihood of about 1-1.5% of India's population. Another 0.5% of the population will be supported by the ancillary effect of BPO. Thus, at best, 2% of India's population will be affected by the BPO industry. In sheer GDP terms, assuming India's GDP to be about US$600 bn by 2010, 4% of the GDP will be contributed by BPOs. As put by Kiran Karnik in a recent interview, "In the broadest terms, it is the customer service industry and from the point of career growth too, there are numerous opportunities. Above all, presently we are just tapping 2% to 3% of the total BPO market. And by 2009, we project that the BPO industry alone will generate about $20 bn-$24 bn revenue from the present $3.6 bn." These numbers show sufficient promise to spark the "prosperity chain", wherein, the capital generated through this industry is invested back in other industries not only domestically but also globally to generate a virtuous cycle of investments and profits.

But, this is also an industry where change looks like the only constant. Much in the way of the core IT industry where the change in technology, systems, programming languages, platforms, hardware/ software, etc., has already been accepted as a way of life for the products as well as the people involved. The BPO industry is also witnessing a continuous change in terms of the client requirements, domains in which BPO solutions/services are offered, value propositions and delivery models.

Outsourcing has a fairly long history of evolution by now. There have been various forms and figures and models and propositions which have been tried and tested. The value propositions that have stood firm the test of time so far can be broadly categorized as below.

Business Process Outsourcing

Business process outsourcing involves the full transfer of responsibility for routine organizational functions such as transaction processing, policy servicing, claims management, HR, finance, and compliance to the outsourcing company. The outsourcing provider then administers these functions on their own systems to agreed service standards and at a guaranteed cost. Some of the BPO contracts call for performance-based payouts, tying vendor payments to business performance or overall cost savings.

Business Process Offshoring

Business process offshoring is the transfer of business tasks (medical transcription) or business processes (call centers) with the primary focus being cost reduction. The interaction is conducted over telecom networks and the Internet. Offshoring, typically includes tasks like transaction or accounts processing, credit card processing, call centers, translation, and transcription. Most of this work can be sent without the need for in-person interaction.

Business Application Outsourcing

This is seen where Company A (vendor) rents applications to Company B (user). Increasingly, corporations are renting applications like customer relationship management, e-business, enterprise resource planning, systems maintenance and troubleshooting, messaging and collaboration, etc. The basic value proposed in this model is to relieve the corporation from day-to-day management activities and lower the Total Cost of Ownership (TCO). Here, the outsourcer provides the mission-critical enterprise application hosting and management service, which often forms the backbone of the client's operational systems and consequently determines their performances. The outsourcer hosts the software solution ensuring a preset level of performance and reliability, which is monitored by a pre-defined and agreed upon contract like the Service Level Agreements (SLAs). This is also termed Application Service Provider (ASP).

Multi-Sourcing

Multi-sourcing is the management and distribution of different business processes among multiple BPO vendors. For instance, HR processes are outsourced to one best-of-the-breed vendor. Logistics are outsourced to another. IT development and maintenance are given to another vendor. Risk mitigation is a primary driver behind multi-sourcing.

Shared Services (or Insourcing)

Shared services, a form of "internal outsourcing," enables corporations to achieve economies of scale by creating a separate internal entity within the company to perform specific services, such as payroll, accounts payable, travel and expense processing. A typical shared services initiative takes advantage of enterprise applications and other technological developments, enabling the company to achieve further improvements to quality in processes, such as finance, accounting, procurement, IT, and HR. At the core of shared services is the idea that new technologies offer the opportunity to (i) make better use of scarce skills, (ii) provide information and services more efficiently, and (iii) reduce the cost of administration."

Then, location-wise the delivery models are:

- Onshoring — outsourcing to another company within the same country.
- Near shoring — outsourcing to a country nearby.
- Offshoring — outsourcing to another country, which does not qualify as near-shore.

Considering these basic delivery models, three main types of operational models can be identified:

- Captive processing centers.
- Third-party providers.
- Joint ventures (build, operate, and transfer).

Captive centers undertake business processing only for their own multinational businesses. These can be formed as part of the shared services model also. Some examples are HSBC (Hyderabad), American Express (Delhi), British Airways (Mumbai), Citibank (Chennai), and Dell (Bangalore).

The third-party providers, who are also the second operation model, supply other companies with outsourcing services. These companies include Nipuna (a subsidiary of Satyam), MsourcE, 24/7, Spectramind, and Daksh, which resemble Internet software service firms that complete IT systems set-up projects for various companies.

The Joint Venture (JV) model is the third operational model often used in offshoring. In a JV, better known as a build, operate, and transfer model, two entities own the operation. For instance, in December 1998, Satyam Computers entered into a joint venture with an affiliate of GE Industrial Systems for providing engineering design services, software development, and system maintenance services. In early 2003, Satyam sold its interest in this JV after an affiliate of GE exercised its option to purchase Satyam's interest for $4 mn.[1]

The Evolving Nature of Value Propositions

The industry has been maturing, and witnessing success and failure of certain models. During the fast-growth stage, the industry has offered almost every old or new entrant some arena to boast about their strength and flex their muscles. But, as the maturing stage has set in, just boasting the volumes/cost/impressive clientele muscles are not being viewed as enough. The clients are looking for uniqueness, something that can add value to their core business, something that can transform their business. Here comes the call for the new but traditional BPOs, some of which are quick enough to respond to it. In an effort to move up in the value chain, the Indian BPO units are looking beyond voice and accent businesses to improve both spread as well as margins. Sources say non-voice processes are fast becoming a serious business model for BPOs. Lately feeling that non-voice processes may contribute a major part of the outsourcing revenue, several Indian BPOs have forayed into the non-voice aspects of the outsourcing business. "In about five years, non voice based businesses will account for 15-20% of all business in most BPOs" (Nasscom). Sanjay Kapoor, president and CEO of Teletech India, said, non-voice processes have emerged as a significant value

---

1 *www.bpoindia.org*

addition to the BPOs, which also get a chance to expand their employee base through the new model. So, here came the new wave of KPO. Pipal Research, Exevo and Pangea, specialize in providing outsourced web-based consultancy in market research and legal services. According to Manoj Jain, CEO, Pipal Research, diversification into non-voice processes should help BPOs increase the return on infrastructure via multiple-shift staffing.

If BPO and KPO could not help transform businesses of Fortune 500 companies, Business Transformation Outsourcing (BTO) is planning to deliver exactly that. Welcome to the world of BTO!

Business Transformation Outsourcing

Business transformation outsourcing involves the transfer of responsibility for all back-office functions as well as a comprehensive business change management process to an external vendor, and is a natural extension of the more tactical BPO model. The objective is to maximize the long-term benefits of the BPO operations, resulting in a comprehensive business transformation (or overhaul). Transformation outsourcing is a forward-looking strategic tool for change and not a tactical issue, which has a simple logic: big gains in performance only come about through business transformation.

Vendors that started with call centers have tried hard to change that business to either a BPO or a niche KPO. They are now planning to enter the BTO sector. The entire industry is making this shift to a BTO model now as clients are asking for more value addition, and they also want to know what else their outsourcing vendors can do for them. Be it Wipro BPO, Satyam Computer Systems' Nipuna Services or IBM Daksh, all have adopted the latest mantra, which is embedded in transformation of client businesses. IBM and several others call it BTO, while HP has named it as integrated services offering —providing both the IT and BPO services to clients.

Regarding the transformation, Randy Walker, General Manager, Asia Pacific BTO, IBM, told *Economic Times,* "BPO was based on labor arbitrage. But now clients want business performance improvement and not just savings on wage difference due to shifting work to India. BTO is the answer for that." In India IBM Daksh has over 10,000 staff many of whom are now engaged in offering

BTO services. IBM has 24 BTO units worldwide, 17 in Asia and 12 in India. At the Indian centers, customer relationship management and finance and accounts practices are the core areas through which it delivers to clients globally.

IBM Daksh's BTO clients include Bharti Tele-Ventures, Pioneer Corp., Johnson Controls, Kodak, Mitsui Life Insurance and Dun & Bradstreet. Wipro BPO, that started reducing focus on voice-related tasks last year, does BTO for four of its 38 clients. According to Mythily Ramesh, Vice President, Customer Acquisition, Wipro BPO, "The process outsourcing game has now changed to continuous improvements that vendors can give to clients. Instead of just doing a single process like finance and accounts or HR, the client is looking at both IT and BPO, which is a business transformation from vendors." So, for a Fortune 500 oil and gas major, Wipro Technologies is doing the SAP rollout, while the BPO arm is executing the HR, finance and accounts and procurement processes. For a US-based oil retailer, Wipro BPO developed a business model to cut down distribution loses and also executed the processes.

So, this way, the new value propositions of BTO are beating the world of business processes into a unique shape. Perhaps we are graduating towards a world of business where companies will not do anything other than what they are having core competencies in, and there will be companies which will have their core competencies in transforming and managing other company's all non-core processes. This can bring about a win-win situation to both the sides of the clients and the service providers and will perhaps prove to be a boon to the business domain in the long run.

(Tapati Bandopadhyay is a Faculty Member, The Icfai Business School, Bangalore. The author can be reached at chatterjee_tee@yahoo.com).

4

Multi-Sourcing
Managing a Portfolio of Deals

Peter Munro

Forget everything you think you know about outsourcing. The promised results are not materializing and while companies continue to ink deals, they're not the mega deals of the past. Today's contracts tend to be smaller and shorter. As outsourcing deals change so must a company's approach. It is time to think of outsourcing as you do a product portfolio—with different strategies for different deals.

Bank One Executives had just hammered out a $2 billion IT outsourcing deal with IBM and AT&T, called the Technology One alliance, it was heralded as a groundbreaking partnership that would not only help Bank One cut costs but also increase innovation and market share. Top managers were elated; industry watchers and the media were in a flurry. That was 1998, by 2002, both the agreement and the partnership were falling apart. Bank One was describing the contract as vague and refusing to pay for improvements necessary to make the deal work. Just three years into the contract, Jamie Dimon, then CEO of Bank One, pulled the plug. "It hadn't worked out," he told an industry group, explaining that from now on Bank One would control its own destiny.[1]

[1] Bob Evans, "Business Technology: Outsourcing on Outs at J P Morgan Chase, Wal-Mart," *InformationWeek*, 20 September 2004.

Other mega outsourcing deals were careening toward similar fates. Sainsbury's scrapped a 10-year IT outsourcing deal three years early; Cable & Wireless prematurely cancelled its $3.3 billion global IT outsourcing contract with IBM, and after just two years, JPMorgan Chase wrote off its $5 billion IT outsourcing mega deal with IBM.[2] All three companies decided to "back source" their services in-house.

These are not isolated incidences. Companies around the world are cancelling mega deals or deciding not to renew end-of-life outsourcing contracts having recognized the stark differences between what an outsourcing deal should deliver versus what it does deliver. And the disillusionment is not reserved for the major IT outsourcing deals either. Companies with vast experience, outsourcing a range of processes and functions, as well as the "bundled" mega contracts involving IT driven processes, are becoming disenchanted with their deals as well.

Why Good Deals Go Bad

Conceptually, the benefits of outsourcing are clear: Companies gain the advantage of size, access to lower labor and facility costs, and improved capabilities and innovations. By outsourcing non-core functions, managers are less distracted and able to focus on the company's most important core functions. In theory, outsourcing is a win-win proposition. Yet more companies are disappointed with their outsourcing results. A survey by AMR Research found that 80 percent of outsourcing deals did not meet the company's expected return on investment. A study by Gartner Group found that, of companies that outsource IT activities, one-sixth did not save any money and half saw their costs go up.

Companies attribute their outsourcing troubles to a supply-side push from providers that prescribe services beyond the organization's needs. Conversely, the providers blame companies for their overly ambitious expectations. This gap can be attributed to the different ways in which companies and providers approach outsourcing. Companies prefer bundling a broad range of different activities together and finding one provider that can handle all of them. Providers want to handle all of a company's activities, but do not want to go to the trouble of tailoring their capabilities, business models or contracts to meet the different requirements of their customers.

---

2 Steve Ranger, "Sainsbury's Scraps Outsourcing Deal with Accenture," www.silicon.com, 27 October 2005.

Clearly the blame falls on both sides. Douglas Hayward, senior analyst at research firm Ovum, sums up the issue, warning companies that, "business benefits don't necessarily follow from IT infrastructure renewal unless the business itself is well run and the two sides are properly connected."

No matter how you slice it, there is dissatisfaction all around. And yet, outsourcing, and increasingly offshoring deals are on the rise. Last year, the global Business Process Outsourcing (BPO) market experienced a 33 percent increase in the volume of deals, according to research analyst firm IDC. Offshoring went from 5 percent of the total outsourcing market in 2003 to 20 percent in 2005. There are more outsourcing service providers and business models today than ever before, and corporations are outsourcing a broader and more diverse range of functions. Gartner thinks the uptake will continue, predicting a 5 to 10 percent growth rate in outsourcing for the coming years.

So how to explain the disconnect of dissatisfaction with outsourcing on one hand and more outsourcing deals on the other? For one thing, there is a difference in how companies are outsourcing. While the total number of outsourcing deals has increased, the size of the contracts is smaller and the duration shorter. According to Datamonitor and Everest Group, the average size of IT and BPO contracts in the first quarter of 2005 fell to $56 million compared to $106 million the same period a year earlier. The average length of an ITO (Information Technology Outsourcing) contract declined from 6.2 years to 5.3 years from 2003 through 2005, while the average length of a BPO contract declined from 5.5 years to 4.8 years during the same period.[3]

Rather than signing mega deals with one or two large outsourcing providers, more companies are "multi-sourcing"—signing smaller deals with multiple providers.

The Move to Multi-Sourcing

With multi-sourcing, companies break up their requirements into smaller activity bundles and pursue a "best-of-breed" sourcing strategy. They look for the best provider with the best capabilities for performing the process or function. Dutch

[3] "Market Trends: Outsourcing Contracts, Worldwide, 2005," *www.gartner.com*, April 2006.

banking giant ABN Amro spent two years planning and implementing an outsourcing deal that involves five offshore providers. The bank outsourced its IT infrastructure maintenance to IBM, application support to Infosys, TCS and Patni, and application development to Accenture.

As with most things, multi-sourcing has its good and bad points. Companies get better service and capabilities from highly qualified providers, and more competitive prices because the providers compete with each other for the work. But they also have to manage the multiple relationships that multi-sourcing spawns: It takes more of everything to manage five or six partners than it does for one big partner. Yet even this downside is not so bad. Many of the outsourcing relationships are straightforward, and although there are more deals, most tend to have fewer difficulties. And from our experience, we know that any relationship-management costs incurred through multi-sourcing are small in comparison to the total benefits that multi-sourcing can deliver.

As Outsourcing Deals Change, So Must the Approach

Corporations can maximize the value from outsourcing by adopting a multi-sourcing strategy—building a network of partners and managing the relationships from a portfolio of different strategies. There are four basic outsourcing strategies, with the strategy of choice depending on the nature of the benefits the company is seeking and the scope of the functions to be outsourced *(see Figure 1).* In other words, a company should never structure an outsourcing deal without first knowing its true strategic requirements and the type of benefits it needs to achieve. Essentially, executives have to answer *why* (should we outsource) before answering *what* (scope and functions), *where* (local versus offshore), *who* (which suppliers) and *how* to outsource.

The four strategies are as follows:

Sourcing services are simplified, short-to medium-term relationships aimed at achieving the best price to deliver straightforward services that have clear deliverables with well-defined specifications. These services include call centers and back-office processes, contract design work, facilities management, warehousing and logistics. They are discrete, have a high level of repeatability

Figure 1: Basic Outsourcing Strategies

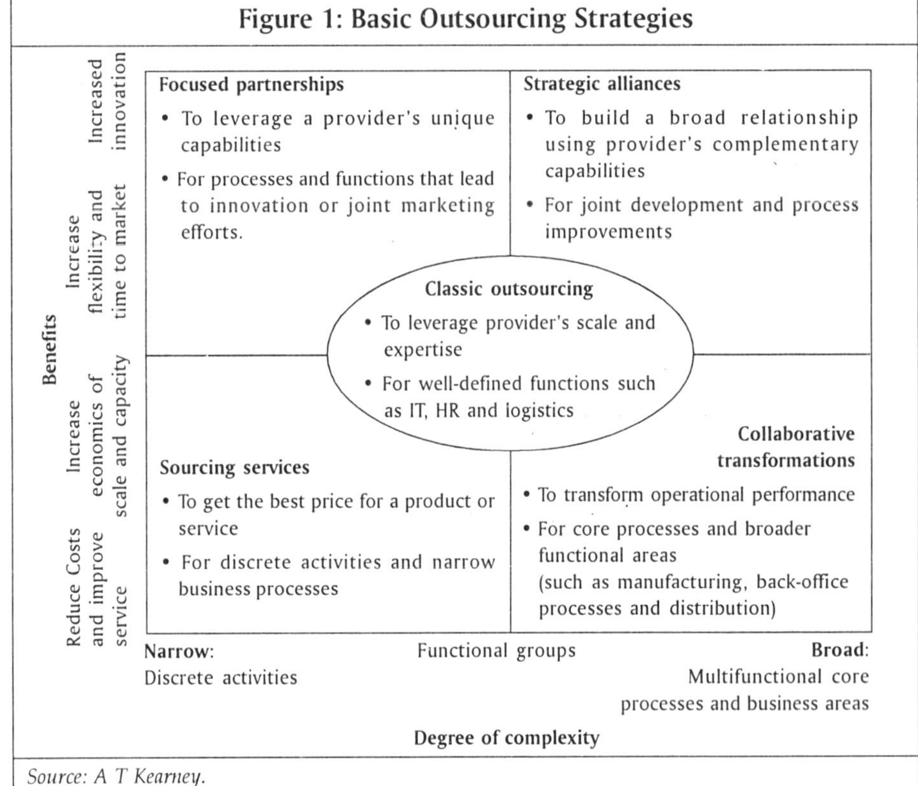

Source: A T Kearney.

and require limited customer contact. It takes about three or four months to finalize a sourcing-services deal and another month or two, depending on the complexity, to shift the activities to the outsourcing partner.

This strategy is a good starting point for companies that are considering outsourcing for the first time, because the risk is manageable and they provide a good learning platform. The downside is that sourcing services is narrow, and when companies begin with this strategy they may inadvertently exclude better options. Companies will be asking *what* should be outsourced before they ask *why*, which, as discussed earlier, is a mistake. The strategy should drive the scope and potential value of the outsourcing deal, which in turn drives the outsourcing or multi-sourcing solution.

Eventually, sourcing services will not be the preferred option, either because cost reduction is not the primary focus, or because the activities being considered for outsourcing are related to other parts of the business and therefore must be viewed in a broader context. Once a company reaches this point, it is time to consider the other three strategies.

Focused partnerships are short- to medium-term relationships with suppliers that possess a unique capability or innovation that the company needs. Such partnerships don't focus on cost reduction, but instead try to support a company's product or service innovations, joint marketing initiatives, or new capabilities development. They may also be helpful in breaking into new markets, as when HP partnered with a contract manufacturer to enter the digital camera market.

Focused partnerships are particularly attractive for established companies that want to free up people and resources to concentrate on more significant developments. For example, electronics firms that typically outsource manufacturing to a single third-party provider are building focused partnerships to outsource manufacturing and design to the same provider. Dell, HP, Siemens, Cisco and Nortel have all signed on with former pure-play contract manufacturers that now include product design among their capabilities. The providers—Flextronics, Solectron, Sanmina-SCI and Celestica—are using their complementary technology expertise, knowledge of sourcing components, and logistics and manufacturing capabilities to help their clients rapidly develop, test and launch new products.

Collaborative transformations are medium-term relationships aimed at gaining access to a supplier's size and operational expertise. In these relationships, you can expect the outsourcing provider to make a significant upfront investment to help improve your operational performance.

Most of the larger IT mega deals are collaborative transformations because the goal is to outsource and improve a troubled IT organization. BPO deals also tend to fall into this category. When an Australasian bank outsourced its mortgage processing operations, the provider helped transform the bank's business by redesigning business processes, upgrading its underlying technology, and progressively cutting costs by more than 20 percent.

DuPont's deal with URS Corporation is another example of a collaborative transformation. URS is helping DuPont meet its environmental commitments at a much-reduced cost, including performing site assessment and feasibility studies, remediation design, and construction management. URS is also managing due diligence on Dupont's property transfers, compliance (permits and regulations) and IT for environmental applications.

Strategic alliances are large, long-term outsourcing arrangements aimed at providing competitive advantage. Automakers perhaps are the best known for building strategic alliances as they outsource key components and systems, R&D, design, production, module assembly and even the design and production of niche models.

In strategic alliances, the basis for competitive advantage often shifts to the success of competing supply chains and, increasingly, these deals are cemented with equity investments. For example, when a shortage of personnel made it impossible for Toyota to support its rapid business expansion, the automaker forged a strategic partnership with rival Japanese automaker, Fuji Heavy Industries (FHI), maker of Subaru vehicles. Both companies are leveraging their development and production expertise, with Toyota buying an 8.7 percent stake in Fuji. Toyota now says it plans to outsource the full redesign of an existing model to FHI as well as a portion of its production.

Another good example is Cable & Wireless, the global telecommunications service provider that formed a strategic alliance with Nortel to support its Voice over Internet Protocol (VoIP) strategy. Nortel provides a broad range of services related to the implementation of VoIP, including planning, design, engineering, deployment, migration, provisioning, service activation and ongoing maintenance and support. The two companies are going to market with a combined end-to-end solution using Nortel's technologies and Cable & Wireless' managed telecommunications service. This relationship should provide Cable & Wireless with faster access to new technologies, accelerate the launch of new services, and reduce the risks associated with launching new products.

Classic outsourcing is not one of the four strategies, but it deserves mention. Although these four strategies can largely replace classic outsourcing, it remains a viable option for companies that do not have the resources to develop leading practices in house, or the critical mass to pursue a best-of-breed approach. It is

Who's Who Among Multi-Sourcers

A few companies and industries stand out for their ability to deploy all four outsourcing strategies simultaneously. The automotive industry has spent decades refining its multi-sourcing mettle. Almost all automotive manufacturers outsource their basic administrative functions, such as accounting, payroll and IT services, while a few outsource their more critical activities, such as designing a new model. Several automakers have built focused partnerships with specialist design firms. Ford, for example, joined with Pininfarina in Italy to produce the Focus and Streetka.

Collaborative transformations are fairly common throughout the industry, especially in manufacturing and logistics. For example, Toyota Australia has an agreement with Patrick Autocare, a leading logistics company, to accelerate delivery times and reduce inventories. Patrick streamlined Toyota's delivery process by performing pre-delivery inspections at the docks along with customs clearance, and reduced inventories by handling final assembly of accessories and sports packs. Other examples of collaborative transformations lie in the extended role that tier-one suppliers, such as Magna International, Dana and Lear, perform for automakers that want more modularity in their vehicles. Automakers regularly outsource research, design, parts sourcing, manufacture and assembly of entire modules to these "value-adding integrators."

Cockpits of cars and transmission systems, for example, are now sold as modules. Magna International took collaboration to the next level by performing final assembly for certain Chrysler models in Austria.

Strategic alliances are becoming more prevalent in the auto industry, although it is certainly not a new concept. Ford, for example, has had an equity stake in Mazda for some 25 years. What's new is the broader basis for collaboration. The alliance between Renault and Nissan, which GM wants to join, exploits both companies' synergies in engineering, manufacturing, sales, IT and procurement. Renault and Nissan have developed common platforms, and are leveraging their best capabilities to renew their model lineups. They are sharing production plants worldwide and distribution in Europe, and have pooled their IT resources and purchasing into two new service companies.

Multi-sourcing is making inroads in retail, as convenience store giant 7-Eleven illustrates. 7-Eleven has adopted the sourcing services model for its more routine functions, such as accounts payable. It formed focused partnerships to develop custom products (with Hershey's and Anheuser-Busch), pursued collaborative transformation agreements to share productivity gains with selected outsource providers (HP), and built a strategic alliance to provide direct-store delivery of fresh goods.

In the pharmaceuticals industry, Wyeth has also stepped up to the multi-sourcing plate. The global pharmaceutical and health-care powerhouse sources, services for its internal IT help desk, manufacturing services (filling and packaging), and parts of its benefits administration process. The company entered into a collaborative transformation deal to manage its clinical trials data—and the provider revamped the process to require fewer people and take less time. Wyeth established focused partnerships with specialists in different treatment areas for the research and

Contd...

Contd...

development of new drugs and therapies. One such partnership, with Trubion Pharmaceuticals, has evolved into a comprehensive strategic alliance for the discovery, development and commercialization of novel bio-pharmaceutical products. In June, Trubion announced that its relationship with Wyeth will culminate in a 20 percent equity stake when Trubion makes its initial public offering.

still a good way to cut costs, improve performance, and enhance flexibility and responsiveness to market changes.

Importantly, companies don't have to choose just one strategy. The box "Who's Who among Multi-sourcers," highlights industries and companies that employ all four strategies simultaneously.

Tailor the Strategy to the Deal

As with most partnerships and alliances, flawed execution—not flawed intent—can compromise a relationship. In multi-sourcing, the outsourcing strategy must be tightly aligned with the overall business strategy, and companies must use different tactics for different relationships *(see Figure 2).* What is not necessary, however, is managing each contract as though it is a central component of the business strategy. Not all partnerships are strategic, requiring elaborate capability assessments, complex incentive plans or relationship building. If they did, the costs of managing multiple relationships would quickly outstrip the benefits.

Yet many companies invest time and resources in micromanaging their least strategic deals, which may be a way to compensate for poorly specified requirements and, therefore, not a good idea. Sourcing services, at its best, requires a broad approach to the supply market. Companies should draw up clear specifications and benefits so that they can contact the most suppliers in the shortest amount of time. Service partners can be procured from around the world using a multi-round, multi-partner negotiation process. Once the company identifies the right partners, contract terms should be straightforward and represent the best balance of price, service and quality. The deal should outline penalties for not providing agreed-upon service levels, include a clause for annual cost reductions, and involve no more than an arm's-length relationship. These deals shouldn't take longer than four months to close.

Figure 2: Different Tactics for Different Strategies

	Sourcing services	Focused partnerships	Collaborative transformations	Strategic alliances
Supplier selection	• Use broad approach to supply market with RFI and RFP	• Select partners based on capabilities	• Select partners based on capabilities and scope of relationship	• Select partners based on strategic fit, shared goals and mutual trust
Procurement approach	• Employ multi-round and multi-partner negotiations, based on clear specifications	• Negotiate with pre-selected partners • Include resource commitment to capture targeted business outcomes	• Negotiate with pre-selected partners, extending transactional agreement to include desired business outcomes	• Negotiate with pre-selected partners, including gaining access to capabilities and understanding strategic priorities
Contract terms	• Achieve balance of best price, service and quality • Apply penalties for non-compliance to service requirements	• Remunerate based on contribution to company's goals; include incentives • Offer cross-subsidies of base products and services and value-add if needed	• Remunerate based on contribution to total life-cycle cost reduction and improvement targets • Offer best price and incentives for meeting joint targets	• Remunerate based on joint business plan, using a variety of mechanisms • Offer significant incentives for exceeding joint goals
Ongoing collaboration	• Lead at the procurement organization • Maintain an arms-length relationship • Exchange transaction and performance information	• Lead at the business unit • Align relevant functions • Share relevant information, including business plans	• Lead at the business unit and involve procurement • Align relevant functions and establish joint improvement teams • Share operational plans	• Lead at the senior executive level • Integrate relevant functions; invite provider's executives to management meetings • Share and jointly develop all relevant plans

Source: A T Kearney.

Quite the opposite, focused partnerships, collaborative transformations and strategic alliances all require significant planning and preparation. No one should go into these deals without first determining what capabilities or innovations the potential supplier can bring to the partnership. After an initial prequalification, negotiations should take place with one to three pre-selected candidates. Contract terms should outline remuneration based on the outsourcing providers' contribution to the company's specific business goals, and offer incentives to exceed these targets. To promote ongoing collaboration, both companies should align their relevant functions and plans. In the case of strategic alliances, it would not hurt for the company to go a step further and actively involve the outsourcing provider in the ongoing management of the business, such as cross staffing or including an executive from the outsourcing provider on its executive committee.

By tailoring the strategy to the specific partner, companies can alleviate much of the complexity, risks and headaches that surround some of the more intricate deals. Of course, planning is key. Some companies make the mistake of not recognizing that the business landscape will change and there will come a time either to adjust the current outsourcing strategy or move to a new one. As product lifecycles, business environments or even corporate cultures change, companies may need to update or terminate their outsourcing deals. This means it's a good idea to build flexibility into contracts either to get out of the deal quickly, or at least adapt to new business realities as necessary.

Five Principles of Multi-Sourcing

A multi-sourcing strategy requires a new mindset and frameworks for overseeing multiple best-of-breed relationships. Because every partnership can have an impact on the larger organization, we devised five basic principles to help companies improve their multi-sourcing initiatives.

Define how each organization will contribute: The most successful outsourcing relationships begin by setting common goals and determining the resources, timing and investments necessary to achieve them. Too often companies go into outsourcing relationships focused on the current state of the activity to be outsourced, and the service levels they expect from the provider. Everyone understands the high-level objectives—for example, to accelerate time to market, or increase market share—but fall down when it comes to defining how to achieve those objectives.

Reward the value-add of each partner: Companies expect their partners to add value and should reward them for doing so. In most outsourcing contracts, companies pay competitive rates for the activities being performed, but fail to factor in payment for the less tangible benefits, such as innovation or improved processes. It is little wonder then, that the intangibles frequently fall by the wayside.

There are a variety of mechanisms, such as reinvestment allowances and gain-sharing agreements, for encouraging partners to focus on the less tangible benefits. The important part is that the remuneration commensurates with the benefits. If a partner's innovative idea turns into a new product, the reward should be comparable to the company's profits derived from the new product. Rewards should also be paid separately from ongoing work and based on targeted outcomes.

At the same time, companies should periodically test every partner's cost competitiveness through benchmarking, or open-book cost models for pricing and adjustments. To maintain some competitive tension in the relationship, always retain the option either to broaden or reduce the scope of services.

Link project planning to procurement processes: A structured process that gives early visibility into new product developments will allow both parties to leverage more effectively their capabilities and benefit from new ideas. Shared visibility will minimize unnecessary duplication of effort, time consuming requalification and iterative RFI and RFP activities, as well as outsourcers' misguided business development and marketing efforts.

Define clear roles and "good" partnering behavior: The best outsourcing partnerships depend on trust and appropriate behavior from both parties. Common complaints from outsourcing providers and corporations are two sides of the same coin. Companies bemoan that providers do not provide sufficient innovation or access to leading-edge capabilities, are not willing to invest in the relationship, will not readily share ideas or intellectual property, and put a premium price on all contract extensions and changes. Outsourcing providers, however, often complain that corporations will milk the provider for information and reuse their intellectual property without due consideration. They say companies are interested only in lowering the cost of services and use (or overuse) the RFP process to play competitors against each other. There is a surprising lack of trust.

If strong interpersonal relationships are key to successful outsourcing partnerships, why are they so difficult to achieve? How can two companies build relationships when mutual understandings and knowledge of each others' capabilities are mainly derived from a few short meetings? How can business priorities be shared when managers at both companies come and go as they cycle through different positions? The answers are in formal secondment programs, such as staff-exchange programs and succession planning. In the strategic alliance between Nortel and Cable & Wireless, staff members hold responsibilities in both organizations simultaneously.

Avoid becoming locked in deteriorating relationships: All partnerships will traverse a natural lifecycle as organizations change and strategic priorities shift. In a merger or acquisition, for instance, a company's capabilities and strategic focus can change quickly, as with the merger of JPMorgan Chase and Bank One. Chase scrapped its $5 billion outsourcing agreement with IBM just 18 months into a 10-year contract. Yet even without such a catalyst, the value of an outsourcing relationship will erode over time as outsourcing partners lose their technology advantage, unique positions and skills, and as investment needs are satisfied.

With this in mind, companies should always be able to reverse or exit an outsourcing deal. This means never sell irreplaceable core assets or eliminate core skills because they are critical for maintaining control of outsourced functions and for acting on outsourcing agreements that have outlived their usefulness.

Making a Powerful Contribution

Whether signing a mega deal with one large provider or numerous contracts with many smaller providers, outsourcing is destined to remain as an essential part of every company's business model. To avoid the common frustrations of outsourcing and to make the most of providers' increasingly impressive capabilities, it is important to take a differentiated approach. In the coming years, the top companies will multi-source, choosing from among four outsourcing strategies for every function or business process that they determine should be outsourced. They will formulate a clear recipe for how outsourcing can deliver a powerful contribution, and draw on all the opportunities to prepare the company for tomorrow's challenges.

(Peter Munro is a Vice President in the Sydney office and leads the firm's financial services practice for Australia and New Zealand. He can be reached at peter.munro@atkearney.com).

5

Captive Business Process Outsourcing Units: Workflow Models

Dipesh Kumar Dipu

This article deals with the growth of the captive BPO model based on the cost structures, operational efficiencies, nature of work to be outsourced, human resources etc. The various models discussed are (i) Software Offshore-Onsite Model, which is followed by the software vendors working with clients offshore outsourcing, (ii) Third Party BPO Model, where outsource service providers work on the billing hour based/number of work-items delivered to the clients. (iii) Dedicated Teams Model is followed in the offshore site where the teams are formed on the basis of skill sets to work for onsite requirements and (iv) Offshore Home Office Model is followed by the parent company as a representative office offshore, which coordinates all the workflow from the home offices to offshore and vice versa working in the foreign country. Finally, the article discusses the success of all these models depending upon research on the applicability of each offshore business unit.

Source: Effective Executive, July 2005.

According to January-February 2005 issue of *BPO Newsline*, a NASSCOM news magazine, the global IT/ ITES Services market has grown from US$1,184 billion in 2002 to US$ 1,322 billion in 2003 and is expected to achieve a turnover of around US$ 2,497 billion by 2008-09 and US$3,3991 billion by 2012. According to NASSCOM, the Indian ITES-BPO industry is likely to grow to US$5.1 billion by 2004-05E. And a big chunk of the market is taken by captive BPO units of companies like HSBC, Citigroup, Goldman Sachs, Merrill Lynch, American Express, Swiss Air, Deutsche Bank, McKinsey and several of the reputed companies.

BPO units have become a strategic tool for maintaining competitiveness. Therefore, operation models and the efficiencies of the captive units have become a decisive parameter based on which the parent companies decide the investment decisions and future of their captive offshore units.

The following models can be envisaged for such captive BPO units to operate upon. The application of any of these models is based on the cost structures, operational efficiencies, nature of work that have been identified to be outsourced, human resource policies and numerous other factors. The models have been discussed as follows:

1. Software Offshore-Onsite Model

This model is an imitation of how software vendors work on their engagements with clients offshore. The software vendors in India have followed this model very effectively to cut costs and effectively manage work from offshore, thereby adding value to the clients by bringing down the billing rates. Historically, software developers from India used to land on the client site and used to work in teams of sizes sometimes bigger than the client strength. The process meant a huge chunk of client's budget on maintaining the software vendor's team on its premises, providing them with all infrastructure needs and paying them higher billing rates. Automation of business process, therefore, used to be a costly process and only those organizations with deep pockets could afford it. Then came the offshore-onsite model and the scenario changed for the better.

A team comprising business analysts and senior project managers with software design skills and maintenance capabilities, with a maximum size of about

10 percent of the total workforce required for the engagement is posted onsite. The responsibilities of team include client interactions, requirement gathering and analysis, development of design specifications and management of delivery from onsite by continuous interaction with offshore team. In maintenance projects, the responsibilities include understanding the problem, identifying the bug or enhancement needs and managing debugging or enhancement by interacting with offshore team according to pre-set Service Level Agreements (SLAs).

In the context of software development, the model has been a big success and has been the reason for enormous success of the big Indian software companies like Tata Consultancy Services, Infosys Technologies and Wipro. The model cuts down costs drastically and means a lower budgetary allocation for IT needs for the client. This has gone on the increase of the market size for the software companies, even though it has reduced billing rates, which could have affected the margins and profitability.

For a captive BPO unit, the model promises a smooth and streamlined workflow and higher utilization for the offshore workforce. Representatives from various teams from offshore can be stationed in the home offices, where their responsibilities will include building confidence level in the home offices, interacting with the home and offshore teams for smooth workflow and fast turnover of deliverables. These representatives will also have responsibilities of identifying work that can be taken offshore, managing utilizations and identifying training needs for offshore resources.

The model promises a great opportunity for operational efficiencies but may end up being slightly costlier. Since a representative onsite will cost more than the offshore, the outsourcing cost may rise. But it will be only slightly so. In turn, it will raise resource utilization from levels of 40-50 percent to about 80-90 percent and higher. Also it will absolve the home managers from the responsibility of packing chunks of their work offshore and will shift the responsibility of work awards to the offshore representative, and develop entrepreneurship. The offshore office will become cost and quality conscious since winning them work will no longer be a responsibility of managers of parent company but will be a function of cost and quality of their deliverables and effectiveness of their representatives onsite. This will enhance the culture of earning work than being awarded work passively.

Figure 1: Software Offshore Onsite Model

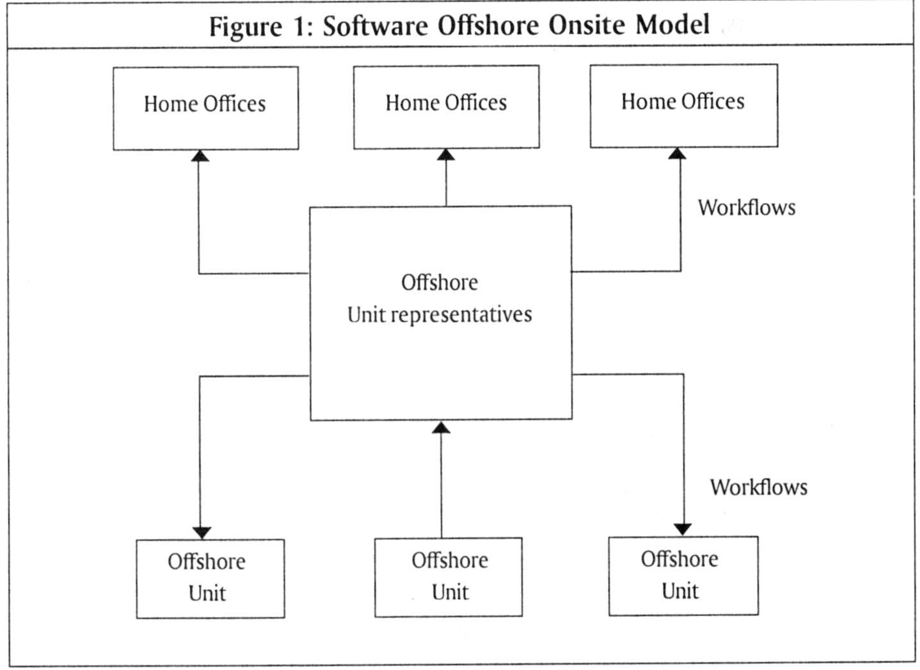

2. Third Party BPO Model

In case of a third party BPO service provider, like Netscribes India, Office Tiger, Adventity, Global Realty Outsourcing (GRO) and hoards of others, workflow is based on pre-set classification of source-able work by their clients and contracts are signed based on either billing hours or number of work-items delivered. The clients who are quality conscious can provide training facilities to the resources of these third party service providers, but are not obliged to do so. The strategic decisions and directions are responsibilities of management of the service providers and client winning forms one of the biggest challenges for them. From human resource perspective as well, job enrichment and career development are the responsibilities of the service providers.

This model of third party BPO can be effectively applied to captive BPO units and is highly effective in process driven outsourcing. The home offices classify work and identify the work items that can be outsourced. Based on the expected volumes of such identified work, the contracts are designed for the pricing of outsourced work, which may also be a parameter to define the profitability of offshore units. Once such a system is defined all the work items of the identified nature are shipped to offshore units, to a common mailbox or to administrative head of the offshore unit, wherefrom the work allocation happens for the workforce. The recruitment, utilization, training and career development of workforce remains the internal matter of the offshore unit with least interference of the home office. The captive offshore unit acts as third party service provider. Apart from high level management and strategic directions, all the responsibilities lie with the local heads.

The model is extremely competitive in terms of price effectiveness and efficiency. Parent company leadership is generally not burdened with the success of such a unit as the work flows naturally due to classification as outsourcing work items. The units in this model can be highly successful if the work items are not very high on knowledge intensity and do not require high level of interaction between home and offshore offices. There are cases of Indian third party companies like Netscribes and Office Tiger who have forayed into high-end business process outsourcing or more commonly described as Knowledge Process Outsourcing, having been successful even in delivery of research oriented work items. Hence, the scope of application of third-party BPO model in case of captive units seems to expand taking a cue from what the third party service providers have been successful at.

Figure 2: Third Party BPO Model

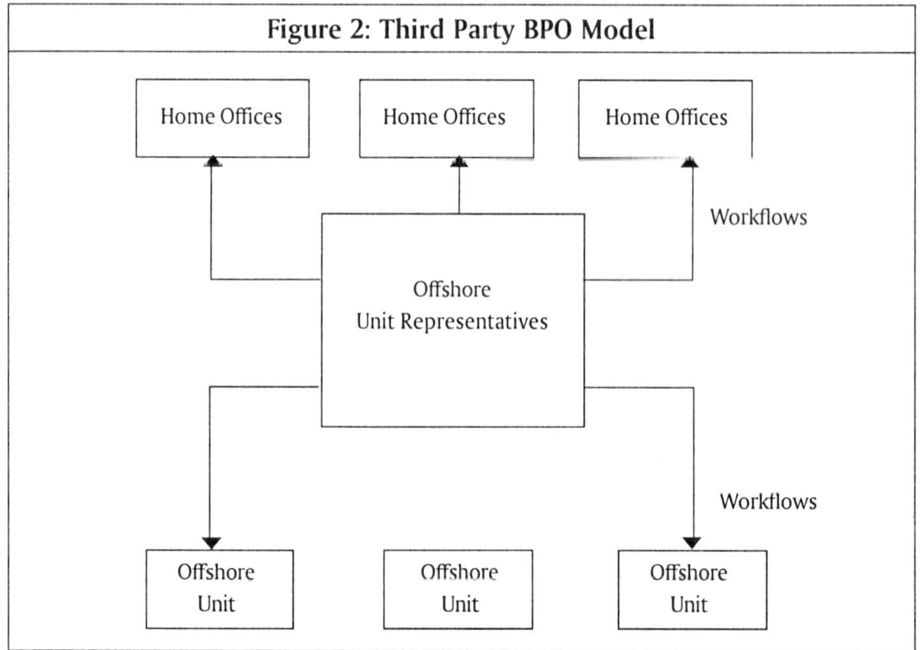

3. Dedicated Teams Model

As the name suggests the offshore offices may have a structure comprising teams that are dedicated to the departments or divisions or offices in different geographical locations and their working, utilization, team-building, career development and training depends on these onsite entities to which they are bound to.

The model is highly effective in cases of work that are knowledge intensive and involve higher levels of communication. The teams offshore develop in the niche fields, if the teams are formed on the basis of skill sets and thus, become a hub for knowledge driven processes. Teams can develop into research support, in client specific needs and for product development for exploring new opportunities. Jobs in such offshore units bring about specialization and growth of the human resources in their chosen fields. Because of close knit ways of working with the home units, the teams develop good inert personal skills and the resources do not remain faceless as can happen in cases of other models.

McKinsey Knowledge Center is an exponent in this model. McKinsey Knowledge Center India Private Limited is a wholly owned company of McKinsey

Figure 3: Dedicated Teams Model

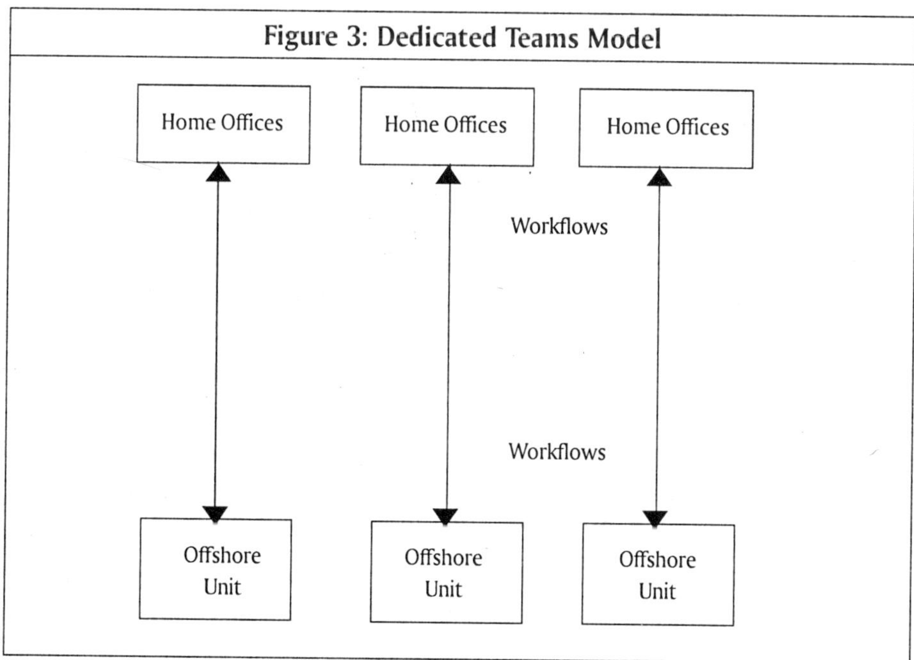

& Company and serves the parent company as a research support. The company has teams tracking various industries and functions, the analysts work in teams with the consultants working on engagements across the world. The teams have developed deep understanding of the industry or the function they work on and the scheme of workflow has helped them to become specialists in their chosen fields. Whereas the Company forms the backbone of research support for the most reputed management consultants, the workforce at the Knowledge Center is a satisfied lot with job enrichment coming from various strategic perspectives from the same industry or function they work on.

4. Offshore Home Office Model

The offshore home office works on the principle of embassies working in foreign lands. The parent company has a representative office offshore, which coordinates all the workflow from the home offices to offshore and vice versa. The representative office, therefore, acts as a nodal point for work requests and deliverables. The representative office may comprise people from home offices as well as offshore units if the units are diverse in their functions or geographies. There exists a cost differential in workforce from offshore units being present on site representing offshore units and resources from home offices representing the parent company offshore, and depending upon the nature of cost differential, one of the two models may be applied by the companies. In a sense, this model is opposite to the software offshore-onsite model.

Earlier, the model was not favored since professionals from the US and other developed countries did not desire to travel to India because of security concerns. But off late, there has been a major shift in the way residence in India is looked at. According to reports in newspapers, there has been a heavy incoming traffic of professionals from the developed countries to various destinations in India. This paradigm shift has made offshore home office model really workable and there can be more companies operating offshore units opting for this model. The model can be favored since it gives the home office representatives to supervise, inspect and maintain good quality control due to thorough understanding of the needs of home offices. The representative officers can help training and development and design of jobs that can keep the human resources motivated. The strategic decisions may, however, still rest with people at the helm of it in the home offices, since the representative officers will generally come from junior or middle

Figure 4: Offshore Home Office Model

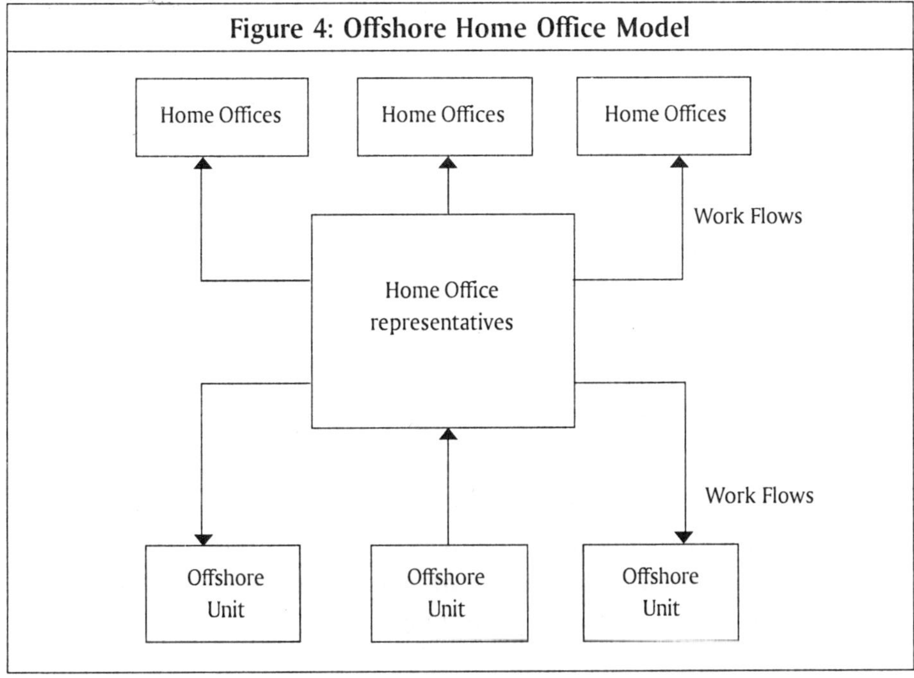

management level with operational and tactical skills.

The success of the models depends upon a thorough research on the applicability of these models in case of each offshore business units. Different models can be applied in the same captive unit if the nature of work differs. The selection of the model greatly depends on cost effectiveness and promised profitability for both the home and offshore units. Inappropriate application of the model, on the other hand, can be devastating in terms of inefficiencies, wastages, de-motivation and chaos. Hence, the application of the models must be a well thought out decision that alone can see the captive units keeping the competitiveness of parent companies high enough to sustain in the cut throat competition in the market.

(Dipesh Kumar Dipu can be reached at dipeshdipu@gmail.com).

6

BPO/IT Bundling
Position Paper

This article details the characteristics of the trend, reasons for emergence of bundling, benefits and drawbacks of bundling, and potential developments in bundling. Bundling means combining at least one tower or more from traditional IT spheres with one tower or more from BPO, in one outsourcing contract. Bundling is increasing as more companies focus on adding business value, rather than merely updating technology for cost savings. ITO/BPO bundling is emerging because major service providers are now able and willing to offer and promote it, having prepared themselves through evolution, acquisition or partnering. Major technology and consulting companies like IBM, Accenture and Capgemini might be best equipped initially to respond to BTO and bundling. Bundling might become more popular and frequent if companies move more strongly toward Business Transformation Outsourcing (BTO) – a merger of business process outsourcing and business process re-engineering.

The emergence of Business Process Outsourcing (BPO) has not only brought smaller outsourcing contract values, but also a trend of "bundling" ITO and BPO in outsourcing relationships. Bundling occurs when a client chooses to include the underlying Information Technology (IT) systems and operations within the scope of a transaction that is principally aimed at contracting for a business function, such as human resources or finance and accounting operations. Technology Partners International (TPI) has observed this trend in its historical metrics, which have often reflected overall industry trends. This position paper explores the characteristics of the trend, reasons for its emergence, benefits and drawbacks of bundling, and potential developments in bundling. Since clients sometimes ask us what they can gain by bundling, we will also indicate TPI's experience in effectively helping clients who want to bundle ITO with BPO.

Predominantly, ITO is bundled with BPO efforts, and not vice versa. We rarely see an ITO requirement move up the food chain to subsume a BPO scope. The business process rules the decision-making.

We find that the bundling client will typically either accept or encourage the alignment of transactional business processes with enabling applications. For example, a client might opt for PeopleSoft as the IT that enables the elected BPO HR process. On one occasion, this decision is driven by the client's legacy; on other occasions, it is driven by the solution offered by the service provider. At yet other times, businesses are bundling a broad set of processes (IT, HR, procurement, logistics, facilities, marketing and sales) under a common "Global Business Services" umbrella. For clarity's sake — as the word "bundling" has been used in other contexts — bundling does not mean multi-tower BPO or multi-tower ITO deals. Instead, it means combining at least one tower or more from traditional IT spheres with one tower or more from BPO in one outsourcing contract. The creation of an integrated shared services operation is often a precursor to the exploration of a bundled sourcing solution.

What Signals the Emergence of Bundling?

As the number of TPI-advised BPO transactions has risen significantly in the recent past (from one in 2001 to four in 2002 to eight in 2003), the number of relationships involving BPO/IT bundling also increased (from zero in 2000 to three in 2002 to five in 2003). To date in 2004, we are seeing that about twenty-two percent of our active BPO transactions include the underlying IT as part of the scope of those deals.

TPI – Advised BPO Deals

	BPO	Bundled BPO/IT
2001	1	0
2002	4	3
2003	8	4
2004YTD	9	2

Source: TPI Databases.

In 2003, TPI worked on 36 BPO transactions, eight of which resulted in signed contracts with a TCV of US$2.75 billion. Of these eight, four (50 percent), involved bundling and those accounted for more than half of the TCV. This trend tells us that the winners in the BPO marketplace are service providers who are adept at leveraging technology solutions as part of their overall offerings.

Within our sampling of bundled contracts, certain characteristics emerge, while others elude. Typically, no one service provider wins a majority of bundling contracts, but the Big Six (Accenture, ACS, CSC, EDS, HP, and IBM) predominate. Most often, one provider assumes both IT and BPO responsibilities in a contract. Global-500 companies and non-Global 500 are almost equally receptive to bundling. The Americas region accounts for most bundling so far, but Asia Pacific and Europe are also represented.

Few other similarities can be found in our sample. Bundling deals with cross sectors: Financial services; manufacturing; telecommunications; travel, transportation and hospitality; media & entertainment; and retail & restaurant sectors have all embraced bundling. ITO components have accompanied all BPO categories—HR, F&A, CRM and Procurement. Bundled deals range widely in TCV: total spend in scope of bundled contracts has ranged from US$38.5M over five years to US$584 million over seven years. Finally, the percentage of the total spend on IT functions has varied from 10 percent to almost 100 percent.

Industrywide, a significant portion of the top outsourcing deals in 2003 also involved bundling, as reported by *HRO Today*: seven of the top 25 HR outsourcing transactions (28 percent) and six of the top 25 F&A outsourcing transactions (24 percent) contained traditional IT elements.[1]

Why is Bundling Emerging?

Bundling is increasing as more companies focus on adding business value, rather than merely updating technology for cost savings. They are also challenging the reason for the existence of the underlying technology assets (people and capital), and looking for the correlation between IT and business operations.

Firms are more often viewing outsourcing as a way of increasing the value of their businesses, rather than simply looking for cost reductions,[2] so they seek solid business results from both IT investments and improved business processes. Further, firms are moving toward the integration of business and technology[3] and assessing IT's value not only in reducing costs but also in enabling productivity and innovation. IT must deliver business value, and that often bridges to transforming business processes. Thus, ITO and BPO converge, and in the process, are sometimes "bundled" in one contract.

Second, although companies historically have generally not sought to implement many IT and BPO functions all at one time, the record shows that when they do, bundling can add efficiencies and economies. A company can bundle to productively and quickly "catch up" with and even "leapfrog" a competitor's existing BPO and IT advantages. In one such case, the competitors of a TPI client had already outsourced the IT and business functions the client sought to outsource. Additionally, the client's SG&A was 30 percent higher than that of its main competitors; therefore, the client wanted to lower costs and start growing again. Bundling provided a possible means to catch up with and even leapfrog the competitor.

Third, ITO/BPO bundling is emerging because major service providers are now able and willing to offer and promote it, having prepared themselves through

---

1 *HRO Today*, December 2003.

2 PA Consulting study, February 18, 2004.

3 A T Kearney study conducted by Harris Interactive, September/October 2002, from "The Road to Business Value: An Integrated Approach to IT Investment," ATK, 2004.

evolution, acquisition or partnering. For example, IBM acquired PwC, an acquisition target that HP earlier had rebuffed. EDS acquired NeoData, which, along with their GM association, boosted their CRM capabilities. Others have partnered well. Officially since 2001, Hewlett-Packard and Accenture have aligned their ITO and BPO strengths, respectively, to provide enterprises with ERP solutions.[4] Hydro One Networks Inc., and ITO provider Capgemini Canada Inc., announced a bundled agreement in February 2002, that required partner Inergi LP to manage and operate existing business processes and technology enabled services for Hydro One.[5]

TPI data on the industry at large reveals that EDS has been the service provider most often involved in bundling, but other "Big Six" service providers are also involved. Of 46 bundled deals industrywide from 2001-2003, 14 were won by EDS; six by IBM; five by Accenture, five by ACS and one by HP. Other non-Big-Six firms account for the remainder.

What Advantages and Disadvantages are Companies Finding in Bundling?

There is more project integration from start to finish, which can enable the efficiencies and economies of bundling.

Optimally, bundling can help clients get to broader outsourced solutions with the optimal service provider – faster, more easily, and more systematically.

There are often more "win-win" opportunities for all potential participants. The larger size of a bundled deal is more attractive to major traditional IT players who are evolving their BPO practices; thus, it can leverage efforts, allow negotiating advantages, and offer greater cost savings for the client.

Clients might also value the chance to select from a broad range of niche players in BPO, who themselves value the opportunity to be part of a larger-scale deal than they might normally encounter.

Bundling enables the business process provider to also own or control the technology used in the process, allowing a more seamless service. Ultimately, we

4 HP PR Release, May 8, 2001.

5 National Post, February 2002.

might expect companies to increasingly relinquish their hold on IT systems and focus more on process results, a trend hat could lead to more bundling.

Bundling typically prompts wider executive participation in shaping a deal. ITO, traditionally the focus of the CIO, joins BPO, more often the province of the CEO, CFO or COO. One research study found that two-thirds of nearly one thousand CIOs studied do not see BPO as important either now or through 2007.[6] Analysts found that, in many cases, CIOs are not included in BPO decisions, and many service providers go directly to business unit executives. Bundling can counteract this trend.

Bundling makes governance, or sourcing management, easier. The client can choose just one service provider "throat to choke," and gain one very committed service provider. The service provider typically wins a larger scope of work than he might with a single-scope deal. He also gains a client who is more beholden, or "locked in." Since bundling requires (or benefits from) stronger loyalties than a single-function deal might, it is important that relationships be clear and effective upfront with well-defined objectives and clear alignment of expectations.

How Might Bundling Evolve?

Bundling might become more popular and frequent if companies move more strongly toward Business Transformation Outsourcing (BTO), a merger of business process outsourcing and business process re-engineering. For example, firms might want to go beyond traditional data centre hosting to request that a service provider guarantee the running and improvement of a customer's non-core business processes. A specific example: Accenture won a 10-year, US$1 billion BTO deal with B C Hydro to bundle IT, CRM and human resources, vowing to save the utility US$250 million during the life of the contract.[7]

Major technology and consulting companies like IBM, Accenture and Capgemini might be best equipped initially to respond to BTO and bundling. Only firms with expertise in both business management and IT can successfully play.

6 Gartner, in Business Wire, March 09, 2004.

7 Meta Group analyst, in Computer Dealer News, January 16, 2004.

Meta Group estimates that, through 2005, business transformation outsourcing will remain more rhetoric than reality, with deals looking more like traditional business process outsourcing, yet having some transformational aspects and cost-cutting results. The research group expects that through 2006 and 2007, transformational services (i.e., application development maintenance, business process outsourcing) will segment along horizontal and vertical business process/services functions. While service providers will attempt to bundle infrastructure with "value" services, clients will demand "line item" pricing by 2008-2009 and expect continuous price declines. If "on-demand" BPO services catch on, the outsourcing industry will migrate to a fully integrated process/technology model (we might consider it "extreme bundling") and utility like pricing will be the norm. The challenge is to separate the hype from reality in developing a consumption-driven model. One of the risks is that IT costs are double counted in the pricing model. The level of sophistication and maturity has to increase in the service provider community for utility pricing to become the norm. TPI is focusing on developing standard unit pricing and definitions for various BPO activities.

Another possible evolution is that, as outsourcing and BPO gain momentum in Europe, as they have in the recent past, bundling might also increase. For now, however, bundling is still more prevalent and growing in the Americas, compared with other regions:

2001: Americas (50 percent)/EMEA (50 percent – off a small base of 2).

2002: Americas (67 percent)/EMEA (25 percent)/AP (8 percent).

2003: Americas (72 percent)/EMEA (28 percent).

(Source: TPI estimates of industrywide BPO/IT Bundling.)

Conclusion

TPI expects bundling to continue selectively as companies become more confident of the advantages of both ITO and BPO and the benefits of bundling the two. For example, as clients learn of the negotiating leverage, as well as the economies of scale and scope of bundling, they will explore or embrace it as an option. TPI is advising in an increasing number of bundling transactions. It has also found more clients seeking to understand how to coordinate and integrate current and future BPO and ITO transactions.

A key decision criterion revolves around the strategic relevance of an enterprise's ERP platform. Is there a need to own and control an ERP infrastructure of one's own choosing? Might the ERP services be better delivered on a pay-as-one-goes basis by bundling the ERP/IT aspects into a BPO or BTO relationship? What of data? Where is the line drawn between a managed BPO/IT relationship and corporate data stewardship?

There is something to be gained by major and niche service providers alike, especially those eager to be part of a bigger game plan than usual. In the future, bundling will increase as major service providers prove ready, willing and able to offer it. It will also increase as clients seek to simplify their sourcing relationships. Further, it will increase as the market matures in terms of pricing mechanisms and service level agreement definitions.

We anticipate that the leading ERP software providers—SAP, PeopleSoft, Oracle, and JD Edwards—will play a role in the changing face of the industry.

We suspect that bundling, in a way, might be emerging as sort of a practice run for (or a precursor of) full Business Transformational Outsourcing.

TPI (with a wide range of experience in BPO, ITO and bundling) is well equipped to help clients discover if and how they can benefit from bundling.

(TPI offers sourcing advisory solutions that support organisational goals to create enduring value, achieve effective transformation, and meet rapidly changing market demands. Since 2000, TPI has advised on more than 25 percent of total contract value awarded in the broader outsourcing market, which includes commercial contract awards each valued at €40 million or more. With 350 advisors to help clients find the right balance of value, speed-to-market and risk mitigation, TPI remains the most sought-after advisory firm in the world. TPI operates in locations including London, Paris, Brussels, Frankfurt, Amsterdam, Houston, New York, Toronto, Sydney, Bangalore and Singapore. For additional information, please visit us at www.tpi.net.)

7

IT Outsourcing Rediscovered
Getting Your Share This Time Around

Ralf Dreischmeier, Peter Balnaves and Anthony Datel

The companies have to focus on eight levers that help them capture greater values from their IT Outsourcing efforts. The companies have to find and follow the value, manage outsourcing service as a lifecycle, not as a transaction, make the bidding more collaborative and competitive, build a partnership, not a contract, pressure-test the economics, manage the organizational change effectively, maintain checks and balances on the outsourcers' access and influence and start working on renegotiation and renewal to capture greater value from their IT-outsourcing efforts. IT outsourcing offers a wide variety of potential advantages such as financial benefits, economic benefits, accounting benefits, performance improvement, and freedom to focus on core competencies. Successful IT outsourcing demands skillful implementation so that the outsourcers can entirely capture the deal's promised value without putting the rest of the business at risk.

Is your IT-outsourcing contract up for renewal? Did the value you thought you'd gain from outsourcing fail to materialize? Or has your business context radically changed? If you answered yes to any of these questions, it's time to look critically at your last IT-outsourcing efforts. Typically, when a deal falls short of expectations, a company has made at least one key misstep:

- Viewing outsourcing as a transaction rather than as a fundamental change in the way the business works.
- Agreeing, without a firm sense of the deal's optimal value, to an arrangement in which the out-sourcer promises to cut the company's costs by a fixed percentage.
- Failing to anticipate and address change management issues surrounding the transition to the out-sourcer.
- Failing to include the costs of transition, management, and termination in the assessment of the deal's value.
- Giving the bidding outsourcers cost data or, alternatively, no information at all.
- Trusting the vendor to find, and pass on, additional cost reductions in the normal course of business.
- Determining how to manage the relationship with the outsourcer *after* the contract is signed.
- Paying insufficient attention to the contract's exit barriers in the hope that the company will never have to take the exit option.

If your company has made one or more of these missteps, chances are you left a considerable amount of money on the table. You may also have needlessly restricted your company's ability to adjust its strategy and respond to changes in the competitive environment. Take heart, though: you're not alone. Although IT outsourcing has been around for years in different guises (the latest of which is *on demand),* few companies have mastered its planning and execution. Indeed, many companies continue to make decisions that needlessly destroy or reduce business value, often in shocking ways.

We think it's time companies played smarter. To that end, we have identified eight levers that can help them capture greater value from their IT-outsourcing efforts. These levers can also be useful in broader initiatives that involve Business Process Outsourcing.

Lever 1: Find and Follow the Value

Outsourcing offers a wide range of potential advantages. They include financial benefits (cash benefits through lower operating expenses and non-cash benefits through asset transfers and removal of depreciation from the balance sheet); economic benefits (the ability to turn fixed costs into variable ones); accounting benefits (write-downs and restructuring charges); performance improvement; freedom to focus on core competencies; and improved capabilities (access to advanced technologies or expertise).

But outsourcing shouldn't be the default choice, nor should it be seen as a cure-all. A few companies go so far as to outsource almost all their IT, seeking immediate cost savings or a solution to a problem they can't seem to fix on their own. This is typically a sign of desperation more than of shrewd judgment. Other companies decide to outsource specific functions without a strong business case for doing so. Many of them never quite know how successful they've been, since they weren't sure what potential value they stood to gain in the first place. We recently worked with a financial institution that had outsourced several functions in an effort to cut $20 million in IT costs. We found that while the company did hit its savings target, its outsourced IT costs were still 2.5 times those of best-practice institutions. The company had really shortchanged itself.

To understand what you can reasonably expect to gain from outsourcing, you must analyze your particular situation in light of your economics, those of your potential providers, and your business needs. Carefully consider costs—especially the less obvious ones, such as transition, management, and termination costs. Indeed, the difference between a deal's perceived value and its real value, which does factor in such costs, can be substantial. (See Exhibit 1.) We've found that if outsourcing doesn't save at least 30 percent of your current costs, it probably won't cover enough of the transition, management, and termination costs to be worthwhile.

Exhibit 1: Consider All Costs When Making Outsourcing Decisions

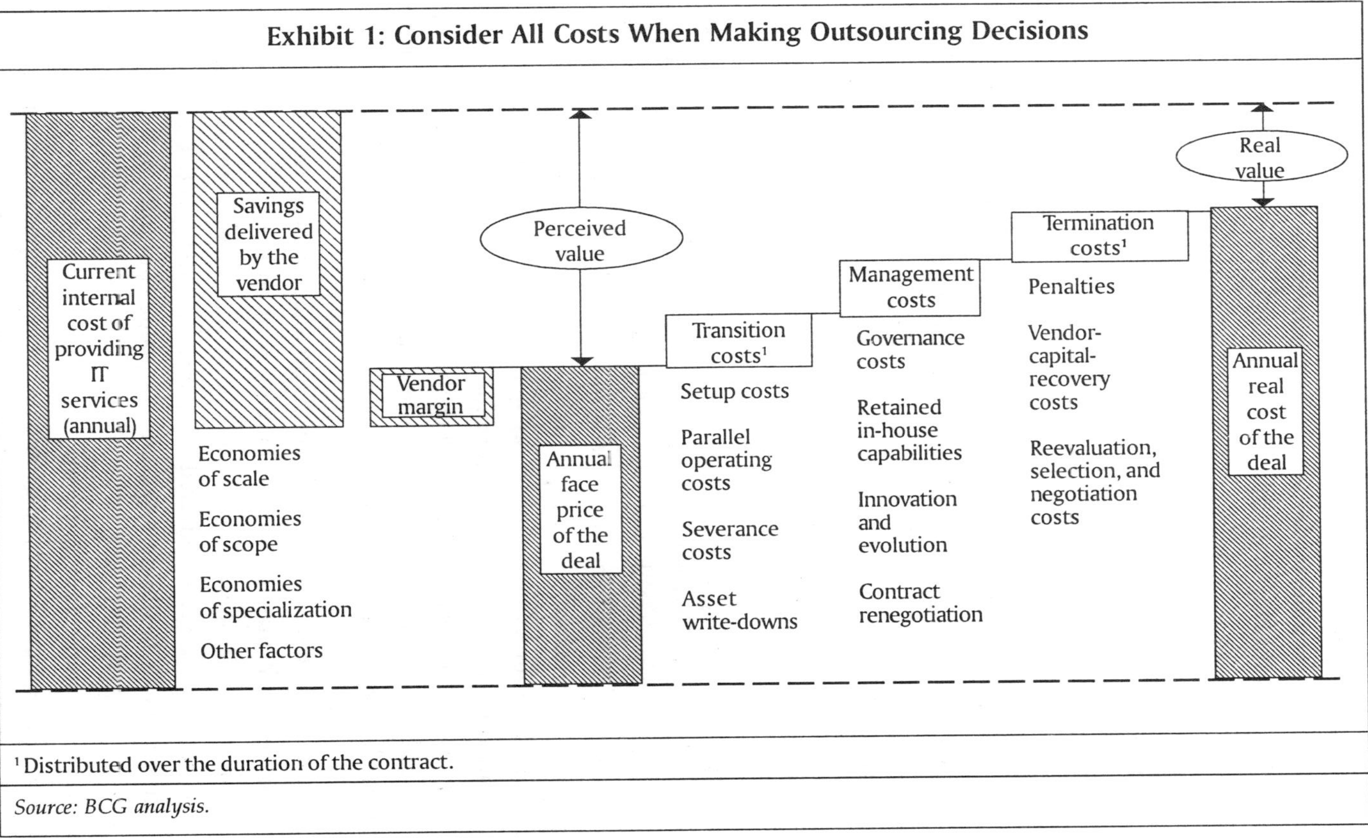

[1] Distributed over the duration of the contract.

Source: BCG analysis.

You should also consider alternatives to outsourcing. Especially if your company is large, you might be able to capture similar scale economies to those of an out-sourcer by consolidating your data centers. Finally, recognize that not all IT functions lend themselves to outsourcing. Application development, support, and management, as well as infrastructure, are good projects for outsourcing. IT strategy, governance, and architecture, on the other hand, should never be entirely outsourced; and choosing which parts to outsource, if any, should be done with great care.

Lever 2: Manage Outsourcing as a Life Cycle, not as a Transaction

Not surprisingly, many companies and their advisers focus intensely on the *sine qua non* of an outsourcing agreement: the contract. An over emphasis on the legal transaction, however, can severely handicap you by drawing attention away from other elements essential to capturing the most value from outsourcing. (See Exhibit 2.)

To manage an outsourcing relationship successfully over its entire life cycle, we recommend that, as a first step, you clarify your IT-sourcing strategy, specifying what you hope to accomplish and why and how it fits into your company's business strategy. If outsourcing is on the agenda, you should establish an active cross-functional governance team comprising senior managers from the business, IT, and human resources departments, as well as from any shared-services or process functions. This team will determine the value to be captured from outsourcing and be responsible for ensuring that it is indeed captured over the life of the deal. The team will also determine the scope of the effort and the schedule for the internal transformation that will be required.

Another critical responsibility of the governance team is to establish an organization that will manage the outsourcing relationship. This organization will perform a variety of tasks over the course of the relationship with the outsourcer: compare services delivered with those of best-practice companies; leverage the contract's flexibility to ensure that value continues to be delivered and that your company's evolving business needs are met; and work to maintain negotiating power and reduce exit barriers so that your company will be well positioned to choose from a wide range of outsourcing options in the future. This relationship-management organization should be formed *before* the contract is developed so that the group's staff has a sense of ownership in the vendor selection decision and the terms of the agreement.

Exhibit 2: Always View IT Outsourcing as a Life Cycle, Not as a Transaction

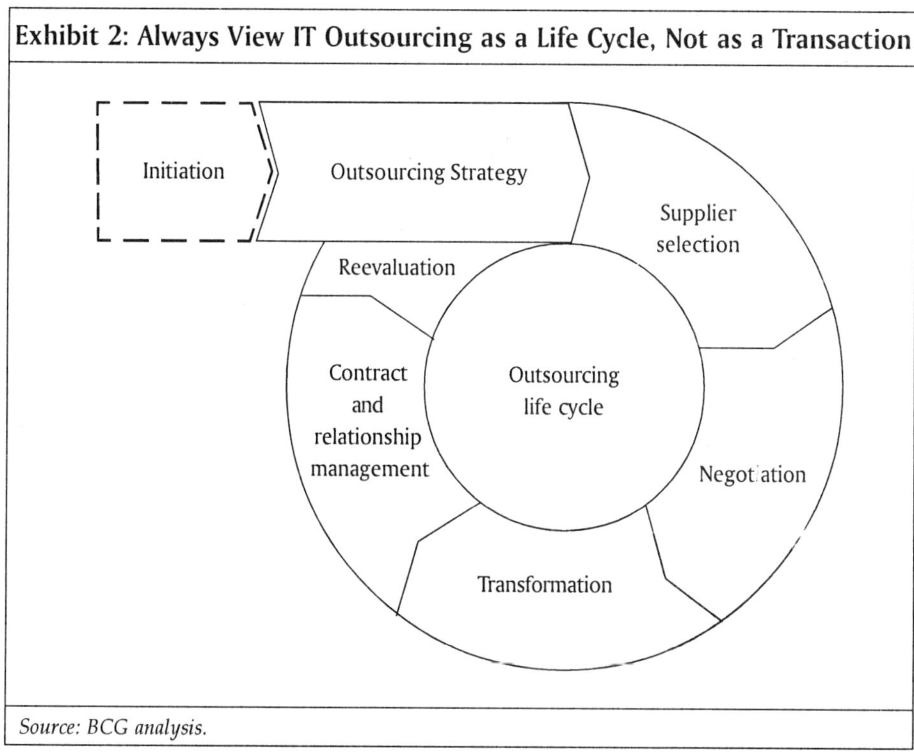

Source: BCG analysis.

Only by managing the outsourcing relationship comprehensively over its life cycle, from strategy through re-negotiation and renewal, will you be able to capture its promised value.

Lever 3: Make the Bidding Collaborative and Competitive

Conventional wisdom holds that a competitive bidding process is critical to realizing maximum value from negotiations with outsourcers. We have found, however, that the bidding also needs to be *collaborative.* Work individually and closely with all competing vendors to help them build cost models and pricing proposals from the bottom up. Use each vendor's expertise to help design the best solutions for IT, human resources, pricing, financial engineering, and other essential functions of your company. Then leverage those solutions across all bidders to improve the proposals and raise the level of the competition.

Do not, however, disclose your costs. If you do, bidders will simply lop off a fixed percentage based on what they think it will take to win your business. Instead, be honest about your business environment, infrastructure, and requirements, and help bidders build their models on the basis of *their* scale and labor costs plus a reasonable profit margin. This will increase the transparency of the economic value created by outsourcing, as well as the share of that value that each vendor proposes to keep for itself.

Lever 4: Build a Partnership, not a Contract

An open, collaborative bidding process will also give you insight into the culture and values of each bidder.

This is critical because you will need to work closely with your chosen outsourcer on a number of complex issues. You may even have to renegotiate the deal because of an unforeseen event, such as a merger or an acquisition. Hence, you need to choose a provider whose culture and staff are compatible with your own.

Lever 5: Pressure-Test the Economics

Outsourcing contracts are often negotiated on the basis of static or simple straight-line growth projections. This is a recipe for disaster. Business conditions – your demand for IT resources, and the market value of those resources can change substantially over time, so the pricing must be able to adapt to those contingencies predictably and cost-effectively.

It is therefore critical that, before negotiation, you assess your upside and downside risks, and use scenario analysis to model the effects of those risks on pricing. Carefully evaluate the use of caps, floors, and options to ensure that you are not giving away value to the outsourcer and exposing yourself to price and volume risk. If you try to negotiate these details after the contract is in place, you'll find you have little real leverage. We recently helped a large technology-products distributor, negotiate highly favorable terms with a vendor by using this type of analysis. The distributor's business cycle was extremely volatile; by pressure-testing the economics, we helped it identify specific risks and put in place a contract that included pricing and volume mechanisms to scale capacity up and down where necessary.

Also make sure that your contract reflects the generally downward trend of technology prices. Hardware and, in some circumstances, software prices continue to fall over time. The implicit unit costs of technology should be dropping in your contract as well.

Lever 6: Actively Manage the Organizational Change

Many companies pay insufficient attention to the "soft side" of changes brought on by outsourcing. As a result, the economics of even the most compelling deals often unravel as shadow IT increases, critical expertise is lost, and business operations are put at risk.

For an outsourcing effort to succeed, business and IT staff must accept the changes involved and adapt to them. To ensure that this happens, you must actively shape and manage expectations, emotions, opinions, and both formal and informal communication. A linch-pin of this effort is getting early buy-in from key stakeholders. They typically include senior and other important IT staff and, on the business side, senior managers from the center and the respective business units. (You will need business representation not only if you're outsourcing application development, management, and support but in many cases even if you're outsourcing infrastructure.) As you begin to refine the scope of the outsourcing effort, you should conduct a quick and anonymous poll to determine how ready, willing, and able these stakeholders are to accept and implement the changes needed. Then you can focus on converting the skeptics and supporting the champions.

Recognize at the outset that achieving lasting organizational change can be a long, difficult, and emotional process, especially when jobs and careers are at stake. Knowing where you are in the process and what to anticipate will help you prepare, ride out the ups and downs, and ultimately capture the value you expect.

Lever 7: Maintain Checks and Balances on the Outsourcer's Access and Influence

Some cutting-edge organizations have begun to judiciously outsource parts of their core IT capabilities, such as IT strategy and architecture. We helped a financial services institution that was seeking a step-change improvement in its

IT capabilities enter into a novel arrangement with an outsourcer that agreed to help seed many of the company's IT functions with its own staff over three to five years. The goal was to transfer expertise permanently to the financial services company, leaving a self-sufficient IT organization behind. The effort is meeting expectations, and the IT organization's increased capabilities are winning it new respect from the rest of the business.

A potential drawback of giving an outsourcer this degree of access, however, is that the outsourcer's true value added can become increasingly difficult to gauge. The bigger an outsourcer's role and the more entrenched it becomes, the more influence it can have over your future sourcing decisions, especially if you have shed critical expertise and capabilities. It is therefore essential that you safeguard certain skills and ensure contractually that the benefits you stand to gain from outsourcing outweigh the sourcing risk you are taking on. For example, the financial services company described above, specified an endpoint to the relationship and secured itself a guaranteed annual savings of nearly 20 percent.

Lever 8: Start Working on Renegotiation and Renewal

It's never too early to think about renegotiation and renewal. If you aren't considering exit strategies even as you're working on defining the scope of the effort, you may find yourself trapped—not only at the end of the contract but from the moment it's signed.

Maximizing the value of IT-outsourcing efforts requires deep economic and organization-specific business analysis. Only this type of scrutiny will generate the robust quantitative valuations essential to designing a plan that is feasible, given the culture and context of your business. Applying a series of templates to your situation and needs, and comparing vendors' cost estimates with roughly equivalent "benchmarks" to arrive at contract prices, is a recipe for failure.

Successful IT outsourcing also demands skillful implementation so that you can fully capture the deal's promised value without putting the rest of the business—and its ability to use IT strategically and operationally—at risk. The levers presented here will help you to be successful.

And it's important for you to succeed. After all, if you don't continue to reduce the "lights on" costs of IT and improve overall IT productivity, the money left over for discretionary IT spending will continue to shrink. If you can't be a partner for the business when it needs to change strategy or rapidly transform some aspect of its operations, who will? Your out-sourcer? Think about that.

(Ralf Dreischmeier is a Vice President and Director in the London office of The Boston Consulting Group. He can be reached at dreischmeier.ralf@bcg.com

Peter Balnaves is a Manager in the firm's Los Angeles office. He can be reached at balnaves.peter@bcg.com and

Anthony Datel is a Manager in BCG's Boston office. He can be reached at datel.anthony@bcg.com).

8

Global Outsourcing
BPO to KPO – The Way Ahead

Priya Angle

This article explains the outsourcing and offshoring models, and the shift of the industry from BPO to KPO industry. It also narrates how the Indian BPO/KPO industry can specialize in the emerging areas of the industry, such as engineering services or remote education, and develop a distinct advantage over others in the context of increasing competition.

"Where the mind is without fear and the head is held high;

Where knowledge is free;

Where the world has not been broken up in fragments... My Father, let my country awake."

– Rabindarnath Tagore

Way back in 1835 Lord Macaulay made the English language compulsory in India with the objective of breaking Indian affinity for local languages. A century later, English speaking Indians are driving the Business Process

Source: Icfai Reader, May 2006. This paper was presented in the National Conference on Global Competitiveness 2006 held on January 13, 2006 at The Icfai Business School, Kolkata and published in the seminar proceedings.

Outsourcing (BPO) industry. Availability of highly skilled, low-cost, English speaking manpower has contributed to the flourishing BPO business in the country.

The BPO sector is not only generating employment for young India; it is also providing significant disposable income in the hands of a growing and spending population—facilitating an improvement in the standard of living of the country's citizens. What, therefore, becomes important is: Whether this sector will be able to sustain itself? It is essential that the BPO sector does not disappear like many dotcom companies a few years ago, in which is know as the dotcombust.

The mercurial rise of the BPO sector, however, has been accompanied with its own set of problems. Issues such as increasing attrition levels, necessity to scale up rapidly, and billing pressures in the wake of increasing competition both internally and externally are being discussed in various forums. New laws are being enacted, market participants are experimenting with new business models and issues pertaining to quality and confidentiality are being addressed.

This article attempts to understand the BPO model as it exists today and explores initiatives that are required to be taken up proactively in order to maintain the country's competitive advantage in the years to come.

The topics that would be covered are listed below:

- Outsourcing vs. Offshoring.
- Benefits of Outsourcing.
- Moving up the Value Chain—The possible alternatives to graduate from BPO to KPO.
- Future Prospects.

Pulitzer Prize winning author and columnist with the *New York Times,* Thomas Friedman had said, "My father used to tell me: Honey, finish your breakfast; children in India are starving." He goes on to say that in today's times he has to tell his children: "Do your maths well, else children in India will make you starve." This dramatic change in the way the world looks at India of the 21st Century has been brought about by a large pool of educated, innovative English

Figure 1: Estimate of Money Spent on BPO Activity in 2005

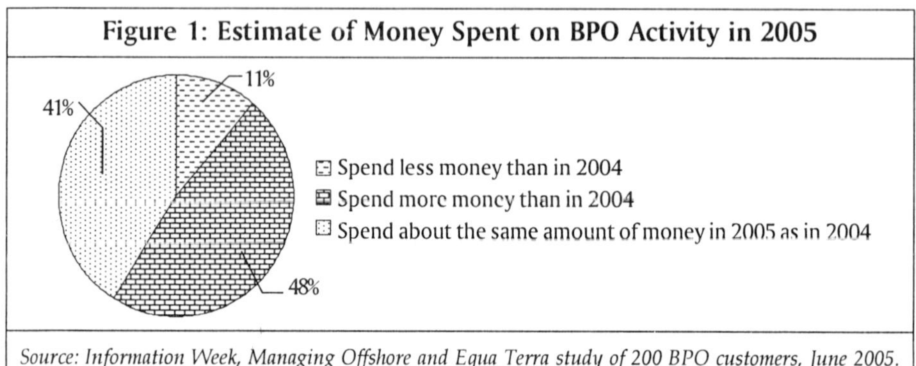

Source: Information Week, Managing Offshore and Equa Terra study of 200 BPO customers, June 2005.

speaking Indians—who are grabbing opportunities that are available world over through what is known as Outsourcing. India's immensely skilled population is its asset—unmatched by any other country in the world, in present times. (See Figure 1)

Outsourcing and Offshoring

What do we understand by the term outsourcing? How is it different from offshoring? For how long will India be able to maintain an advantage in the global outsourcing space? What needs to be done to ensure that we as a nation are able to sustain our competitive advantage for a long time in the future? An attempt is being made to address the above mentioned issues.

Outsourcing is hiring another company to do some of your work. It is getting non-core, non-value adding activities done from another service provider. Offshoring, on the other hand, is moving some of your operations to another country with qualified labor and cheap input costs. Terms like global sourcing, right sourcing, inter-sourcing and blended sourcing are often used to denote offshoring. In case of offshoring, the entity that seeks to relocate some operations to another country would have managerial control over the operation being set up in foreign location, unlike outsourcing.

The Y2K syndrome first gave a major impetus to the process of relocating activities in the mid-1990s. Functions related to IT still constitute a major chunk of total outsourced businesses in the world. Many firms also saw the benefits of setting up call centers, customer support centers, business transaction processing, and customer transaction processing in a foreign country like India. An English speaking population facilitated this.

Outsourcing other businesses like insurance claims processing, equity research, middle office functions like finance, accounting and human resources are also becoming well established as the confidence of overseas clients in this mode of functioning has been built up. The graduation from low-end office support tasks to carrying out high-end jobs is happening not purely due to an English speaking population, but due to availability of highly qualified manpower, capable of applying knowledge to fulfill tasks related to these functions.

BPO to KPO

The shift from outsourcing standardized, non-value adding business processes that are repetitive in nature (Business Process Outsourcing) to outsourcing of value-adding business that largely depend on domain knowledge (Knowledge Process Outsourcing) is what India needs to focus on.

The line of distinction between BPO and KPO is difficult to establish. BPO primarily constitutes outsourcing of non-core, non-value-adding tasks to destinations with distinct cost advantages in terms of cheap labor. KPO on the other hand would encompass outsourcing some of the core activities of an organization to locations where qualified manpower exists—the objective being highest quality at the best possible price. (See Figure 2)

Figure 2: Share of India in the Global BPO Market

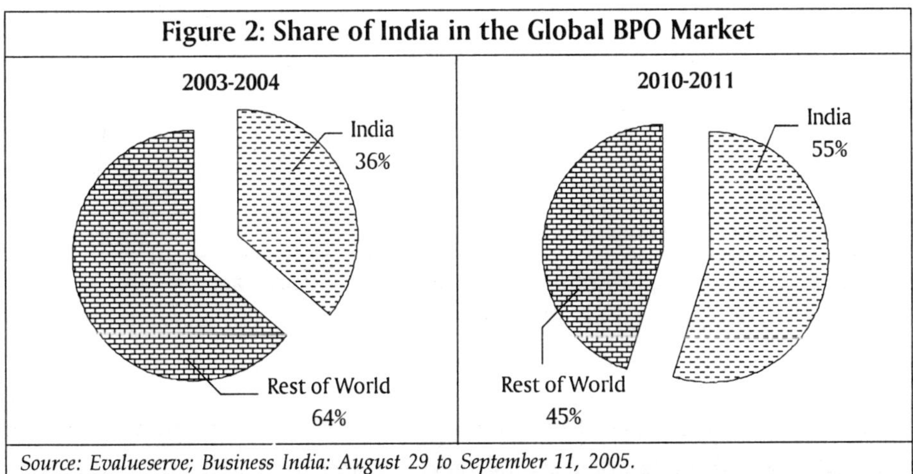

Source: Evalueserve; Business India: August 29 to September 11, 2005.

Outsourcing Advantages

The outsourcing business has grown manifold primarily because it enables corporations to:

a. Focus on Core Competencies.

b. Reduce Operating Costs.

c. Access Vendors' Resources and Expertise.

d. Enhance Productivity and Quality.

e. Unlock Capital.

Figure 3 lists all the benefits of outsourcing as stated by companies who have outsourced some of their activities.

Figure 3: Wide Range of Outsourcing Gains

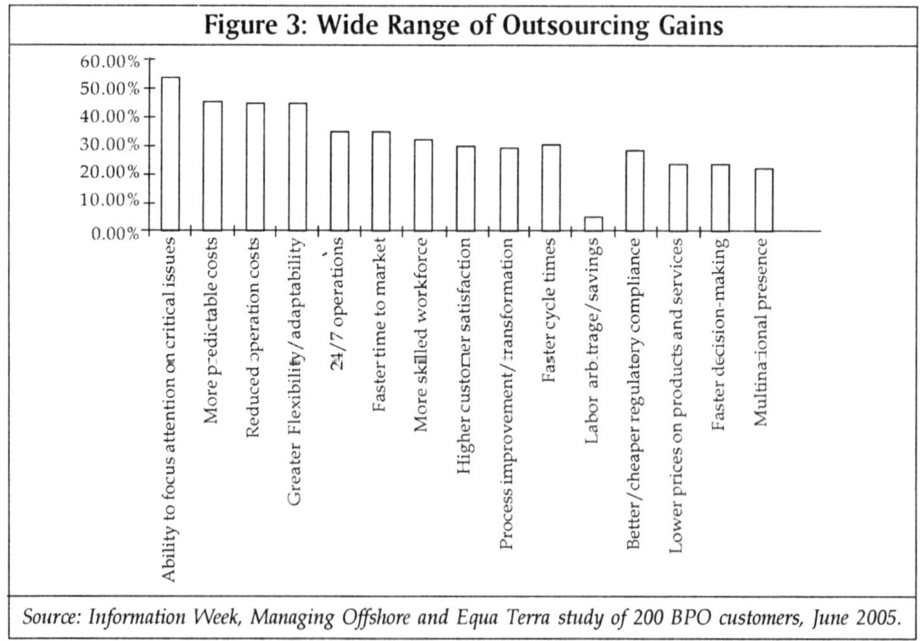

Source: Information Week, Managing Offshore and Equa Terra study of 200 BPO customers, June 2005.

A few years ago, outsourcing was preferred to offshoring. Of late, however, more and more companies are choosing to retain control and ownership through wholly owned subsidiaries—especially with respect to financial services.

According to a Deloitte Research Report: Eighty percent of the world's large financial institutions (market capitalization greater than $10 bn) are working offshore, while 50% of the smaller firms (market capitalization less than $10 bn) have moved some operations offshore. It has been estimated that by the end of 2005, $210 bn cost base would move to offshore locations with an average cost saving of $700 mn for top 500 financial firms.

Initially, offshoring was driven by the need to cut costs. However, in recent times, corporations have realized that they can hire workers who are more skilled than those in their domestic countries at a lower cost, thus achieving the twin objectives of high quality and low-cost.

Moving up the Value Chain: Possible Alternatives

Although India enjoys the number one position as a low-cost destination for outsourcing, competition is fast catching up. Countries like China, Czechoslovakia, Vietnam and the Philippines are becoming popular for low-end work like call center services and maintenance. In the wake of threats being posed by these nations it is imperative that India excels in providing certain categories of services. Such a focus on specialization will ensure that India does not lose its footing in the global outsourcing space. According to NASSCOM (National Association for Software and Service Companies) President Kiran Karnik: "In the coming years, companies in the IT software and services sector will have to move up the value chain. Companies specializing in intellectual property rights, IT infrastructure management and HR business process outsourcing will be able to drive a good price for their services."

A few areas where India could have a distinct advantage through specialization are discussed below:

- **Engineering Services (Non-IT)**

  Corporations world over are reexamining product development life cycle in order to exploit the benefits of outsourcing a few services. This enables corporate entities not only to reduce costs but also to reduce time-to-market. According to AMR Research's 2004 BPO survey 15% of the companies in the manufacturing sector had hired outsourcing companies to handle a part of their research and engineering activities. An additional 10% of companies with similar businesses had indicated their preferences to outsource a part of their research and engineering activities by the end of 2005. As the market for outsourced engineering services expands, India can tap the opportunities that will be thrown up.

- **Software Product Development**

  India can establish expertise in software product innovation capitalizing on its vast pool of engineering talent and the support that is given by the government to entrepreneurial initiatives in IT domain. A NASSCOM-McKinsey study estimates that product and technology services will grow to $8-11 bn by 2008. Currently, India's share in global software product development market is only 0.20%. Since the country has already built up the reputation and credibility as a software services nerve center of the world, the time is ripe for Indian companies to move up the value chain by offering high-end software product development.

- **Procurement Outsourcing**

  Procurement outsourcing encompasses outsourcing of all direct and indirect resources needed by any firm. The resources that need to be procured could range from computers to home décor. Procurement Outsourcing can be Broadly Classified as:

  a. **Contract Compliance:** In this type of outsourcing, knowledge of specific terms and conditions of contracts is necessary. Ability to negotiate the terms and conditions of the contact, analyze the cost-benefit ratio between parties to the contract, and the expertise to work out the conditions for payments are essential.

  b. **Assisted Buying:** This type of outsourcing would require the outsourcer to take a decision with respect to the kind of products to buy on best possible terms to best fit a given need. Knowledge about the sector, the different players, different products and prices would enable the service provider to take such decisions.

  c. **Financial Requisition:** In this type of outsourcing, financial and accounting professionals would be required to use their domain knowledge to identify business needs and negotiate appropriate deals.

- **Remote Education Market**

  NASSCOM estimates the potential of the remote education market at $15 bn by the year 2008. Under the remote education system, teachers in India, each students in foreign countries on various subjects with the aid of information technology. In the US alone this market is worth $3 bn annually. A few firms like Career Launcher have already made forays into the remote education market, where their teachers conduct mathematics tutorials for students in the US.

- **Pharmaceuticals and Biotechnology**

  India is the largest exporter of antibiotics to the US. Sixty manufacturing facilities of Indian drug makers have been approved by the Food and Drug Administration (FDA)—the highest outside the US. With its highly educated talent and low-cost of operations the Indian Pharmaceutical sector is set to provide generic drugs to the world at affordable prices.

  The Indian pharmaceutical challenge, however, will not be restricted to low-value generics. High-value R&D skills are also being developed in right earnest. The flow of venture capital into this segment, and successes achieved by a few companies is proof enough that this industry has realized the importance of high-end R&D for long-term survival.

  Ranbaxy, for instance, sold its novel, once-a-day antibiotic drugs delivery technology to German drugs giant, Bayer, for $65 mn. Indian pharmaceutical companies both big and small are making their presence felt in cutting-edge fields such as recombinant DNA vaccines and R&D in stem cells. In 1990s, Shanta Biotechnics had stunned the world scientific community with its recombinant DNA-based vaccine—the first of its kind from a developing country. Another firm, Bharat Biotech, is developing third generation hepatitis B vaccines in collaboration with the Indian Institute of Science.

- **Health Tourism**

  A few estimates state that Indian KPO services in healthcare services will bring revenues to the tune of $5 bn by 2008. This is hardly surprising. Indian medical colleges and physicians are attaining prominence world over.

In 2003, for the first time ever, surgeons from Chennai's Apollo Hospitals simultaneously performed two complex procedures using the "latest generation sirolimus-eluting stent." This procedure was viewed live by 2000 interventional cardiology professionals who had gathered from all over the world at Europe's EURO PCR conference. According to United Press International, Indian hospitals already treat 150,000 patients every year. This number is only going to increase in future. It is not just cost savings (between 200% to 800% in some cases) but also availability of the best doctors in the world that is driving such a wave.

Indian hospitals have identified cardiology, oncology, minimum invasive surgery and joint replacement as priority areas to be outsourced.

Outsourcing healthcare services is also becoming a high priority area for Indian pharmaceutical companies. The hospital set up by Wockhart(s1), for instance, has treated patients insured by US private health insurers—Blue Cross and Blue Shield. It is also in talks with Britain's National Health Service to outsource treatment of British patients to India.

Pharmaceutical giant Ranbaxy too has plans of building up a network of pathology labs across India, Middle East, and Asia—all networked with Indian hospitals, at a estimated cost of $200 mn.

The Figures 4 and 5, and Table 1 would help one understand the importance of the Business Process Outsourcing (BPO)/Knowledge Process Outsourcing (KPO)

Figure 4: Components of the KPO Market in 2003-2004

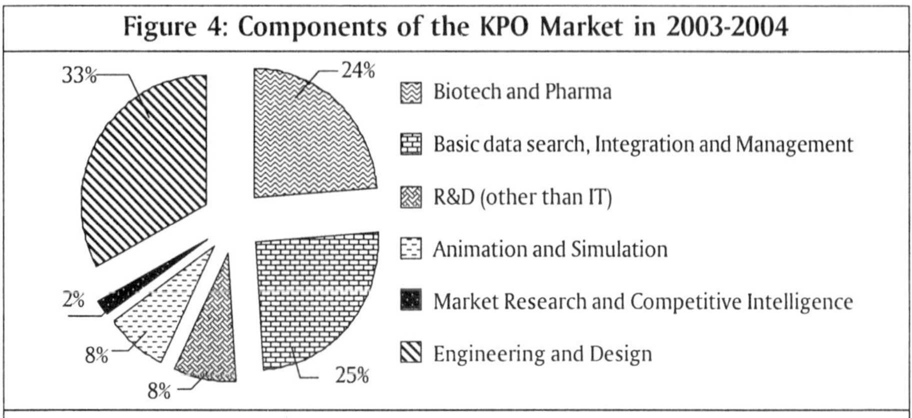

Sources: Nasscom Strategic Review 2005 & Evalueserve Business India, August 29 to September 11, 2005.

Figure 5: Components of the KPO Market in 2010-11

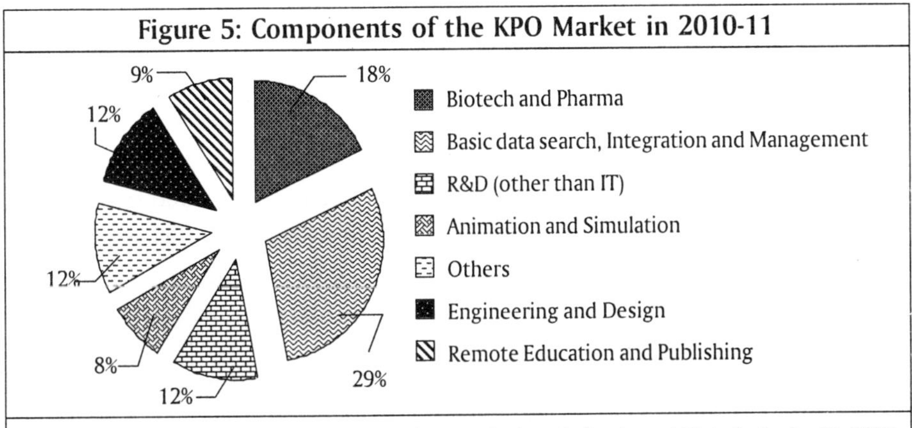

Sources: Nasscom Strategic Review 2005 & Evalueserve Business India, August 29 to September 11, 2005.

Table 1: Number of US Jobs Moving Offshore

Job Category	2000	2005	2010	2015
Management	-	27,477	117,835	288,281
Business	10,787	61,252	161,722	348,028
Computer	27,171	108,991	276,954	472,632
Architecture	3,498	32,302	83,237	184,347
Life Sciences	-	3,677	14,478	36,770
Legal	1,793	14,220	34,673	74,642
Art, design	818	5,576	13,846	29,639
Sales	4,619	29,064	97,321	226,564
Office	53,987	295,034	791,034	1,659,310
Total	102,674	587,592	1,591,101	3,320,213

Source: US Department of Labor and Forrester Research, Inc. All numbers are rounded.
The Rising Elephant ... by Ashutosh Sheshabalaya.

market in the years to come. In the year 2003-04, the size of the global KPO market was estimated to be $1.20 bn. The share of India in this was about $0.67 bn. However, by the year 2010-11, the global KPO market is likely to grow to $17 bn, with India accounting for 71 % of the total KPO business — a staggering $12 bn share.

The Challenges Ahead

Outsourcing in India has largely been a private sector activity. The lack of government intervention to some extent has been the secret of outsourcing success in the country. However, moving forward, the investment made in state-of-the-art outsourcing centers needs to be matched by public investment in infrastructure. Airports, roads and utilities are necessary to enable people to work more efficiently and live comfortably in outsourcing locations. Both the government and the industry need to work together if outsourcing is to remain India's growth engine.

Another aspect to be ensured is that the Indian education system produces people who are suitable to be employed by multinational corporations. Merely adding graduates and postgraduates to the workforce without ensuring that this segment of the population is competent enough to be absorbed in industry would lead to dangerous socioeconomic issues. In many outsourcing locations like Bangalore, problems such as rising wages and high attrition rates amongst BPO/KPO and IT professionals point towards constraints on supply of talent. Such a shortfall is going to increase in future. To overcome such a situation, the numerous mediocre universities in the country need to be raised to the standard of the very best—a tough and time consuming task.

Goldman and Sachs has predicted that "India has the potential to deliver the fastest growth over the next 50 years with an average rate of more than 5% a year for the entire period". It does not require in-depth analysis to infer that "outsourcing" is going to contribute significantly to such a growth in the Indian economy. However, both the private sector players and the government need to give their undivided attention to the key issues, namely:

- Human Capital Issues.
- Focus on Infrastructure.
- Higher R&D Budgets.
- Moving up the Value Chain.
- Quality Control Systems like TQM and Six Sigma.
- Thinking Global.
- Customer Relationship Management.

Tackling these issues is the real challenge before India. It is a challenge, which neither the government nor the private sector alone can overcome. The people of India—individuals, public sector undertakings, private enterprises, need to collectively work towards eliminating the deficiencies that exist. Once that happens, India without doubt, will be a global KPO hub—a driving force in the world economics. As a nation we need to have faith in our abilities. As Mahatma Gandhi has said: "Men often become what they believe themselves to be. If I believe I cannot do something, it makes me incapable of doing it. But when I believe I can, then I acquire the ability to do it even if I didn't have it in the beginning."

(Priya Angle, CFA, PGDBA, Faculty Member, The Icfai Business School, Pune. She can be reached at priyaangle@ibsindia.org).

9

Business Process Outsourcing
Innovation and Growth Strategies

P Sivarajadhanavel

Global competition is the most important issue facing top decision makers in some of the world's largest companies today and companies today are focusing their resources on their core competencies as business strategies to compete profitably in a global market. There are three different BPO business models—transactional, niche, and comprehensive models, as strategies of business success. Now the companies have started concentrating on product innovation which helps their clients to reduce their product introduction cost by 30 to 50 percent. It also facilitates flexibility product pricing and designing the product to fully exploit the market capabilities and technology innovation. Today outsourcing industry is moving towards a high level of specialization with great competition from low-end process to high-end process jobs like knowledge process and analytical process outsourcing jobs. Outsourcing industry is focusing on creating high revenue growth opportunities through its services in research and development (R&D) and other areas like legal process, research, product innovation, equity research, consulting and market research.

Today Business Process Outsourcing (BPO) function happens worldwide with the objective of reducing the operational cost of the product and to bring more product innovation and efficiency in the service offerings to the customers through expertise service. Globally outsourcing was earlier dominated by big players like IBM, CSC, EDS, Accenture and ACS. Now the trend has changed, as more outsourcing companies have started their operations with more competitive offerings than the major outsourcing firms could offer to their clients. With more than $100 billion contracts to be renewed in the next two years globally by the major outsourcing firms, they fear that a major share of the outsourcing contract will shift towards other outsourcing services. The outsourcing service providers mainly affected will be IBM and EDS, as both are estimated to share a contract size of $50 billion in the outsourcing industry. New outsourcing service providers are concentrating on their core competencies rather than on other areas, and this is what the outsourcing companies too are expecting from the service offers. Moreover, products and services offered by them are more innovative and flexible to suit the needs of the outsourcing clients.

In the multiple outsourcing landscape, companies have started to outsource their activities to more than one client for different functional activities. This gives the outsourcing companies the great opportunity of getting benefits from different service providers. For example, ABN Amro Bank planned its outsourcing deals with five major offshore outsourcing companies of different service outsourcing like IT infrastructure with IBM, application support service with Infosys, Patni and TCS and application development with Accenture. This could provide a greater advantage to ABN Amro in getting services from specialized service providers. The prospect of Indian outsourcing is challenged by the growing competition from global players. This could have a major impact on the current growth trend of the Indian BPO industry, but the global delivery capabilities with multiple features will be a competitive advantage for Indian BPOs in the global market. The next move by a global BPO industry in creating competitive advantage over rival firms will be product innovation like innovative delivery business models, creative designing of their work flow models by reducing the project run time and cost of service marginally over the competitors, and flexible services to suit the clients base.

Core Competencies of Outsourcing

Business outsourcing is not a new practice; it has become the routine strategy of a company to outsource the services to get them done better than they can do on its own. The primary focus of the industry is to cut down the cost and to improve the performance of the output quality and profitability considerably. The business strategy of the company is to concentrate on its core activities and to outsource the remaining activities to the low cost third party service providers.

The competent strategies are success factors for each business organisation as they make a difference in the service offered to their business clients. Normally BPO companies frame their business models to suit the clients' demand so that they make their business successful. Each BPO company has got its strength in a particular area like product development, customer service, documentation, consulting and knowledge process, value creation, product promotion, technical service, and support service. The companies work on the domain space in which they have an advantage over their competitors. Today business has become more riskier especially in the outsourcing industry. Companies look for vendors who can provide quality services at low cost i.e., cost and quality competence have become essential factors in the outsourcing industry. The American industries look for competent vendors from outside countries who can increase the financial performance of their business through their competent workforce.

Organizations interested in outsourcing have to concentrate on the core activity of their business functions and outsource other activities like data management, documentation, processing, telemarketing and HR services to third party service providers who are competent in outsourcing activities. Even today the pharmaceutical companies depend on third parties' outsourcing service for 40 to 60% of their R&D activities. Through outsourcing, companies get more successful new drug products at cheaper rates, which could be more competitive in the market. But in most of the outsourcing projects, spread of advanced processing technology provides full speed and cost advantage to the contract service providers. The technical ladder of any offshore or onshore activities is significant in intellectual outsourcing activities such as knowledge processing and analytical processing. With the broad technical advantage of the outsourcing company and its technical expertise, companies have a greater global competitive advantage in providing innovative products and services to suit the clients' business needs. This enables them to withstand global competition.

It is also important for the companies to stay focused on their objectives and goals. They have to carefully choose a strategy that supports the unique competitive strength of the resources available to them. In order to protect the core competencies, companies have to invest in identifying their competitive strengths. In the process of enhancing their competencies, companies need to shift their outsourcing projects towards becoming more strategic rather than go by the operation momentum of the business. For the growth of the business, companies need to follow the strategic business models, which would go through their core competencies. Strong company growth can be achieved when companies focus on their strength instead of the activities, which gain short term business growth. Also, the business strategy should be assessed frequently, as this helps to serve the clients' needs better than competitors Table 1 explains some of the core

Table 1: Core Competency/Outsourcing Decision Example

	Growth requirements	Company's position	Require ownership/ control?	Supply options available?	Out sourcing benefits	Decision
Strong sales force	❖	■	Yes	Yes	❍	Develop existing
Well recognized brand	■	❖	Yes	No	❍	Leverage/ protect
Innovative technology	❖	❖	No	No	❖	Leverage/ protect
Low cost manufacturing	❍	■	No	No	❍	Outsource
Distribution channel	■	❍	No	Yes	❍	Keep in-house
Reputation for quality	❖	❍	Yes	No	■	Develop new
IT operations	■	❍	No	Yes	❖	Outsource

■ Strong ❖ Medium ❍ Weak

Source: www.deloitte.com, Core Competencies and Strategic Outsourcing Achieving Competitive Advantage.

competencies and outsourcing decision requirements like sales force, brand, manufacturing cost, distribution channel and quality.

Business Models

Outsourcing is the business strategy of the company to get things done in the best manner to achieve high quality. Today the outsourcing service providers follows the best business models in serving the clients' activities. There are many models which could accelerate successful outsourcing, but the three popular models of outsourcing, are transactional, niche and comprehensive business models, which are considered the best among the BPOs. Table 2 on business models of outsourcing details the advantages of the BPO business models in serving the clients' business.

Table 2: Business Process Outsourcing (BPO) Business Models

BPO Business Model	Transactional	Niche	Comprehensive
Number of processes	Transactions only, typically for 1 process	2-4 processes	10+ processes in a function; sometimes more than one function
Invest in client assets?	No, migrate everything to their system	Yes – but modest dollars and personnel take-on	Yes – significant dollars and employee take-on
Hire client's people?	No	Yes – but usually & lt; 50	Yes, usually & gt; 100s and often in the 1000s
Locations	Work at provider's location; very low headcount at the client site – typically account managers and sales people	Mixed, people at both client and provider locations	Mixed, people at both client and provider locations
Geographic spread	Multi-country	Domestic (& gt; 80% of revenue) with some international (typically Europe)	Global
Contract duration	1-2 years	3-5 years	7-10 years
Contract value per year	$1-5 million a year	$5-10 million a year	$50-$100 million a year

Contd...

Contd...			
Business model	Offload transactions from client, use provider's software	Make processes more efficient – reduce costs, raise service levels	Make functions more effective, introduce best practices
Accountability	For the transaction processing	For process outcomes	For cost savings for the entire function plus business outcome
Risk-holder	90% of the risk is still on the client, 10% provider	50% client, 50% provider	30% client, 70% provider
Metrics	Per transaction	Based on outcome	Based on outcome
Source: Business Process Outsourcing (BPO) Business Models - www.xicom.biz			

Typical examples of the outsourcing process include payroll, credit card processing, billing, bills payable and receivable and workforce management, all of which require more than one function. All these functions are handled under the different business heads of the investment clients' business. Business models are designed based on the following aspects of the business process—investment clients, locations, project time, project value, accountability and risk of the business. Generally, all business models are carried out to reduce the transaction cost of the business and to increase the efficiency of the offshore/onshore business process.

A transaction service provider handles a single transaction process of the outsourcing activities, because outsourcing with its too many processes complicates the transaction process, which will affect its productivity. For example, in the payroll process, they only cut the checks and they do not take over all functions of the department. The contracts are for one or two year period and the contract value of these projects is low. Transaction processes have many advantages, but the more fragmented the process outsourced, the greater is the risk associated with the client's business. But 90 percent of the risk is within the client's place and the service provider has minimum effect on the client's project.

The second business model of outsourcing is the Niche Model, which provides services for many processes focusing on employment and workforce management. Niche service providers carry the project, which can have a contract period of three to five years with a contract value of \$5-10 million. The business risk is shared by clients and the service provider equally, but the only difference is that the clients invest the capital, whereas the service provider only hires the human capital require for the process. The service provider is responsible for the outcome of the business.

The comprehensive business model service provider handles all the transactional and administrative process functions of HR and finance departments, which amount to nearly 22 processes in HR and 33 processes in finance[1]. The projects under this model are global projects, which are carried out over a period of 7-10 years and the project contracts are valued at over $100 million a year. They carry on the projects at their own risk by buying the clients' assets. 70 percent of the project risk is carried by the service providers. Comprehensive business models have been there in BPOs for less than two-three years. It has to go a long way to prove its success.

Some of the other common BPO business models include delivery models, (Example: CRISIL subsidiary Irvena) associate models, and project based delivery models. The associate model used in serving an investment bank client is similar to onshore associates. Usually for this project teams are formed as associate groups which work on building financial models in maintaining the stock portfolio of the investment banks. In the project based models, a research executive works on the research projects, and helps to provide valuable data for the business product in a short period of time.

Product Innovations in BPO

The BPO industry has been growing rapidly, especially in terms of innovating new ideas, which reduce cost and improve the quality of service through new techniques. Any business has to come up with new product innovations to be successful. But BPOs have several products, which provide their business clients the maximum benefits. The key success of all BPO services is cost reduction and rapid process change for the business requirements. Generally, outsourcing is a bundle of techniques, transformation skills and operational skills, which provide maximum pivotal advantage for the service provider over their competitors. The frontline improvement in technology and continuous technological transformation is the main factor contributing to new products.

BPOs operating for financial products have been continuously updating their technology as the process has automated with the advanced techniques of financial

---

1 Business Process Outsourcing (BPO) Business Models-*www.xicom.biz*

data processing, and analysing and modeling techniques for routine data processing projects as these services require repetitive data processing. Specifically the BPO models adopted for the process of mutual funds and invest banking projects, mortgage processing and insurance claim processing require great efficiency and standardization. But the insurance claim processing in outsourcing still lacks in efficiency. But research and development (R&D) requires a high level of product innovation, which is a major trigger for outsourcing. The level of product innovation in R&D, Knowledge Process Outsourcing (KPO) and Analytical Process outsourcing (APO) needs more of product innovation.

The demand for outsourcing is increasing with growing number of American companies outsourcing their manufacturing requirements to low cost locations like India, China and Philippines to increase the profit ratio of their business. Initially outsourcing started in the manufacturing sector and has now spread to R&D services, where the companies outsource product innovations to third party service providers who get it done at a low cost. With the maturity of the industry, customers look for more innovative products from service providers which include product differentiation from their competitors, low costs for their product with quality, and more service facilities for their products. Moreover, product design has been given more importance by the original equipment manufacturers.

Capital One Financial Corporation used innovations for marketing its consumer products like credit cards. It had developed a portfolio of solutions, which focus on the consumer needs. It had formed a small group of serving teams to understand the needs of the consumers and it created innovations to market its financial products successfully and gain more business, achieving 20 percent growth for five consecutive years. It followed a Customer Service Marketing (CSM) system, which adopted technologies for marketing its products to the right customers. Information technology had become the lifeblood of Capital One. "Technology and business are one and the same," said Donehey, Capital One. The CSM technology gives customer data profiles and their relationship with the banks. This helps to identify customers' needs from the existing data when they make calls to the call centers. When the customer informs loss of his credit card the CSM system automatically informs the representative card seller and registration service. Through this system Capital One serves 14.9 million card users through

Figure: The Offshore Innovation Network

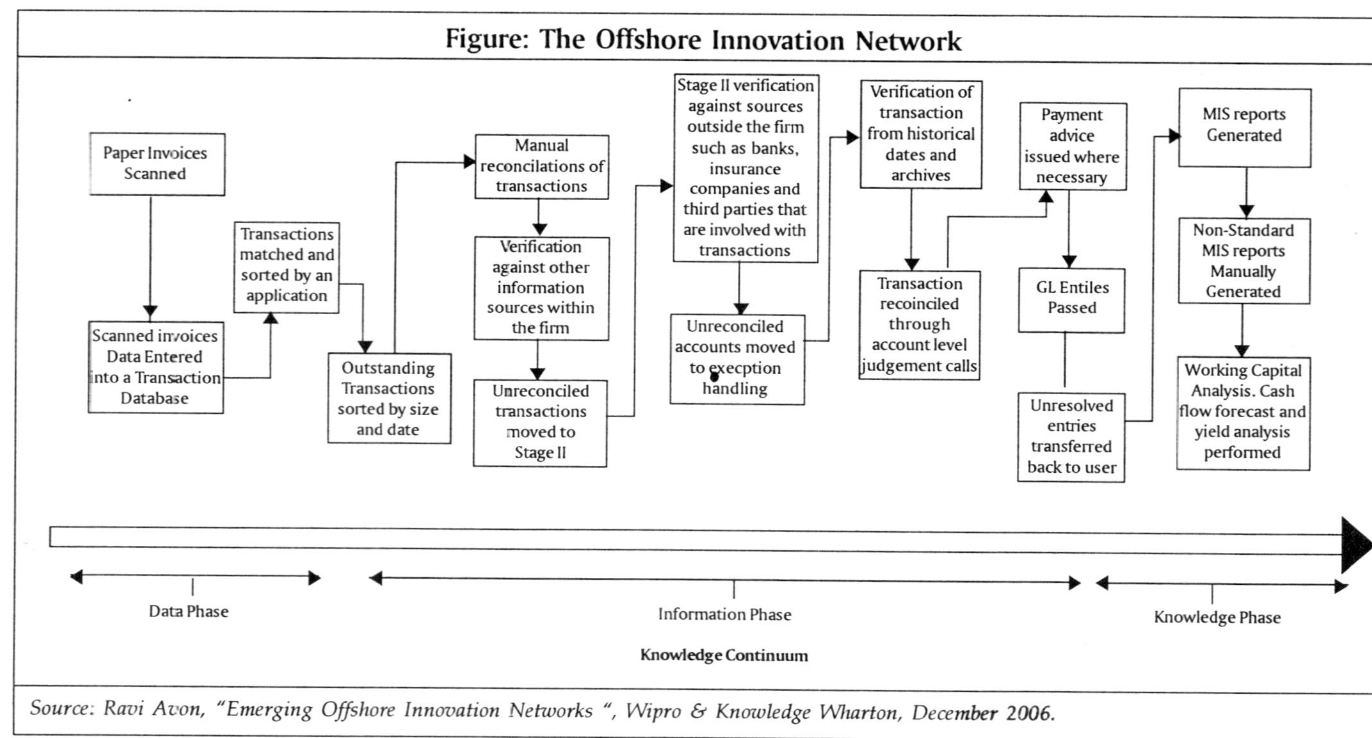

Source: Ravi Avon, "Emerging Offshore Innovation Networks", Wipro & Knowledge Wharton, December 2006.

2,200 representatives. The advantage of the system is cheaper and faster service of clients.

The outsourcing industry is dominated by Indian companies. The Indian BPO has been more innovative in serving onshore and offshore clients with the increasing growth of IT technologies. NASSCOM has introduced product innovation awards to promote Indian BPOs, which has drawn a good response from companies. Product innovation can happen in on shore or offshore outsourcing. For example, in the offshore outsourcing of network processing, a customer's reconciliation statement requires a different transaction process. Starting from the customer database sorting to MIS report generation for customer accounts in the reconciliation process different processes have been followed. (Refer Figure)

Low-End to High-End Outsourcing

BPO companies have started moving from low-end jobs towards high-end outsourcing jobs. Companies in India have started their high-end BPO operations mainly in Knowledge Process Outsourcing (KPO) and analytical processing. This provides more opportunities for American investment bankers to diversify their growth into consulting and financial portfolio operations. The economic boom has brought more R&D jobs to countries like India and China in huge volume. Indian companies now serve the top investment bankers in the analytical process and data modeling activities in offshore and onshore outsourcing. According to Booz Allen Hamilton R&D, spending in India has grown to 17 percent in 2006 compared to 5.2 percent and 2.3 percent in US and Europe respectively. Indian companies like Wipro, TCS, and Infosys have been successfully doing consulting work for the Western nations.

Manufacturing and pharma industries outsource high-end jobs to the third party service providers in the areas of product design, innovations, and research activities as they realize the importance of production innovation to sustain in the global market. Indian automotive companies like Bajaj Auto, TVS Motors, and Force Motors spend 2 percent of their sales revenue for the R&D process. Through outsourcing their high-end jobs to expertise, they are successful in releasing new products to match the demand in the market. With the growth of information technology in India, the high-end outscurcing jobs are done successfully, as global companies are turning towards Indian companies for high-end research. The worldwide market for Knowledge Process Outsourcing (KPO) is estimated to grow at the rate of 46 percent and it is estimated to touch US$17 billion by 2010. Currently India holds 60 to 70 percent of the market share in the knowledge industry. Other upcoming areas in the high-end jobs are equity research and legal process. As the mutual fund industry is booming it is an added advantage to the KPO industry involving portfolio and equity research activities.

Future Growth Opportunities

The market for the outsourcing industry is growing continuously. In the future outsourcing activities will be more competitive as more regions getting involved in the business will bring more competitiveness. Actually this would bring down the market share of the Indian companies and also other developed countries' shares. The countries in Africa are now successfully entering the BPO business with low-end jobs like billing, documentation and process jobs. But the high-end jobs like consulting research and development, report generation, industrial and company analysis are handled by the mature companies in the developed nations of the BPO services. Revenue growth from outsourcing is expected to grow constantly as more players are getting involved. Legal Process Outsourcing (LPO) requires more expertise in handling. Outsourcing the legal activities is more risk prone but outsourcing to countries like India costs 80 percent less than outsourcing in US and UK firms. US alone has a market potential of $25 billion. Indian LPOs can target more US based projects. This would fetch revenue of $1.5 to $2 billion for the Indian industry and the industry would require more than 33,000 lawyers to achieve this growth. Currently India holds 3-4 percent and this is expected to grow to 6-7 percent by 2010. Knowledge Process Outsourcing (KPO) is the future of the outsourcing business as the industry is expected to have an annual growth rate of 36 percent till 2010. India continues to be a leader in knowledge outsourcing.

(P Sivarajadhanavel is a Faculty Associate at Icfai Business School Research Center, Chennai. He can be reached at sivaraj_mba@yahoo.com).

References

1. "More Competition, Selective Outsourcing—Shift in Trend to Impact Big Six Dominance: TPI," *Business Line,* Feb 15, 2006.

2. Robert Weisman, February 11, 2007, "Outsourcing Expands to Cover all but the Core", *www.boston.com*
3. Robert C Baldwin, CMRP, Editor, "How Core Is Your Competency?" *Maintenance Technology magazine.*
4. "Secret of Organizational Success—Business Process Outsourcing", 2004-07-01.
5. Penton Media, "Bundled Outsourcing: Proceed with Caution".
6. Tony Hallett, 28 April 2005, "Outsourcing your core competencies", *CNET Networks, Inc.*
7. "BPO: Driving Major Shift in Business Module," *The Economic Times General Management Review.*
8. NASSCOM showcases product model innovations for Innovation Awards 2006, *www.prdomain.com*
9. Pete Engardio and Bruce Einhorn, March 21, 2005, "Outsourcing Innovation First came Manufacturing. Now companies are farming out R&D to cut costs and get new products to market faster. Are they going too far?", *www.businessweek.com*
10. Zinnov, "Outsourcing: Product Innovation from India".
11. *Business Wire*, April 5, 2005, "Outsourcing and Product Innovation Offer Growth Opportunities in North American Lighting Controls Market", *www.findarticles.com*
12. Ravi Aron, "Emerging Offshore Innovation Networks", *Wipro & Knowledge Wharton,* December 2006.
13. *www.moneycontrol.com*
14. *www.sethassociates.com*
15. *www.cio.com*
16. *www.irevna.com*

10

Emerging Outsourcing Destinations

Sandeep Varma

Today many new, expanding outsourcing destinations took root beyond India as a result of the rise in labor costs and employee turnover rates in India. Companies had started transferring outsourcing assignments to other parts of the globe like Mexico, Vietnam and Chile. Though India remains to be the most preferred IT outsourcing destination, with $17.7 billion in software and IT services exports in 2005, compared to $3.6 billion for China and $1 billion for Russia, Indian outsourcing industry is still growing at a faster pace compared to other outsourcing destinations. Many new outsourcing destinations have come beyond India as a result of rise in the labor costs and employee turnover rates in India. Companies have started sending outsourcing assignments to other parts of the globe. The other major emerging destinations in the globe like China, Vietnam, Mexico, Philippines, Brazil, and Chile's entry into BPO business with fast growing developments in the infrastructure and improved human resources are discussed. But moving of outsourcing into developing countries like Vietnam or China can also pose big risks, such as insurmountable language and cultural differences, geopolitical instability, and the risk of stolen intellectual property.

In 2005, India was an IT outsourcing powerhouse, with $17.7 billion revenue in software and IT services exports, compared to $3.6 billion in China and $1 billion in Russia[1]. India's outsourcing industry was growing at a faster pace than that of Russia and other outsourcing centers. But as labor costs and turnover rates began rising in India, companies started looking out for cheap labor. As a result, many new outsourcing destinations emerged and started growing at a fast pace. The ever increasing labor cost in India resulted in the emergence of many new destinations for outsourcing. "Ninety percent of all outsourcing deals in the market today have been structured around cost improvement only[2]," opined Linda Cohen, Vice-President, Gartner.

Many companies including Accenture, EDS, IBM Global Services, and Genpact had invested in building global networks, comprising operations in various cities aimed at giving customers a mix of worker skills and labor costs. "Today we are about 35% in high-cost locations, such as the US and Britain; 20% in medium-cost locations like Spain, Ireland, and Canada; and about 45% in low-cost locations like the Philippines, India, China, and Eastern Europe[3]," said Jimmy Harris, global Managing Director, Accenture. It remained to be seen whether India could maintain the competitive advantage over others in the field of business outsourcing.

Emerging Outsourcing Locations

Many new, expanding outsourcing destinations took root beyond India (Exhibits I&II) as a result of the rise in labor costs and employee turnover rates in India. Companies had started transferring outsourcing assignments to other parts of the globe like Mexico, Vietnam and Chile.

China, Dalian

Dalian, a seaport in north east China, was also turning out to be an ideal center for outsourcing. Geography and history were both to Dalian's advantage. It was close to Korea and Japan, and as it was occupied by Japan in the first half of the 20th century, a good number of the labor force spoke Japanese. Having specialized in Application Development, Dalian had high availability of workers proficient in medium-level IT activities. Its proximity to Japan, with workers fluency in the language, made Dalian a strong outsourcing destination for Japanese companies. There were an estimated 100,000 Japanese-speaking people in Dalian and Tokyo was just a three-hour flight away. "Most Japanese feel very welcome in Dalian[4]," said Takashi Ota, a Tokyo-based Senior Manager at NEC Soft Ltd. The major companies who had set up centers there were Genpact, Accenture and IBM Global Services.

Another attraction in Dalian was that labor costs there were lower than in Japan. This ensured Dalian's becoming a center for Application Development for Japanese companies. Some of the US firms also outsourced selected technical work to the port city. General Electric and Nissan outsourced work to Genpact's operations in Dalian. Genpact was the first outsourcing firm to be located in the city in June, 2000. Accenture and IBM Global Services also set up operations there. Some of the Japanese multinationals too had outsourced their technology development functions to set up back-office operations in Dalian. Hitachi, Matsushita, NEC NTT Data, and Sony had call centers or software development operations in Dalian. Dell, GE Capital, and IBM had set up customer-support offices in the city to serve their Japanese operations, while Accenture, Bearing Point, and Hewlett-Packard were providing software to Japanese telecommunication and industrial companies. Japanese outsourcing to Dalian reached $375 million in 2004, almost double the level of 2002. "Dalian is becoming to Japan what Bangalore is to the US[5]," said Chen Ying Sheng, Managing Director of Bearing Point, China Global Development Center. Dalian had roughly 26,000 experienced software engineers, 22 universities and technical institutes. "Dalian has really geared itself up to produce the kind of people with the right skills[6]," said Luke J Yang, practice leader, A T Kearney, Greater China in Shanghai. Dalian's local government offered generous incentives, including a two-year tax holiday on profits and an 80% reduction in value-added taxes. Dalian also had well developed roads and good telecommunication infrastructure.

But the port also had problems. As more multinationals set up back-office support for their Japanese operations in the region, good employees were increasingly poached by other companies. Furthermore, salaries were rising – about 25% every year for some jobs. "The labor market is very cut-throat at the moment, and many vendors complain that as soon as they train someone, someone else steals them,[7]" said Dion Wiggins, Vice President Researcher, Gartner Asia Pacific in Hong Kong. "Software engineers and programmers are easy to recruit, but it's difficult to find project managers and leaders[8]," said Zhang Limin, Chief Technology Officer, Hi-Think. Dalian's revenue from outsourcing was around $600 million in 2006 when compared to India's revenue of $17 billion.

Russia and Romania

"Just three countries, India, China, and Russia, are big enough to become IT superpowers and in terms of geography Russia has a pretty big advantage. In the long term it will be a very good (outsourcing) destination for Europe,"[9]said Dmitry Loschinin, CEO of Russia's largest software development company, Luxoft.

Russia was another major player in the world of outsourcing and was expected to pose a strong threat to India's supremacy in the BPO space matrix. Russia was fast emerging as a new destination in the IT outsourcing market. As per a study done by NeoIT, a California-based consulting firm, Russia was emerging as a strong contender in the IT outsourcing market. As of 2006, Russia was ranked the third largest IT outsourcing market behind India and China[10]. Russian IT companies specialized in high-end software and embedded software product development, which were different from the low-priced software produced by Indian companies. The study also predicted that the Russian IT off-shoring industry was likely to grow at 40-50% in 2007. St.Petersburg was an important educational hub, with a large number of institutions offering relevant courses for developing high-end programming skills. The companies there concentrated mainly on high end software R&D, and embedded software development. "The country can achieve a serious breakthrough in the area of information technology. We simply mustn't waste this chance, especially as other countries have achieved success without such a strong starting position,"[11] said Vladimir Putin, Russia's President.

Until the creation of a Ministry for IT and Communications in 2004, government policy towards the IT sector lacked central coordination. Under the leadership of President Putin, policy-makers had started giving importance to the industry. Russia had planned at least four state-funded techno-parks to be completed by 2010, located in Dubna (a scientific center near Moscow), St. Petersburg, Nizhny Novgorod, and Novosibirsk. The main idea was to create economies of scale and encourage collaboration between businesses and scientific researchers. Each park was expected to receive state funding of $80 million to

$100 million to create the necessary infrastructure. Tax and customs benefits would also be available to companies in the park. The government had also promised to promote the IT industry giving additional tax breaks and promised to simplify taxation procedures. Industry experts were happy about the new measures taken. "The key issue is that the (development) concept was prepared by business, not by the government,"[12] said Valentin Makarov, president of Russoft, the Russian Software Developers Association.

The easy availability of qualified personnel and the city's proximity to Western Europe had made Romania an attractive outsourcing location. Its labor costs were 40%-50% lower than in Western Europe. Companies in Romania specialized in Security Systems Development and software testing. Companies who had set up their operations were Genpact, Wipro, Infosys and Accenture. Primary reasons for companies to outsource to Romania were its good education system, multilingual population and the abundance of technical talent available there. It was expected that if Romania was admitted to the European Union, that would make it even more helpful for companies from Western Europe to do business there. "We're going to where the most cost-effective talent is in the world, but it has to be feasible. It can't be where there are economic, time zones, or language barriers"[13] said Bob Gett, CEO, Optaros[14]. Prague's good infrastructure and proximity to Western Europe made it a good place for companies that wanted easy access to outsourcing providers mainly into IT systems management services.

Mexico and Latin America

For US companies that wanted to outsource, Latin America was an attractive option because of proximity and similar time zones. Infrastructure was also strong in these countries. Mexico, Brazil and Chile were the emerging destinations for offshoring in Latin America. Mexico and Brazil had the critical mass, big clients, and enough educated people. Inauguration of the North American Free Trade Agreement in 1994 made companies on both sides of the US-Mexico border more aware of the benefits of doing business with each other. They coined the term "NearShore", highlighting the proximity of Latin countries to US. "The US was right next door, but we had to offer a differentiated product in order to get their business, we were the biggest in Mexico, but we were very small in comparison to India. If we hadn't come up with something to set us apart, we wouldn't have gone anywhere"[15] said Blanca Treviño, CEO, Softtek, a Mexican software development company.

Mexico had higher labor costs when compared to India but it gained because of its proximity to the US, and the same time zone. Near-shoring in Mexico cost about the same as off-shoring to India. As per industry experts up to 95% of work could be performed off-site in Mexico, compared to just 60% to 65% for clients working with Indian service providers. GE outsourced 90% of its IT work to India, and just 6% to Mexico but as cost of labor was rising in India, Mexico was becoming a worthwhile substitute. "If things continue as they are, India eventually will be charging the same unit cost as Mexico. That's why Indian companies have been hustling to find ways to perform a higher percentage of the work off-site in India,"[16] said Steve Morrison, GE's London-based head of Global IT outsourcing.

Another advantage Mexico had over India was of US legislative restrictions. Certain kinds of projects involving sensitive aviation and energy technology were more likely to be outsourced to Mexico than to India, as India was a nuclear power nation. The availability of skilled labor also made the Mexican capital a good place for software projects that required extensive collaboration with US-based teams. They mainly concentrated on Custom Application Development.

The companies in Brazil had been providing IT outsourcing services to other Brazilian companies for years and as a result of this, there was a pool of proficient labor in Sao Paulo. They mainly concentrated on support and maintenance for enterprise resource-planning systems or software for running a business. Brazil had mature software and the IT industry was attracting companies by highlighting modern infrastructure like airports and highways.

Another major location in South America was Argentina. Argentina had one of the best-educated workforces in Latin America. It was also promoting software development centers, mainly specialized in Open-source Technologies. As a result of the devaluation of the peso in 2002, IT workers were forced to use open-source, or freely available software. Major companies that started operation were Accenture, EDS and Stefanini IT Solutions[17]. "Economies in acute crisis have one major advantage: You can start a new company with a smaller investment and find highly skilled and motivated people very easily,"[18] said Carlos Pallotti, Managing Director for Latin America, DataStream Systems[19] and President of Argentina's

Association of Information Technology Companies. The software industry promotion law, introduced in 2004, gave companies big tax breaks. As a result of this, companies such as Walt Disney, Microsoft, Peugeot, and Repsol had come for Website design and software development. In addition to these companies, Hewlett-Packard, Oracle, Cisco, IBM, America Online, and PalmOne had set up their regional back-office and customer-service operations in Argentina. "The Argentine authorities understand that technology is an engine of growth, which generates competitiveness in the global marketplace,"[20] said Esteban Galuzzi Intel's General Manager for the Southern Cone region.

Santiago, Chile, had the main advantage of educated, IT-proficient workers. The main areas that were being outsourced to Santiago were systems management and high-end software development. Factors that helped Chile emerge as a hub for outsourcing were its economic and political stability and its state-of-the-art telecom infrastructure. Its network of free trade agreements with a number of countries, from the US to China, was an added advantage. Multinationals that had set up in-house outsourcing centers for software development, back-office services, and call centers include Citigroup, Unilever, Eastman Kodak, and Delta Air Lines. The Central American country, Costa Rica was best known for the software development industry, which started with the arrival of Intel, which built a chip-testing facility in San Jose. A number of software development companies were providing services mainly in the financial sector. "International companies can't afford to do all their outsourcing in India. There's a big time difference with the US, it's closer to the trouble spots in the Middle East, and India is a nuclear power,"[21] said Ben Schneider, president of Consulting Outsourcing Management.

One of the fastest growing destinations for outsourcing in Central America was Nicaragua. Various measures had been taken to boost up the outsourcing industry there. The government invested $3 million to build a 500-workstation call center in downtown Managua, the capital. There were training programs arranged to improve the English skills of people. Nicaragua having signed the Central American Free Trade Agreement, had the advantage of free trade agreement with US. While searching for outsourcing clients, the agreement could help. "American companies that want to sign an outsourcing contract prefer to sign it with companies whose countries have a free trade agreement with the US. It's not just a matter of tariffs, but of policies on intellectual property protection and labor rules,"[22] said Ben Schneider.

South East Asia

Emerging outsourcing destinations in the South East Asian region are the Philippines, Ho Chi Minh City and Vietnam (Exhibit III). The Philippines was providing excellent English language skills that played a key role in Business Process Outsourcing. In the coming years, Philippines might become a strong competitor for India in voice-based processes. They were also developing expertise in financial and accounting skills. Indian IT and BPO units began setting up operations in the Philippines mainly due to two reasons – clients wanted a second English-speaking location and attrition/shortage of staff in India started affecting the projects undertaken. Philippines' cultural affinity with the US was another big advantage.

Vietnam was mainly into low- to medium-level applications maintenance and technology support. Its main attractions were cheap labor, costing even less than in India, and workers adept at performing labor-intensive IT support services. Many companies had planned to start their operations in Vietnam. More and more Vietnamese companies started gaining momentum in outsourcing. But the obstacle it faced was the absence of fiber-optic broadband network as a result of which the internet speed was very slow. Another disadvantage was the lack of fluent English speaking people. "One disadvantage of being here is that some people think we work in rice paddies and little grass huts,"[23] said Charles Speyer, Chief Operating Officer, Glass Egg.

Challenges for Indian BPO Industry

> *"India dominates now and will continue to do so in the future because of the sheer scale of skills in the country at low costs. The only exception is China which has become very visible in this space."*[24]
>
> – Sujay Chohan, Vice President and Research Director, Gartner.

India's outsourcing industries had to overcome major challenges to continue their growth and sustain their advantage over other emerging outsourcing destinations. The first major challenge was that the demand growth might slow down.

"Increasingly there is a realization that changing business processes to accommodate large offshore workforces is a difficult, time-consuming task and often produces lower than expected savings,"[25] said Noshir Kaka, principal of McKinsey. The Unions and political opposition in US towards outsourcing had raised concerns about the future (Exhibit IV). Also problems about service quality and security were issues to be tackled.

It was predicted that in the current decade India would face a shortage of qualified workforce. As per the latest NASSCOM-McKinsey study on India's Information Technology and Business Process Outsourcing "India would need a 2.3 million strong IT and BPO workforce by 2010 to maintain its current market share, and a potential shortfall of nearly 0.5 million qualified employees in supply projection was expected." Another area where India was lacking was the absence of large numbers of workers who were fluent in French, German, Japanese and Spanish. This resulted in China and Eastern Europe becoming attractive offshoring destinations for Japanese and Western European companies.

High turnover rates and rapid growth of Indian outsourcing sector have increased the risk of security violations and fraud. Several cases of fraud were reported in India resulting in creation of NASSCOM, the leading industry association, initiating more rigorous background checks for new employees. Saturation, congestion and inflation in the large cities has forced the Indian market to go to tier-three cities including Ahmedabad, Kolkata and Jaipur, which offer lower costs and less competition for resources. Industry experts said that in order to maintain its advantage, India had to improve its infrastructure. Even though this was improving, it was not keeping pace with the rapid growth of the industry. As per Sujay Chohan another way of facing the competition was to emerge as true global players. "Indian outsourcing companies should also think about expanding their brand globally by setting up delivery centers outside of India,"[26] said Sujay. Indian companies, which have opened offices in foreign countries were: Progeon at Czech Republic, ICICI OneSource at Argentina and TCS at different locations like Uruguay, Brazil, Chile, Hungary, China, Australia and Japan.

Ashank Desai, chairman of Mumbai-based Mastek, was of the opinion that one way for Indian companies to maintain their competitive advantage was to upgrade their services by offering more sophisticated back office functions in addition to the basic call center services. "At Mastek we're already looking into merging BPO and IT services so that our clients get double the advantage. We can reconfigure IT used for processing insurance claims to make it more efficient and then process these claims more efficiently for our customers,"[27] said Desai. "Indian vendors depend too much on the US market. India has to make inroads into non-English speaking markets as well, similar to what Ireland has done to successfully service the European market,"[28] said Desai.

Road Ahead

"If you don't have experience and don't do it well, it can negate savings."[29]

Barry Rubenstein, Program Manager
of application outsourcing and offshore services at IDC.

It was estimated that the worldwide offshore BPO market would grow to about $24 billion by 2007 of which India's share would be about $13.8 billion[30]. Some of the new areas in outsourcing were E-governance, Retail Services Outsourcing, Pharmaceutical Research, Financial Services and Healthcare. Along with these new areas in outsourcing there was also a shift in the reasons for outsourcing to India. Cost reduction was no longer the sole motivation. Indian outsourcing companies were concentrating more on value addition with an improvement in productivity and quality.

Moving IT operations into developing countries like Vietnam or China could pose big risks, such as language and cultural differences, geopolitical instability, and the risk of stolen intellectual property (Exhibits V and VI). In 2007, both Russia and the Philippines were expected to grow as outsourcing locations. An overall growth of 25-30% was expected. More and more offshore and nearshore locations were expected to emerge. Mergers and acquisitions of the existing outsourcing companies were also expected to scale up capabilities. Europe was also emerging as a major center for outsourcing. European language speaking countries like Hungary, Czech Republic, Russia, Poland, Bulgaria and Romania were supporting the trend of 'nearshore.' "You keep following the money, but how often are you going to move people around?"[31] said Linda Cohen, Vice President of sourcing research at consulting firm Gartner.

After the great success of Business Process Outsourcing (BPO) in India, Knowledge Process Outsourcing (KPO) and Legal Process Outsourcing (LPO) were coming up. BPO success in India had encouraged companies to outsource their high-tech knowledge based jobs. KPO industry provided domain based processes and business expertise. More advanced and skilled employees were needed for setting up of KPOs. Operational cost saving, pool of talented workforce, infrastructure improvement and favorable government policies were the major factors responsible for emergence of KPOs in India. The main advantage of India was the presence of a technically qualified workforce. The Indian workforce was highly literate and English-speaking. There was a large pool of trained professionals in the fields of IT, Engineering, Education, Law, Science, Finance, Architecture and other competitive fields. The Global Knowledge Process Outsourcing industry was expected to reach US$17 billion by 2010, of which US$12 billion (almost 70%) was India's expected share (Exhibit VII). The KPO sector in India had already taken steps to meet the expected demand. The industry had started employing highly educated and talented people. LPO consisted of a huge range of legal processes, such as patent application drafting, legal research, pre-litigation documentation, advising clients, writing software licensing agreements and drafting distribution agreements. Experts predicted that 79,000 lawyers' jobs were poised to be outsourced from the US to countries like India by 2015[32] and it was believed that the large and increasingly skilled, but low-cost, labor pool would continue to remain India's greatest asset for years to come.

(Sandeep Varma is a Research Associate at Icfai Business School Research Center, Chennai. He can be reached at sandeepvarma78@gmail.com)

Endnotes

1 King Rachael, "Outsourcing: Beyond Bangalore", *http://www.businessweek.com/technology/content/dec2006/tc20061207_164472.htm* , December 11, 2006.

2 Ibid.

3 Ibid.

4 Balfour Frederik and Tashiro Hiroko, "China: Golf, Sushi—And Cheap Engineers", *http://www.businessweek.com/magazine/content/05_13/b3926068.htm*, March 28, 2005.

5 Ibid.

6 Ibid.

7 Ibid.

8 Ibid.

9 "From Russia with Technology?", *http://www.businessweek.com/magazine/content/06_05/b3969420.htm*, January 30, 2006.

10 *http://www.russoft.org/docs/?doc=1298.*

11 "From Russia with Technology?", *http://www.businessweek.com/magazine/content/06_05/b3969420.htm*, January 30, 2006.

12 ibid.

13 King Rachael, "Outsourcing: Beyond Bangalore", *http://www.businessweek.com/technology/content/dec2006/tc20061207_164472_page_2.htm*, December 11, 2006.

14 Optaros is an international consulting and systems integration firm that provides enterprises with online business solutions that leverage the next generation of internet technologies and approaches.

15 Smith Geri, "Can Latin America Challenge India?", *http://lamnews.com/can_latin_america_challenge_india.htm*, February 1, 2006.

16 ibid.

17 Stefanini IT Solutions is a leading provider of comprehensive IT services to the Fortune 1000 companies. Stefanini operates 31 offices in 12 counties with our global headquarters located in Sao Paulo, Brazil.

18 ibid.

19 Founded in 1986, Datastream provides asset management software, integrated procurement, and supporting services to organizations worldwide, including more than 65 percent of the Fortune 500.

20 Smith Geri, "Can Latin America Challenge India?", *http://lamnews.com/can_latin_america_challenge_india.htm*, February 1, 2006.

21 ibid.

22 ibid.

23 Balfour Frederik, "Vietnam's Growing Role in Outsourcing", *http://www.businessweek.com/technology/content/dec2006/tc20061211_099877.htm?chan=globalbiz_asia_management*, December 11, 2006.

24 Bhatnagar Parija," Is India's outsourcing honeymoon over?", *http://money.cnn.com/2005/08/23/news/international/india_outsourcing/index.htm*, August 24, 2005

25 *www.offshoringtimes.com/Pages/2005/offshore_news337.html*

26 ibid.

27 ibid.

28 ibid.

29 King Rachael, "Outsourcing: Beyond Bangalore", *http://www.businessweek.com/technology/content/dec2006/tc20061207_164472.htm* , December 11, 2006.

30 Bhatnagar Parija," Is India's outsourcing honeymoon over?", *http://money.cnn.com/2005/08/23/news/international/india_outsourcing/index.htm*, August 24, 2005.

31 King Rachael, "Outsourcing: Beyond Bangalore", *http://www.businessweek.com/technology/content/dec2006/tc20061207_164472.htm* , December 11, 2006.

32 *http://www.itbusinessedge.com/item/?ci=22676*, November 5, 2005.

Exhibit I: Countries Providing Outsourcing Services

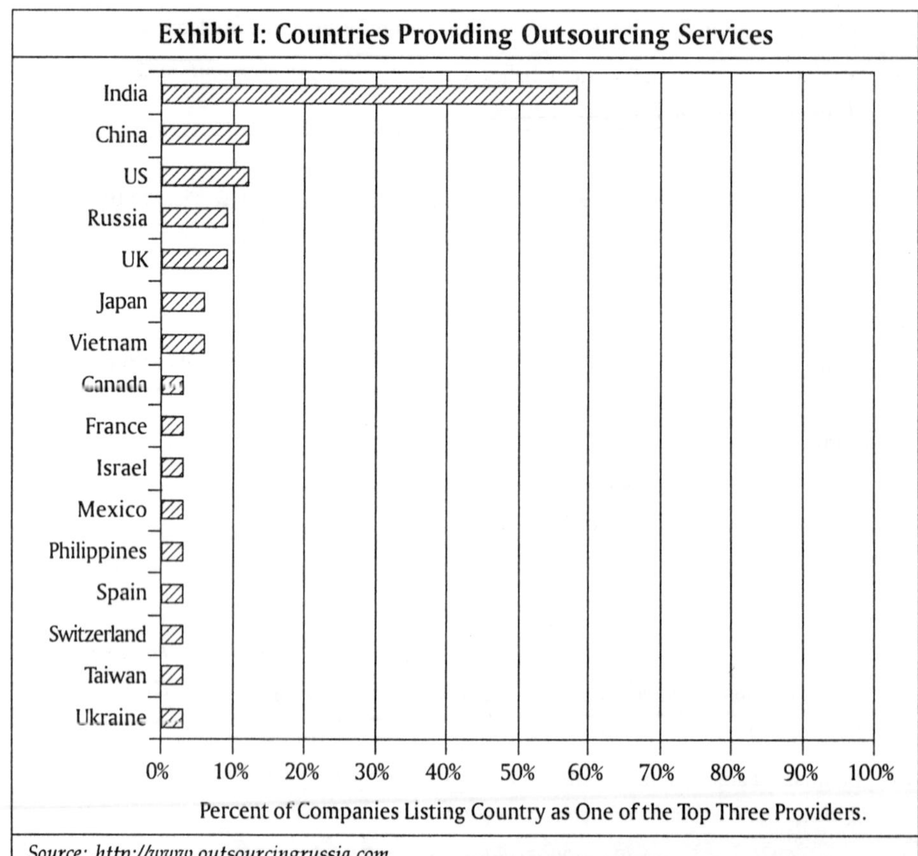

Source: http://www.outsourcingrussia.com

Exhibit II: Global Outsourcing Destinations

Canada
Multiple Process
Eastern Europe
Niche for European Market
Baltics
Nearshoring for Europe
Russia
Software Development
China
North Asia Hub
Philippines
Medical Transcription, Animation
Singapore
Back office to Asia
Australia
Multiple process
Ireland
European Hub
South Africa
Emerging
Mauritius
French English Languages
India
Full ranged

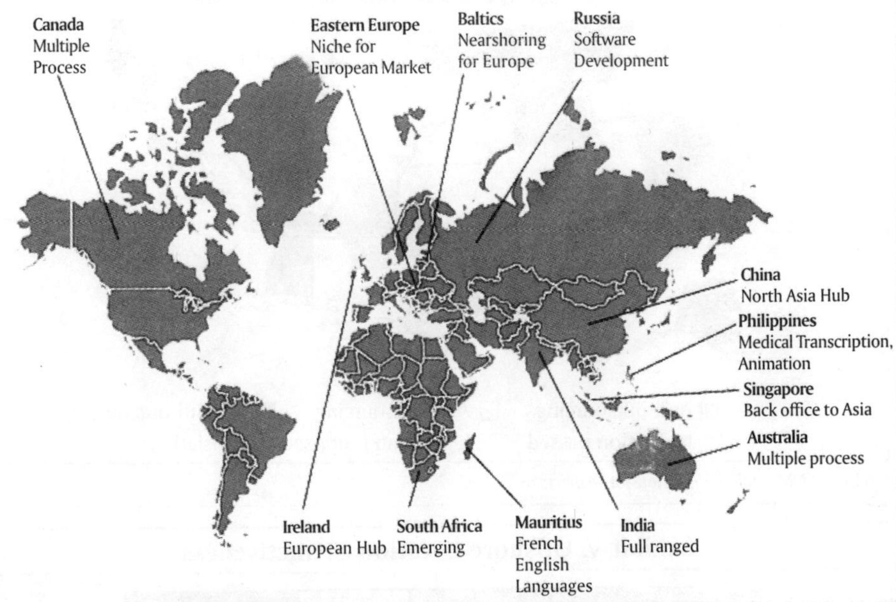

Source: http://www.outsourcingrussia.com/images/global-outsourcing.gif

Exhibit III: Outsourcing Destinations in Asia

China and India Dominate Region, but Other Countries are finiding Niche Positions

India 3.5 2.1
China 3.2 1.8 1.2
Malaysia 3.0 1.1 2.0
Philippines 3.6 1.2
Singapore 1.6 1.4 2.7
Thailand 3.3 0.9 1.5
Indonesia 3.5 1.1
Vietnam 3.5 0.7
Financial Structure
People and Skills avalability
Business enviroment
(*) Indicates overall index ranking
Index ranking
1-10
11-20
21-30
China (2)
India (1)
Thailand (6)
Vietnam (26)
Philippines (4)
Singapore (15)
Malaysia (3)
Indonesia (13)

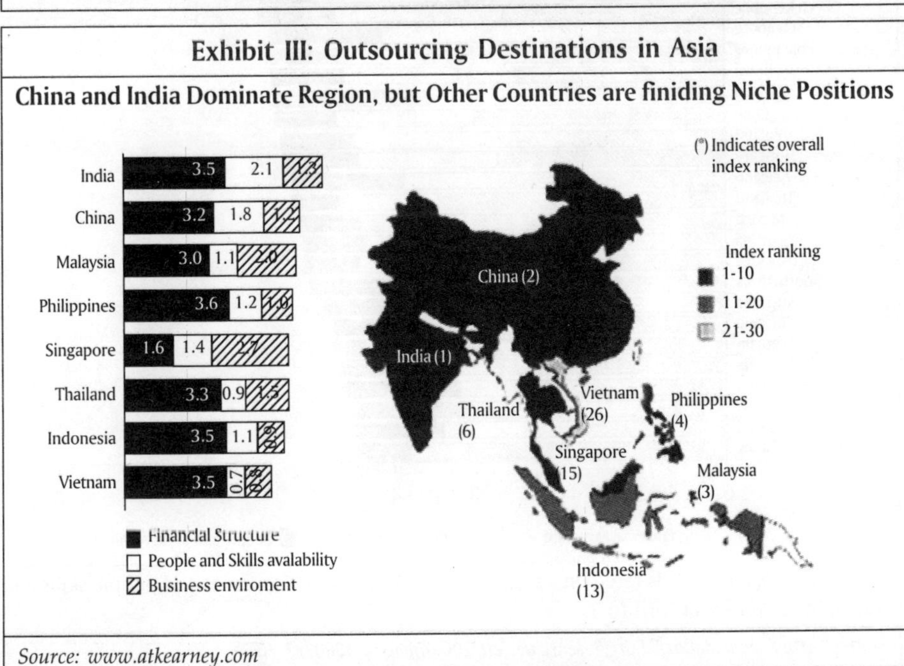

Source: www.atkearney.com

Exhibit IV: Anti-Outsourcing Legislation by US State Governments

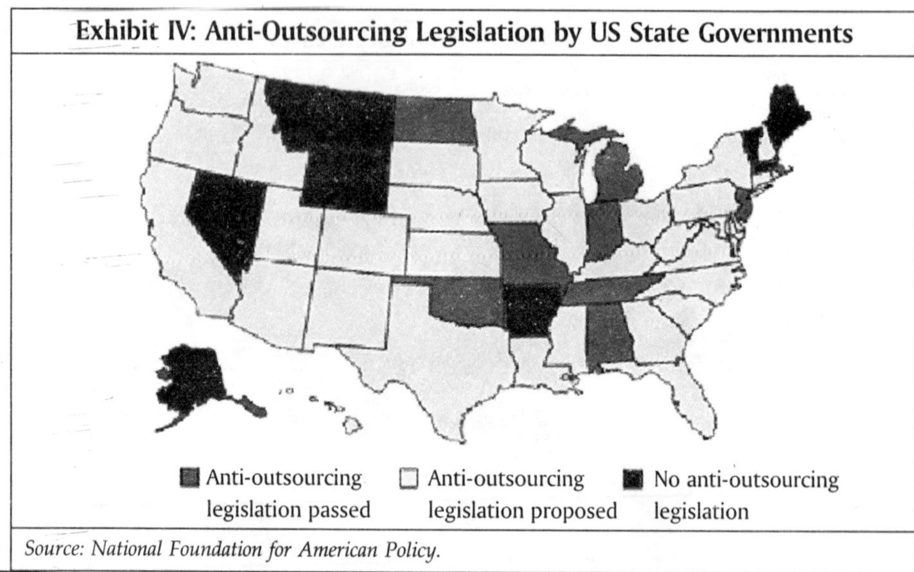

Source: National Foundation for American Policy.

Exhibit V: Offshore Location Attractiveness

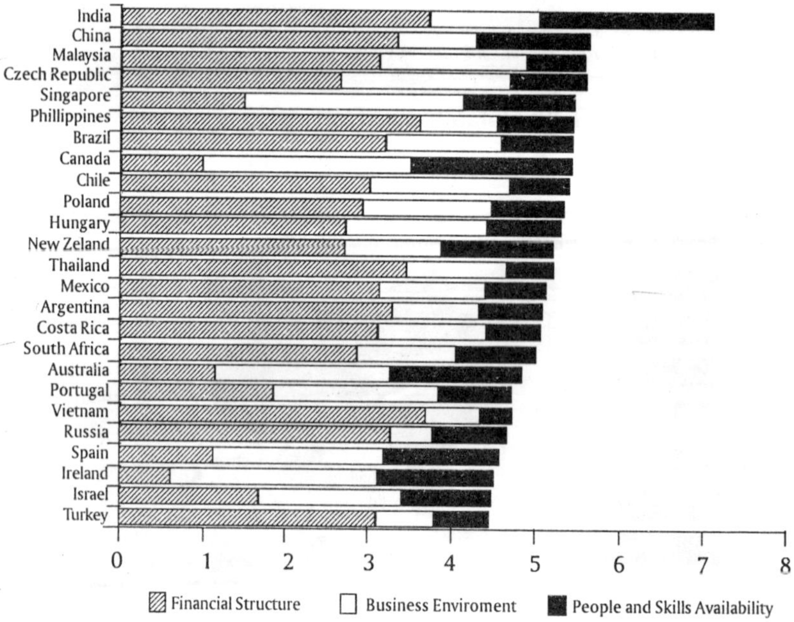

Note: Financial structure is rated on a scale of 1 to 4; Business environment and people skills and availability as on a scale of 1 to 3.

Source: http://www.dallasfed.org/research/eclett/2006/images/el0602c3.gif

Exhibit VI: Outsourcing Location Index					
Rank	**Country**	**Financial Structure**	**People and Skills Availability**	**Business Environment**	**Total Score**
1	India	2.47	2.14	1.26	6.87
2.	China	3.21	1.76	1.17	6.14
3.	Malaysia	2.95	1.12	2.00	6.07
4.	Philippines	3.58	1.16	1.06	5.78
5.	Singapore	1.62	1.44	2.57	5.73
6.	Thailand	3.27	0.94	1.51	5.72
7.	Czech Republic	2.57	1.12	1.10	5.58
8.	Chile	2.73	0.97	1.87	5.58
9.	Canada	1.10	2.03	2.40	5.52
10.	Brazil	2.91	1.36	1.21	5.50
11.	United States	0.54	2.74	2.22	5.49
12.	Egypt	3.55	0.95	0.98	5.47
13.	Indonesia	3.51	1.06	0.89	5.47
14.	Jordan	3.02	0.91	1.43	5.35
15.	Belgana	3.29	0.86	1.11	5.27

Source: www.atkearney.com

Exhibit VII: Global Shift from BPO to KPO

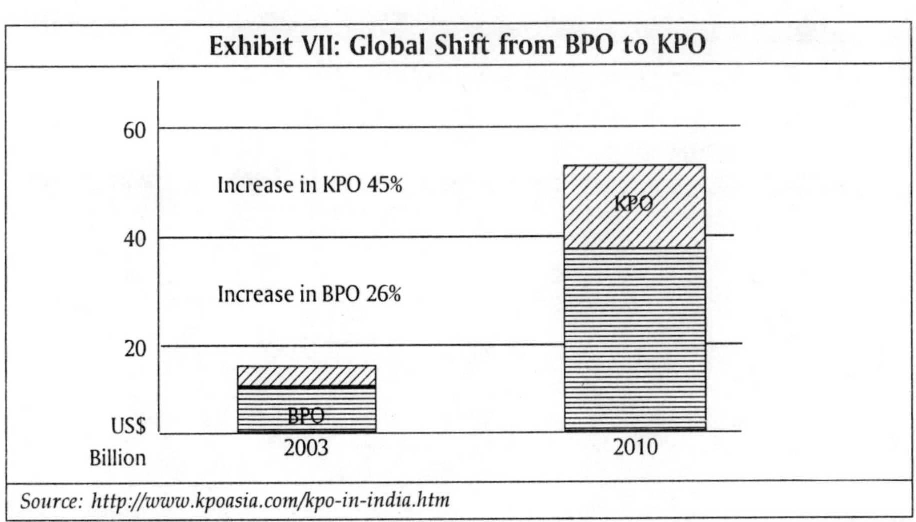

Source: http://www.kpoasia.com/kpo-in-india.htm

Section II

Country Experiences

11

Beyond the Outsourcing Angst
Making America More Productive

Thomas F Siems

For years, American companies have focused on their core competencies and contracted out the other activities which could be accomplished better, faster and cheaper by specialized external providers. The best companies keep costs low and boost productivity by doing what they do best and outsourcing the rest to outsource service providers at low cost locations. The wider offshore outsourcing of white collar jobs and the recent increase in offshore of high-end knowledge work has been followed by a surge in anti-outsourcing legislation by US State Governments. The protectionist policies devised by US also entail significant economic costs. As a technological powerhouse, with skilled workers and adept managers, the US should strive for the most complex and rewarding tasks, while other countries specialize in the routine, labor-intensive tasks. The key to the US economy's future lies in maintaining a flexible labor market, where resources can flow from declining sectors to emerging ones. The outsourcing of jobs by US companies to poor countries is inevitable. It had saved $11 billion in 2004 by outsourcing to India alone.

Source: Federal Reserve Bank of Dallas, Economic Letter, Volume 1, Issue 2, February 2006.

Outsourcing is not new. For years, American companies have focused on core competencies and contracted out activities that could be accomplished better, faster and cheaper by outside, specialized providers. These vendors may be across town, elsewhere in the country or on the far side of the world.

The motive has always been to remain competitive. In today's business environment, profit and even survival depend on making constant improvements throughout supply chains by lowering costs and improving quality, designs, cycle times and processes. Through specialization and trade, businesses develop important competitive advantages that help them become more flexible and innovative in rapidly changing markets.

Indeed, the best companies keep costs low and boost productivity by doing what they do best and outsourcing the rest.[1]

Even when it involves foreign workers, outsourcing benefits individual companies. Many Americans, however, express a deep unease over reports of firms' "exporting jobs" and displacing domestic workers by moving jobs to India, China or other up-and-coming nations.

The concern is understandable. Job losses are painful, especially when they are related to global economic forces beyond individual workers' control. As reports of outsourcing grow, many Americans are advocating policies designed to preserve existing jobs and industries. But many economists – including such notables as Milton Friedman and Jagdish Bhagwati – discourage these efforts as harmful to the overall economy.[2] They argue that outsourcing increases efficiency and productivity and leads to competitiveness, innovation and ever-larger market opportunities.

Knowledge Workers at Risk

One reason today's overseas outsourcing generates heat is the wider swath of occupations being performed offshore. Computers, software, the Internet and fiber-optic cables form an infrastructure that allows businesses to break apart activities and redistribute them elsewhere – increasingly to knowledge workers all over the world. Digital technologies and inexpensive telecommunications have created an efficient and effective information superhighway: Strings of zeroes and ones can be moved to Bangalore, Beijing or just about any place in seconds.

White-collar activities such as processing accounting data, performing standard financial analyses, writing routine software and maintaining call centers are no longer exempt from international competition. With an Internet connection and specialized skills, individuals and companies in the remotest ends of the earth are able to compete and collaborate in today's global economy.

How many knowledge jobs are affected by offshore outsourcing? Data on outsourcing's effect on employment are limited, but one estimate puts the total number of US white-collar jobs moving overseas at 832,000 through 2005, nearly triple the figure through 2003 *(Table 1)*. In another five years, the total could rise to 1.7 million; in a decade, to 3.3 million. We should keep in mind, however, that the US has added 18 million jobs in the past 10 years. Total employment rose to nearly 135 million workers in early 2006, so the offshore outsourcing estimates represent a relatively small part of a growing economy.

Table 1: Offshoring of US Jobs to Low-Wage Countries

	Estimated by		**Projected by**	
Profession	**2003**	**2005**	**2010**	**2015**
Art, design	2,500	8,000	15,000	30,000
Architecture	14,000	46,000	93,000	191,000
Business	30,000	91,000	176,000	356,000
Computer	102,000	181,000	322,000	542,000
Legal	6,000	20,000	39,000	79,000
Life sciences	300	4,000	16,000	39,000
Management	3,500	34,000	106,000	259,000
Office	146,000	410,000	815,000	1,600,000
Sales	11,000	38,000	97,000	218,000
Total	**315,300**	**832,000**	**1,679,000**	**3,314,000**

Note: Numbers are cumulative and have been rounded.

Source: "Near-Term Growth of Offshoring Accelerating," by John C McCarthy, Forrester Research Inc., May 14, 2004.

The recent increase in offshore relocation of knowledge work has been followed by a surge in anti-outsourcing legislation by US state governments *(Chart 1).* According to the National Foundation for American Policy, more than 300 bills have been introduced over the past two years to protect American workers against outsourcing to other countries.[3] The Constitution's commerce clause constrains the states' power to interfere with business, so many of these proposals are limited, often covering only companies doing government work.

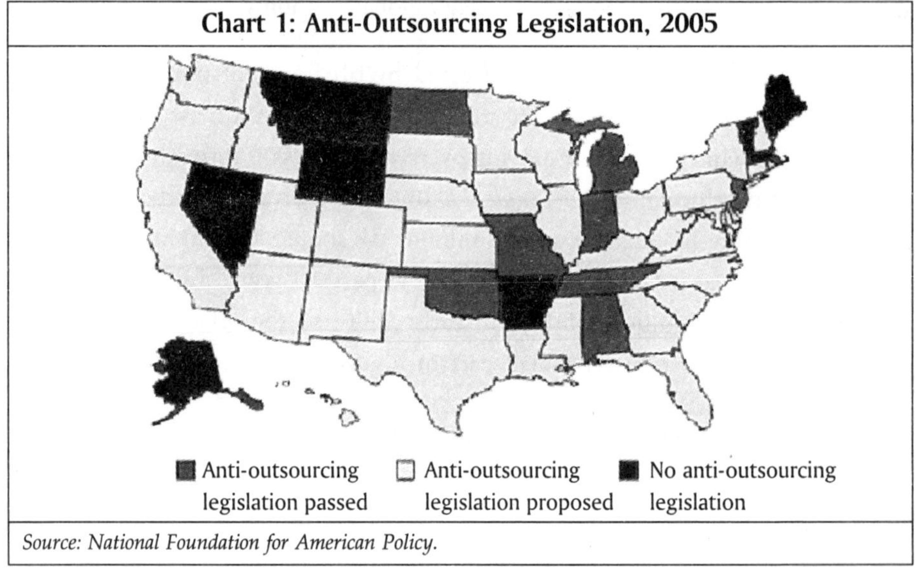

Chart 1: Anti-Outsourcing Legislation, 2005

Source: National Foundation for American Policy.

Outsourcing is fundamentally a trade phenomenon, and empirical evidence suggests protectionist policies entail significant economic costs. They result in higher prices for consumers and declining domestic and global competitiveness. The economy also loses the productivity gains that would have come from shifting resources to their best uses. Trade barriers do long-term harm by short-circuiting healthy economic evolution.[4]

Protectionist measures rarely save jobs. A generation ago, American angst focused on foreign competition's impact on manufacturing employment, particularly in automobiles, steel and textiles. We passed laws to restrict imports. Despite trade restraints and domestic-content laws, manufacturing jobs continued to decline even as overall employment rose. Most significant, some of the biggest job losses have come in autos, steel and textiles.

Saving existing jobs exacts a price. Countries that impose laws aimed at easing the burdens of job loss tend to have lower per capita incomes *(Chart 2).* World Bank data indicate that many countries impose huge burdens on employers who lay off workers – the equivalent of 165 weeks of pay in Brazil, 112 in Turkey, 90 in China, 79 in India. All are poor countries. High firing costs rob economies of their vitality by discouraging companies from hiring new employees in the first place. While generous severance is helpful to the displaced workers, it makes societies poorer by slowing job creation and dragging down labor productivity.

Chart 2: Job Security and Income Per Capita

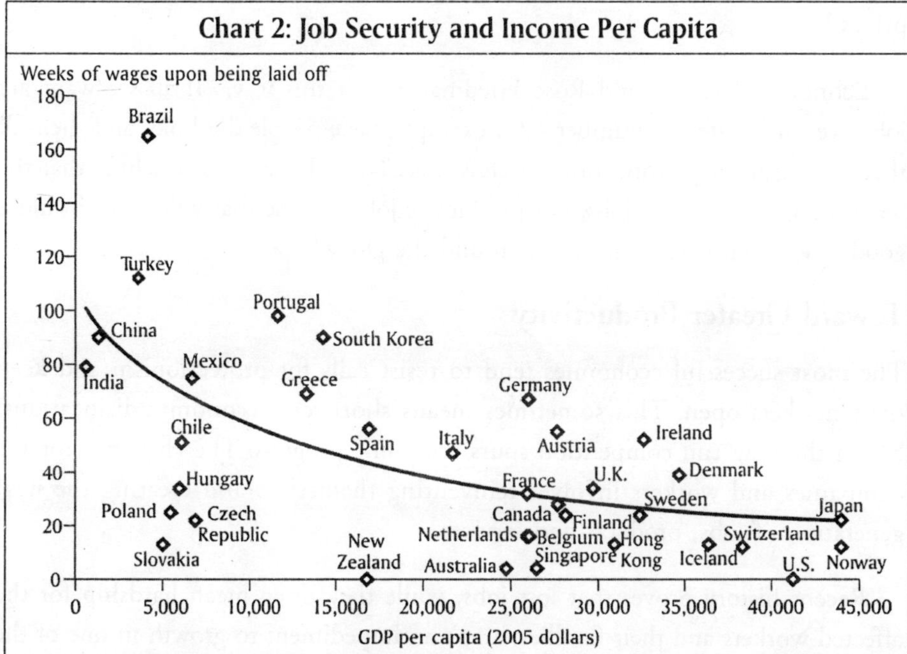

Note: A similar relationship is obtained using purchasing power parity adjustments for GDP per capita. James J Heckman and Carmen Pagés, in "The Cost of Job Security Regulation: Evidence from Latin American Labor Markets," NBER Working Paper 7773, June 2000, obtain parallel findings using 1995 GDP data for Latin America.

Sources : World Bank, World Development Indicators Database; World Bank Group, Doing Business 2006.

By contrast, countries with lower burdens on firing are usually richer. The United States, for example, mandates no severance at all, allowing companies to determine their own policies. Giving companies a freer hand in staffing decisions allows firms to pare payrolls quickly in response to changing market conditions, and it reduces the risk of hiring and forming new businesses. This labor market flexibility encourages efficiency, productivity and economic growth – all of which contribute to higher incomes.

Outsourcing often creates employment uncertainties because it's not always immediately apparent where the new jobs will materialize. History tells us, however, that job creation outpaces job destruction in the long run. If the US had tried to hang onto the jobs of its past, we would be far poorer today. Living standards would have stagnated, and American consumers would be paying higher prices.[5]

Economists Milton and Rose Friedman put it this way, "If all we want are jobs, we can create any number – for example, have people dig holes and then fill them up again or perform other useless tasks." The Friedmans conclude that the real objective is not just jobs, but productive jobs – those that will result in more goods and services for consumers around the globe.[6]

Toward Greater Productivity

The most successful economies tend to resist calls for protectionism and keep their markets open. This sometimes means short-term economic dislocations, but in the long run competition spurs economic progress. The challenge for US companies and workers involves reinventing themselves and creating the next generation of jobs, products and services.

Recent history proves that lost jobs, while they often mean hardship for the affected workers and their families, aren't an impediment to growth in one of the world's most resilient, dynamic and flexible economies. From 1980 to 2005, US workers filed 118 million claims for unemployment insurance *(Table 2)*. Many others lost their jobs, of course, but either didn't qualify for benefits, weren't unemployed long enough to file claims, or quickly transitioned to new jobs. It's hard to find the total number of displaced workers, but it surely would be more than 150 million.

Despite all the job losses, the economy performed quite well. Total employment over the same 26-year period rose by 44 million. At annual rates, unemployment fell from 7.2 percent to less than 5 percent today. Productivity increased by 72 percent.

Table 2: The Churn: Recycling America's Labor					
Year	Initial claims*	Dec.-to-Dec. net job gains*	End-of-year employment*	End-of-year unemployment rate (percent)	Productivity (index, 1980=100)
1980	5,850	267	90,936	7.2	100
1981	5,419	(52)	90,884	8.5	102
1982	7,033	(2,128)	88,756	10.8	101
1983	5,294	3,454	92,210	8.3	105
1984	4,484	3,877	96,087	7.3	108
1985	4,702	2,500	98,587	7.0	110
1986	4,529	1,897	100,484	6.6	113
1987	3,897	3,150	103,634	5.7	114
1988	3,704	3,237	106,871	5.3	116
1989	3,950	1,938	108,809	5.4	117
1990	4,616	309	109,118	6.3	119
1991	5,363	(857)	108,261	7.3	121
1992	4,905	1,157	109,418	7.4	126
1993	4,117	2,785	112,203	6.5	127
1994	4,076	3,853	116,056	5.5	128
1995	4,298	2,154	118,210	5.6	128
1996	4,223	2,793	121,003	5.4	132
1997	3,858	3,358	124,361	4.7	135
1998	3,810	3,003	127,364	4.4	139
1999	3,563	3,172	130,536	4.0	143
2000	3,590	1,948	132,484	3.9	147
2001	4,869	(1,763)	130,721	5.7	150
2002	4,852	(535)	130,186	6.0	156
2003	4,823	112	130,298	5.7	163
2004	4,114	2,097	132,395	5.4	168
2005	3,985	1,976	134,371	4.9	172
Total	**117,924**	**43,702**			
Avg./ month	**378**	**140**			

*Establishment survey, data in thousands. Claims are for unemployment insurance.

Sources: Bureau of Labor Statistics; Federal Reserve Board.

Per capita real gross domestic product shot from $25,309 to $41,257. The average work-week fell by nearly two hours to 33.7, and average household real net worth more than doubled to $431,000. All this was accomplished, by the way, with relatively little economic downtime. Since the beginning of 1983, the United States has had just 16 months of recession, fewer than any other major country *(Table 3).*

Table 3: Economic Downtime, 1983–2005

	Recession	
	Months	**Percent of time**
US	16	5.8
UK	22	8.0
Australia	23	8.3
Canada	24	8.7
Italy	25	9.1
Austria	36	13.0
Spain	42	15.2
France	42	15.2
Sweden	43	15.6
Germany	70	25.4
Japan	82	29.7
New Zealand	85	30.8
Switzerland	87	31.5

Sources: National Bureau of Economic Research; Economic Cycle Research Institute.

Increasing productivity – getting more for less – is key to business success and the ultimate source of higher living standards. Sometimes greater productivity means automating processes and replacing workers with improved technologies. Sometimes it entails adding resources to work on high value-added activities. Sometimes it involves moving non-critical work to lower-cost providers.

Today, global firms increasingly use outsourcing to redeploy and redirect staff to higher value-added activities. Farming out some tasks frees up talent to work on new products and new ideas. It creates greater worker flexibility and allows firms to put the right resources in the right places at the right times.

Competition gives companies the incentive to move production to lower-cost locations. Large segments of the textile industry left New England for the Southeast; more recently, textile plants in the Carolinas have closed as companies shift production to other parts of the world. Automobile manufacturers sent a lot of their parts and assembly work to Mexico in an effort to compete with Asian rivals. The electronics industry has developed a global supply chain, and it takes components from a hodgepodge of nations to build computers and other gadgets.

Laptops, for example, are assembled in Mexico with memory chips and display screens from South Korea; cases, keyboards and hard drives from Thailand; graphics chips from Taiwan; and batteries from any number of Asian countries. The microprocessor, the machine's highest valued and most complex part, is still made in the United States. This is the future of business – a global integration of production, where countries do what they do best, dictated by David Ricardo's principle of comparative advantage.

As a technological powerhouse, with skilled workers and adept managers, the US should strive for the most complex and rewarding tasks, while other countries will specialize in the routine, labor-intensive tasks. Globalization doesn't just mean increased competition; it opens opportunities for cooperation.

Outsourcing creates partners, not rivals. For example, India has historically been viewed as an attractive place to do knowledge work because of its low production and labor costs, talented and skilled workforce, and English-language proficiency. A T Kearney Inc., ranks India as the most attractive offshore location for doing business *(Chart 3),* particularly for call centers and data processing operations. Among the US companies expanding their presence in India are Dell, Sun Microsystems, Ford, General Electric and Oracle.

The key differences between India two decades ago and now are two-fold: (1) the role that technology has played in quickly and inexpensively subdividing and moving work, and (2) the nation's willingness to remove regulatory burdens and attract foreign firms to establish operations there. The availability, affordability and speed of today's technologies allow Indian workers to instantaneously provide highly competitive services to organizations around the globe. And since the new era of fewer regulatory burdens began in 1991, foreign direct investment into India has increased dramatically *(Chart 4).*

Chart 3: Offshore Location Attractiveness

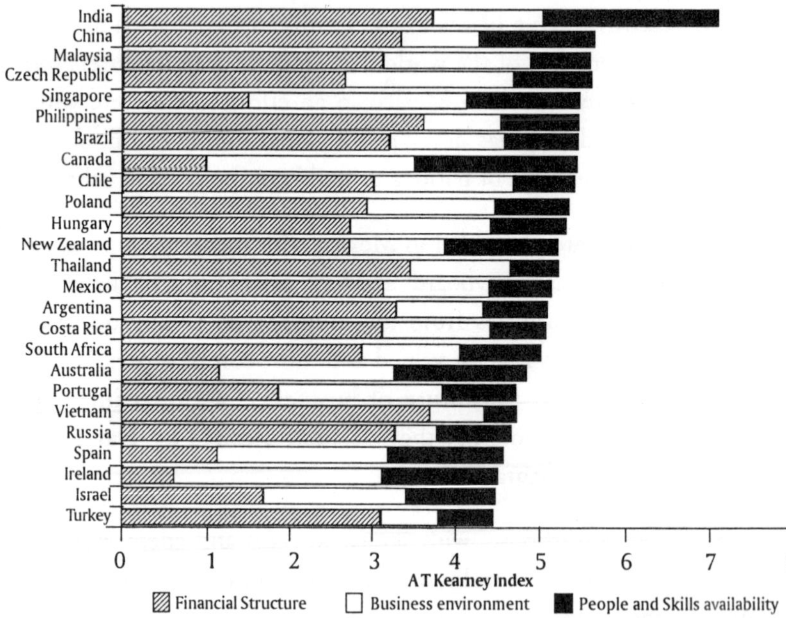

India
China
Malaysia
Czech Republic
Singapore
Philippines
Brazil
Canada
Chile
Poland
Hungary
New Zealand
Thailand
Mexico
Argentina
Costa Rica
South Africa
Australia
Portugal
Vietnam
Russia
Spain
Ireland
Israel
Turkey
0 1 2 3 4 5 6 7 8
A T Kearney Index
Financial Structure
Business environment
People and Skills availability

Note: Financial structure is rated on a scale of 1 to 4; business environment and people skills and availability are on a scale of 1 to 3.

Source: A T Kearney Inc.

Chart 4: Foreign Direct Investment into India

Billions of US Dollars
6
5
4
3
2
1
0
-1
'72 '76 '80 '84 '88 '92 '96 '00 '04

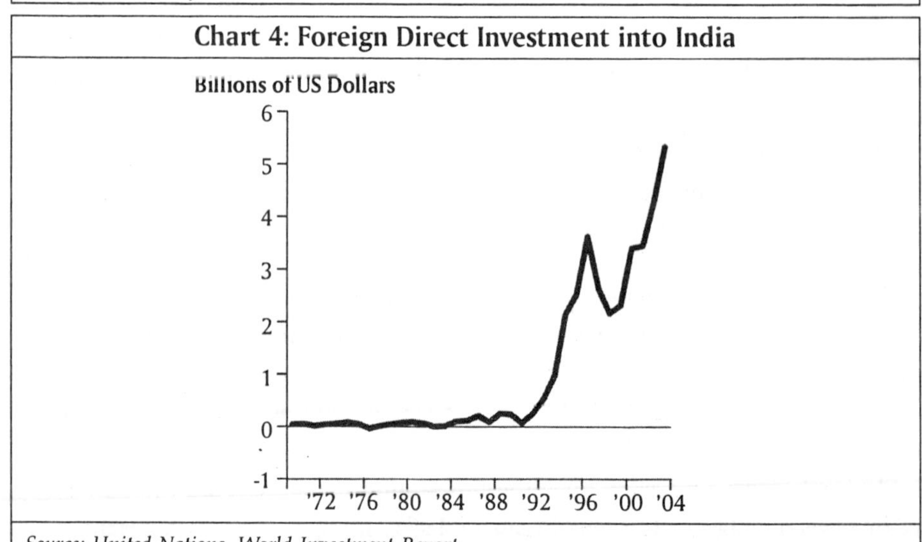

Source: United Nations, World Investment Report.

History has proved the power of letting global competition run its course: Many better, higher-paying jobs have been created as new ideas and technologies replace older ones. The key to the US economy's future lies in maintaining a flexible labor market, where resources can flow from declining sectors to emerging ones. Innovation and entrepreneurship depend on it. Job losses and other unsettling aspects of the process can't be ignored, and society can consider policies to make economic change less burdensome. Preparing workers for new opportunities through retraining and education is often mentioned as an alternative to protecting existing jobs.

Outsourcing's Future

Offshore outsourcing presents complex and often divisive issues, but it is unlikely to wither away. The market pressures that create incentives for outsourcing will not abate. Our economy, however, is resilient and flexible. The long-run evidence on employment-turnover patterns demonstrates that offshore outsourcing results in overall economic gains, such as lower consumer prices, better products and higher productivity growth.

Like other trade, offshore outsourcing can have negative impacts on some jobs and wages, while affecting others in a positive way. These structural changes influence where jobs are located and what tasks workers perform. While policy can address ways to help displaced workers gain the necessary skills to compete in the global economy, it also can encourage Americans to embrace change and adapt to globalization's effects on the changing nature of work.

We have a choice. Saving specific jobs and industries inhibits innovation and short-circuits the next round of new jobs and services, raising prices for everyone.

Accepting the challenge of competition, however, takes a longer-run view. It leads to innovation and ever-larger market opportunities and, in the end, true productive job creation and a lower cost of living. Indeed, the secret to faster growth and greater prosperity lies in allowing individuals and businesses to do what they do best – and outsource the rest.

(Thomas F Siems is Senior Economist and Policy Advisor in the Research Department at the Federal Reserve Bank of Dallas. He conducts economic and financial research to

develop a comprehensive understanding of globalization, including how new ideas (technologies and policies) impact productivity and economic growth. Siems is also a senior lecturer in the Engineering Management, Information and Systems Department in the School of Engineering at Southern Methodist University and an advisory board member of the Cato Institute's Project on Social Security Choice. He can be reached at tom.siems@dal.frb.org).

Note: The author thanks Julia Carter and Timothy J Schaaf for assistance in research.

Endnotes

1 A prelude to this article is "Do What You Do Best, Outsource the Rest?" by Thomas F Siems and Adam S Ratner, Federal Reserve Bank of Dallas Southwest Economy, November/ December 2003, pp. 13-14.

2 The debate over outsourcing is clearly framed in "The Muddles over Outsourcing," by Jagdish Bhagwati, Arvind Panagariya and TN Srinivasan, *Journal of Economic Perspectives,* vol. 18, no. 4, Fall 2004, pp. 93-114.

3 "Outsourcing Saves Money," by Stuart Ander son, *State Legislatures Magazine,* June 2005, and "Outsourcing Attacks Not Over," by Stuart Anderson, *National Review,* February 11, 2005.

4 Interested readers are directed to "In Defense of Globalization", by Jagdish Bhagwati, New York: Oxford University Press, 2004.

5 Job anxieties brought on by offshore outsourcing highlight the tension between efficiency and distributional concerns. See "A Specific-Factors View on Outsourcing," by Wilhelm Kohler, *North American Journal of Economics and Finance,* vol.12, issue 1, 2001, pp. 31-53, and "What Does Evidence Tell Us About Fragmentation and Outsourcing?" by Ronald Jones, Henryk Kierzkowski and Chen Lurong, *International Review of Economics and Finance,* vol. 14, 2005, pp. 305-16.

6 "The Case for Free Trade," by Milton Friedman and Rose Friedman, *Hoover Digest,* no. 4,1997.

Outsourcing the American Dream

– George J Bryjak

Economists Ashok Bardhan and Cynthia Kroll of the University of California at Berkeley estimate that in July 2003 between 25,000 and 30,000 IT (information technology) positions were outsourced to India. According to the Bureau of Vital Statistics, since 2001 "more than 500,000 people in IT professions in the United States have lost their jobs". The website of the nationally syndicated business program "Lou Dobbs Tonight" lists over 300 outsourcing US companies.

These figures are just the beginning. A study of 400 of the nation's top 1,000 companies concluded that by 2006, between 35 and 45 percent of current full-time IT jobs will be sent overseas. Using Bureau of Labor Statistics data, Bardhan and Kroll estimate that of the almost 128 million workers in the US, 11 percent-or just over 14 million individuals are at risk of having their jobs outsourced.

IT positions will follow the millions of manufacturing jobs already lost, only at a more rapid pace. As Matthew Slaughter of Dartmouth College notes, "IT work will move faster because it is easier to ship work across phone lines and put consultants on airplanes than it is to ship bulky raw materials across borders and build factories."

Significantly lower labor costs are the primary rationale for this job exodus. While telephone operators in the US earn an average of $12.57 an hour, in India they make less than $1.00, Payroll clerks take home less than $2.00 an hour whereas their counterparts in the US average $15.17 an hour. *Business Week* reports, "Soon, offshore accountants may do everything but on-site audits." Medical billing may become the first occupational category to all but disappear.

Some outsourcing advocates contend that shipping jobs overseas is a way of redistributing wealth from rich to poor countries, a potent mechanism for creating a democracy-oriented middle-class in developing countries. However, the reality of the situation belies such "noble" intentions. Between the late 1970s and late 1990s, the CEO to workers salary-ratio in the nation's top 100 corporations increased from 47 to 1, to approximately 1,000 to 1.

What will happen to US wo rkers sacrificed to outsourcing? Job-slashing corporations argue that displaced workers will secure employment in the next wave of economic development. They claim that just as agriculture was supplanted by manufacturing, which in turn gave way to the computer information revolution, today's corporate casualties will find employment in the coming stage of economic progression.

Unfortunately, it's far from clear what that next economic phase will be and when it will occur. Few experts anticipate the materialization of a "white knight" industry to save the day. If such an enterprise does become (reality, how long, before newly created positions are sent abroad, the cycle repeat itself?) Data indicate that when people change jobs as a result of global competition, their wages typically decline, at least initially. For too many outsourced workers, "retraining" for future employment will be a simple matter of learning to say, "Would you like to supersize that order?"

Bardhan and Kroll speculate that surviving outsourced occupations could face a "downward adjustment of salary and wages" making them internationally competitive once again. In this scenario, the domestic IT industry would bounce back, but at a significant loss of purchasing power for workers.

Other than outsourcing corporations, the only segment of the economy benefiting from job flight are organizations linking labor exporting companies to overseas workers. One such service provides an "online outsourcing price quote" formula for how much money will be saved as a consequence of job transfer. "As the world stampedes toward outsourcing," their ad reads, "don't get trampled." Let us "help you navigate efficiently in this new frontier."

The ramifications of outsourcing are staggering not only for individuals whose positions are terminated, but also for the larger society. Unemployment and "underemployment" (working below

Contd...

Contd...

one's level of skill and training) will contribute to a shrinking tax base, as already financially burdened city, county, and state governments cut back additional personnel and services. In a nation where 15 percent of the population has no medical coverage, that figure can only increase as most people secure health insurance through their employment. Fewer good paying jobs will be available to college and technical school graduates as the societal opportunity structure is diminished.

High-tech cities such as New York, Boston, San Jose, and San Francisco are certain to be the big losers, while rural areas crippled by the loss of family farms have little chance of economic improvement. Suburbs with an employment base of "back office" activities (customer service personnel and medical transcribers, for example) can expect to see their labor force shrink.

What are the chances of checking this employment exodus? While manufacturing jobs were leaving in droves, union membership and power declined steadily. There is no reason to believe that white-collar workers, the vast majority of whom have little if any history of collective organization, will create a viable movement to halt this trend. In addition, corporate America and its conservative allies have successfully demonized unionism, linking worker solidarity to that most "evil" economic system-socialism. Secretary of Education Rod Paige referred to the National Education Association, one of the country's largest teacher's unions, as a "terrorist organization." In a clumsy apology that revealed Paige's sentiments toward workers' organizations, Paige said he was referring to the union, not the teachers.

At the national level, neither Republicans nor Democrats have shown any inclination to deal with this problem. Both parties are more or less committed to "economic globalization" and job outsourcing is only one aspect of this phenomenon.

Perhaps the outsourcing of jobs from rich to poor countries is inevitable. However, the consequences for those on the losing and receiving ends are not. By one estimate, US companies will save $11 billion in 2004 by outsourcing to India alone. A portion of that money combined with enormous industry profits would go a long way toward prolonged unemployment and health benefits as well as job creation for outsourcing victims. Congress person Tom Lantos of California argues that the aim of globalization should be the maximization of benefits for workers in both the developed and developing worlds. However, in a corporate "democracy" such as the United States, there is little chance of realizing that goal.

(George Bryjak is a Professor of sociology at the University of San Diego. He can be reached at bryjak@verizon.net).

Source: http://zmagsite.zmag.org, April 2004. © George, Bryjak. Reprinted with permission.

12

BPO Fuels European Outsourcing

This article describes how Europe is embracing BPO. It examines how BPO has emerged and observes which industries and processes tend to lead to BPO growth in the region. It also explores some unique factors that have inhibited or encouraged BPO in Europe. TPI measures (which exclude government contracts) show that as outsourcing has grown in Europe, so has BPO as a part of it. TPI believes that Europe is likely to sustain and even increase its BPO growth, especially if the region promotes it via a few "poster children", examples of large, successful BPO contracts by top European companies. Finally, the article details how service providers are competing for BPO business.

Europe has seen significant growth in outsourcing in 2004, especially in Business Process Outsourcing (BPO). While TPI data shows that the sustained year-on-year growth of outsourcing in Europe can be attributed equally to Information Technology Outsourcing (ITO) and BPO, the recent pace of commercial European BPO deals has accelerated dramatically, fueling the region's total outsourcing growth. In the first three-quarters of this year, Europe accounted for a larger share of an expanding BPO pie.

The Americas, as a region, has not slowed in BPO business as much as Europe has grown at an increasing velocity. In fact, in absolute terms, BPO award volumes in the Americas continue apace – award values in the first half of this year equaled those from all of 2003. In relative terms, however, Europe has gained considerable market share in number of deals and in TCV. Europe is making its mark in BPO and sustaining it.

This paper describes how Europe is embracing BPO. It examines how BPO has emerged and observes which industries and processes tend to lead BPO growth in the region. It also explores some unique factors that have inhibited or encouraged BPO in Europe. Further, TPI measures show that governments and Financial Times Europe (FTE) 500 companies have had a leading role in Europe's BPO growth and might logically continue to do so. Finally, the paper will explore how service providers are competing for BPO business. With more than 35 experienced, European advisors working in the area, TPI is prepared to meet client needs as the region expands its use of both ITO and BPO.

The Growth of Both Outsourcing and BPO in Europe

In 2002, Europe's outsourcing Total Contract Value (TCV) was about one-fifth that of the Americas. By 2003, it stood at over one-half. TPI believes that European transaction values, about three-quarters of Americas' values year-to-date, will ultimately approach those of the Americas for all of 2004. This trend toward equalization comes through dramatic European growth, not any decline in outsourcing in the Americas.[1]

TPI measures (which exclude government contracts) show that as outsourcing has grown in Europe, so has BPO as a part of it. By the third quarter of 2004, Europe accounted for slightly more (22) BPO deals in the broader market than the Americas did (21) in transactions valued at greater than US$50 million. This represented almost 48 percent of the number of transactions (compared with nearly 46 percent for the Americas). The TCV picture to date in 2004 is reversed, with Europe accounting for about 41 percent of the total TCV (compared with 54 percent for the Americas).[2] Today, BPO assignments make up more than 30 percent of TPI's European workload.[3]

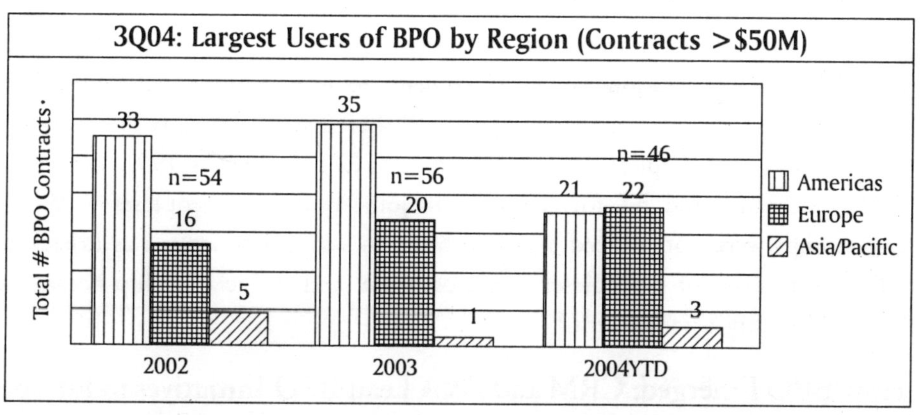

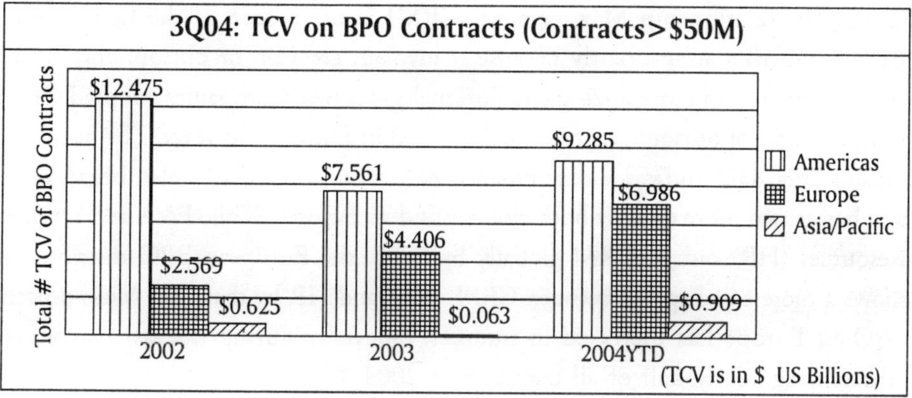

How BPO Emerged: Shared Services Centers Paved the Way in Europe

Initially, many European companies – often more conservative than their American counterparts – wanted to emulate the results of outsourcing without embracing outsourcing completely. To that end, they set up shared services centers. These centers consolidated discrete business processes (e.g., accounts payable) that had been managed locally into stand-alone centers servicing whole regions or even all regions. This allowed the shared services centre to emulate a commercial relationship with its "customers."

Although many such centers have been very successful in saving costs and improving processes, they often serve as a precursor for outsourcing that provides truly commercial, legally enforceable service level agreements and contract terms. Shared services centers are good candidates for driving corporate sourcing agendas.

A major example of the transition from shared services to outsourcing involved British Telecommunications (BT). BT reorganized around functional, rather than geographic lines in 1991, creating a single HR shared-services facility that installed PeopleSoft as its Enterprise Resource Planning (ERP) platform in 1997. In August 2000, Accenture and BT formed a 50/50 joint venture, e-peopleserve. When cost savings were not realized and new business was not generated as expected, BT sold its share of e-peopleserve to Accenture, and the relationship became a full outsourcing arrangement.[4]

How BPO Emerged: CRM and F&A Lead BPO Initiatives in Europe

Customer Relationship Management (CRM) is often seen as the first type of BPO companies adopt, partly because it involves creation or outsourcing of call centers rather than reorganizing core internal processes. Companies adopted CRM from the start of outsourcing both globally and in Europe. However, TPI historical outsourcing data[5] indicates that Finance & Accounting (F&A) also began early and has grown more quickly both globally and in Europe. While F&A and Human Resources (HR) outran CRM globally by 2003, the European BPO distribution shows a more equal spread between CRM, F&A and HR by that year. Multi-process BPO in Europe has increased in number, especially during the last two years, representing nearly half of all contracts in 2004 YTD.

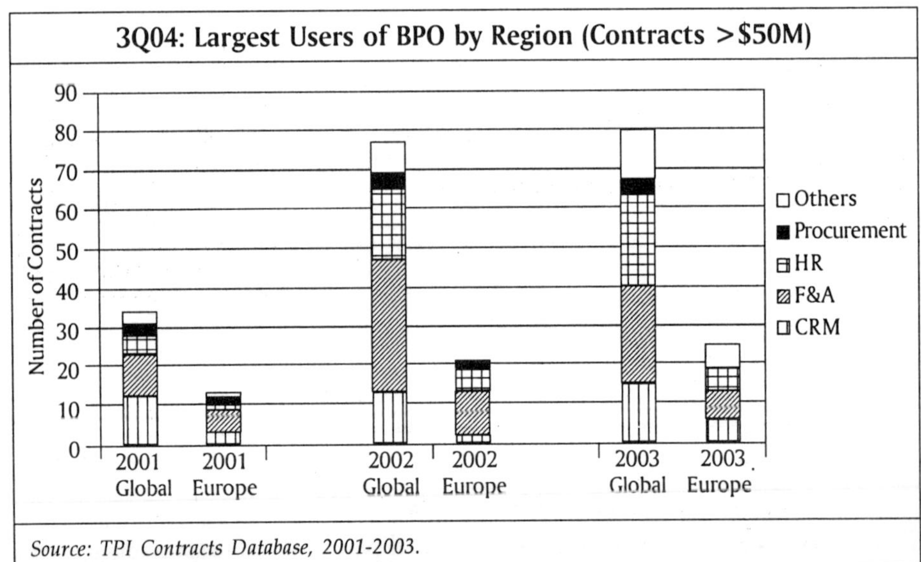

Source: TPI Contracts Database, 2001-2003.

Contracts awarded to IBM by Procter & Gamble, to EDS by Infineon, and to ACS by General Motors Europe, have significantly increased the number of European employees receiving HR services from third-party providers.[6] TPI expects the CRM activity that marked the initial BPO push in Europe to continue or increase, but also anticipates a number of significant F&A, Procurement and HR deals by European Blue Chip companies in upcoming quarters.

How BPO Emerged: Financial Services Led BPO in Europe

Financial Services organizations have spearheaded BPO in the Americas and Europe, partially because companies in this sector more readily perceived the potential for a substantial return on investment through outsourcing. Banking and insurance are highly regulated industries that can find BPO helpful in keeping processes transparent. In addition, they can embrace outsourcing as a way to surmount huge competitive pressures and as a tool for achieving the synergies envisaged by corporate mergers. Measured both by number of deals and their TCV, Financial Services dominated the European BPO growth picture during the past two years. Energy and Manufacturing run a distant second and third, while Retail has gained on Manufacturing during the first half of 2004.[7] BPO market analyst NelsonHall observes that substantial insurance and banking BPO activity accounts for the prevalence of Financial Services in the past 6-12 months.[8]

NelsonHall anticipates that HR BPO will grow in Europe's manufacturing, banking and government sectors and that F&A BPO will develop in the telecom, retail and manufacturing sectors.[9] The analysts note that the government sector has recently demanded a mixture of services, and that central government appears to be replacing local government as a BPO consumer.[10]

Unique Factors Shaping Growth: European Complexity and Labor Restrictions

Although Europe has followed and capitalized upon some of the lessons learned by early BPO adopter, the Americas, the pace of European BPO adoption is largely shaped by the more multifaceted and complex nature of the European market, compared to the more homogeneous Americas market. Because it is less complex, the Americas region has traditionally adopted BPO on a larger scale, faster.

Europe is not one single market but a grouping of smaller markets. The European Community alone comprises some 25 nations that differ vastly in culture, economy, language and receptivity to outsourcing. With 15-20 different languages in Europe, BPO contracts that involve, for example, employee self-service, can become more complex and time-consuming from the outset. As a result of such complexities, BPO tends to be adopted in Europe on a country-by country basis more often than a regional basis. This can represent a challenge to the service providers who have traditionally performed well in the Americas. They sometimes find that they succeed in one European country but not another.[11]

Further, in many European countries, outsourcing service providers must accommodate both stringent labor laws and tax provisions. For example, in the EU, the cost of Value-Added Tax (VAT) on the service provider's services must be factored in.[12] As a result of these regulations, the cost of transferring jobs and responsibilities in some countries can be high, but still affordable. The costs strongly impact service provider selection and the use of existing personnel.

BPO Growth in Continental Europe Follows the United Kingdom's Lead

Most European countries outside of the United Kingdom have tiptoed into adopting outsourcing in general and BPO in particular. While the United Kingdom led the way in European BPO deals, Northern European countries, especially Germany, Benelux and the Scandinavian countries, are increasingly adopting BPO.

In 2003, the United Kingdom accounted for 78 percent of the BPO TCV in Europe. Switzerland, Benelux, Italy, Spain, the Nordics and Germany represented most of the remainder. In the first half of 2004, the United Kingdom accounted for 52 percent of European BPO contract value, half Germany, Switzerland and Benelux accounting for most of the remainder.[13]

Several factors explain the shift:[14]

- The Continental European headquarters of major multinationals are increasingly adopting back-office BPO.
- BPO adoption in Germany has been led by a receptive banking sector.

- UK local government BPO activity decreased sharply from June 2003-June 2004.

BPO activity in Continental Europe tends to be dominated by the financial services sector (middle-office outsourcing emphasis) and the manufacturing sector (Back-office outsourcing emphasis). The BPO market in the United Kingdom has traditionally been dependent on the government and financial services sectors.[15]

Undoubtedly, the area will continue to represent a substantial portion of the BPO pie, as BPO is "the fastest growing IT sector in the UK."[16] However, executives in Continental Europe profess an increasing interest in and comfort with outsourcing in general, which should positively impact BPO in particular. In general – nearly seventy percent of 400 respondents in Morgan Stanley's European IT Spending Survey (June, 2004) expect to outsource more in 2004 than they did in 2003.

TPI is experiencing a similar evolution in its overall outsourcing work in Europe. Two years ago, nearly 60 percent of TPI's European revenues were from billings in the United Kingdom. Today, that portion is 25 percent of total European revenue. If one factors in a more than doubling of the total size of European outsourcing during the same period, TPI has not only held its UK position but also created a truly European business of tangible scale[17].

Financial Times Europe 500 and Governments Spearhead European BPO Growth

Major companies and governments are quicker than other large, medium or small institutions to adopt and lead BPO in Europe. Twenty-two FTE-500 companies account for 36 of the 84 (43 percent) completed corporate BPO transactions of more than US$50M from 1991-1H04. These 36 transactions were worth a total of US$11.8 billion, or 50 percent, of the total corporate BPO TCV for the period. Of public sector contracts, 70 completed European BPO transactions of more than US$50M were for government clients and were worth a TCV of US$28.5B.[18]

Half of the 36 FTE-500 BPO deals were awarded by top 50 FTE companies. This could signify that top companies in Europe more readily feel the heat of

Completed European BPO Deals of > S$50M for 1991 – 1H04

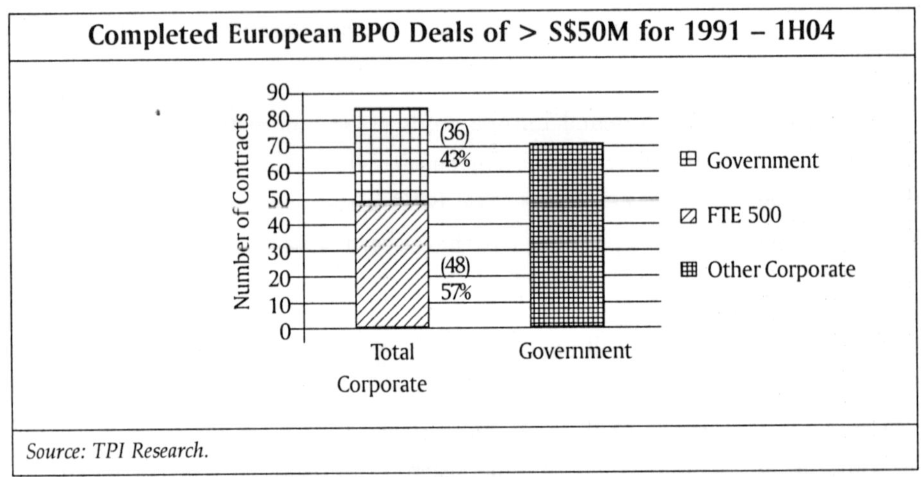

Source: TPI Research.

global competition and, understanding the benefits global competitors gain from outsourcing, feel motivated to outsource.

Several FTE-500 companies awarded multiple contracts. BPO can be a tough undertaking for the uninitiated; however, for those with experience, it has proven to be manageable, attractive and worth repeating.

In the recent quarter, more small and mid-sized companies that are not in the FTE-500 have begun adopting BPO in Europe.

Service Providers Enable European BPO Growth

Major global service providers are aggressively targeting Europe. Thirteen service providers competed for and won BPO transactions in Europe in the first three quarters of 2004. Of these, Accenture and IBM have been particularly successful. By the last quarter of 2003, Capgemini had joined IBM, Accenture, EDS and HP in winning more than US$1 billion in European outsourcing revenue.[19] European companies appear to be most receptive to providers who can demonstrate quality, resilience and stability.[20] These companies have top-level relationships and an established network with Western European organizations that can give them an edge.

The indigenous European service provider market, although less mature than the American, has also made headway in European BPO. Some pan-European players, like LogicaCMG and Atos Origin are moving into this space, but more on a niche transaction-processing basis. UK-based service providers Capita (Public Sector, Insurance), Xchanging and Liberata are also joining the fray. Capita and Xchanging benefited early-on from recognizing that BPO is not a sub-set of IT services, but a wholly different business with different client expectations and critical success factors.[21]

Using a global service delivery model is more complex and has been embraced more slowly in Europe. Twenty percent of all outsourcing transactions in Europe had an offshore element compared with 69 percent globally.[22] Moreover, it can sometimes be hard to make a compelling case for BPO without an offshore element. Offshore outsourcing is often the starting point for simple, commodity customer-management services. The low level of European offshoring could signal that the initial BPO projects in Europe are relatively complex.[23]

The availability of Eastern Europe and Ireland as near-shore sources of service delivery helps European companies overcome the reluctance to consider offshoring. In Eastern Europe, compared with India, a company can easily find an educated labor force that speaks French, German, Italian and/or Spanish.[24] Eastern European resources will also continue to be valued for their ability to overcome cultural or regulatory constraints. Several TPI-advised BPO transactions are evaluating service offerings delivered from Spain, Poland, and the Czech Republic. Ireland is reviving somewhat from three years of strong outsourcing competition with China, India and Eastern Europe. Ireland is waging a government-sponsored marketing campaign that de-emphasizes lower costs as it promotes its workforce's brainpower, ability to work at all levels of business processes and flexibility. The country is English-speaking, Euro-compliant, and easily accessible to both the United Kingdom and the Continent.[25]

Finally, Indian-headquartered service providers are establishing their own beachheads in Europe and are still able to provide cost advantages there. Wipro has the most "local" structure in Europe. Infosys, HCL Technologies, Tata, Satyam and NIIT have established a full-scale services presence in Europe during the past few years. All have learned that a strong onshore presence is needed, especially to penetrate markets such as Germany and France.[26]

Conclusions

TPI believes that Europe is likely to sustain and even increase its BPO growth, especially if the region promotes it via a few "poster children," examples of large, successful BPO contracts by top European companies. TPI executives cite a few or all of the following as potential catalysts for BPO growth in Europe:

- HR, F&A and Procurement begin to take on the CRM pace-setter.
- More continental European countries adopt BPO.
- Indigenous service providers make a stronger showing.
- Near-shore service delivery succeeds.
- More FTE-500 companies and medium-sized companies adopt BPO.

TPI does not advocate any specific form of sourcing. However, in helping companies determine the right sourcing strategy, TPI advisors have witnessed what some European organizations have gained from adopting BPO:

- Cost reductions.
- Operational efficiencies.
- Greater flexibility and ability to respond to changing global market conditions.
- Increased competitiveness.
- Improved business processes.
- Ability to grow (by improving time-to-market, for example).
- Support for merging or regrouping.[27]

When ten new members joined in May, the European Union became a trade and legal alliance of some 450 million people, with economic output approaching that of the US, Europe looks forward to rival the Americas in coming quarters as both a provider and user of BPO.

(TPI offers sourcing advisory solutions that support organisational goals to create enduring value, achieve effective transformation, and meet rapidly changing market

demands. Since 2000, TPI has advised on more than 25 percent of total contract value awarded in the broader outsourcing market, which includes commercial contract awards each valued at €40 million or more. With 350 advisors to help clients find the right balance of value, speed-to-market and risk mitigation, TPI remains the most sought-after advisory firm in the world. TPI operates in locations including London, Paris, Brussels, Frankfurt, Amsterdam, Houston, New York, Toronto, Sydney, Bangalore and Singapore. For additional information, please visit us at www.tpi.net).

Endnotes

1 1Q04, 2Q04 & 3Q04 TPI Index Data.

2 3Q04 TPI Index Data.

3 Duncan Aitchison, August 12, 2004.

4 BPO Case Study, NelsonHall, April 2004.

5 TPI Contracts Database, 2001-2003.

6 #BP52L, IDC, April 2004.

7 2Q04 TPI Index, European version, slide 11.

8 John Willmott, NelsonHall, August 12, 2004.

9 "Global BPO Contract Analysis & Future Opportunities," NelsonHall, January 2004.

10 John Willmott, NelsonHall, August 12, 2004.

11 *Businessworld*, April 21, 2004.

12 *The Banker*, July 1,2004.

13 NelsonHall, "Global BPO Contract Analysis & Future Opportunities," January 2004, and NelsonHall, "BPO Contract Activity and Market Developments: H1 2004," July 2004.

14 John Willmott, NelsonHall, August 12, 2004.

15 John Willmott, NelsonHall, August 12, 2004.

16 *The Times* (London), June 8, 2004.

17 Duncan Aitchison-TPI Update, July 2004.

18 TPI Data, 1991-2004 YTD.

19 #Q52L, IDC, March 2004.

20 *Businessworld*, April 21, 2004.

21 NelsonHall, "BPO Contract Activity and Market Developments: H1 004," July, 2004.

22 *Newswire (VNU), April 22, 2004.

23 John Willmott, August 12, 2004.

24 *Businessworld*, April 21, 2004.

25 The International Herald Tribune, June 5, 2004.

26 IDC, #PR01 L, February 2004.

27 Duncan Aitchison, "Insider Insight: Outsourcing, Shore Thing," *Accountancy Age*, June 10, 2004.

13

Outsourcing and Information Management: A Comparative Analysis of France, Italy and Japan in Both Small and Large Firms

Alessandro Innocenti and Sandrine Labory

This paper compares outsourcing processes in France, Italy and Japan in large scale and also small scale firms. It is shown that outsourcing has increased over the last two decades in both small and large firms in all three countries and that mainly in the last decade the tendency has been to increasingly involve some of the suppliers in product development. We interpret this evidence by means of a cognitive framework related to the activity of information management. Specifically, we show that the more the relationships among suppliers and users are characterised by two-way communication, decentralised information processing, and accordingly balanced contractual power, the more the incentives to create knowledge and to innovate autonomously are guaranteed.

1. Introduction

Subcontracting and, more generally, productive outsourcing has diffused in all industrialised countries in the last thirty years. Attention to this phenomenon arose in the field of organised vertical markets in which vertical co-ordination by large firms has been progressively substituted by decentralised network of suppliers, governed by principles of lean production and just-in-time. Outsourcing has also been the more significant source of downsizing in local systems of small firms, implying that small firms remain small.[1] The result has been the growth in the informative and strategic interdependency among firms with numerous implications, ranging from the fragmentation of labour markets to the intensified use of information technology.

Industrial economics has proposed various explanations for the diffusion of outsourcing. The bureaucratic costs of the large, integrated company have been outlined (Chandler 1962), as well as the incentive and the information processing costs (especially Aoki 1988). When products become increasingly differentiated and renewed, the best strategy appears to focus on core competencies and let other firms deal with the production of other parts, maintenance of machines or distribution (Clark and Fujimoto 1991, Cusumano and Takeishi 1991). Thus, disintegrated firms have been shown to be more efficient in terms of lower costs or higher productivity by Aoki (1988) and Asanuma (1989) for the Japanese case, Coriat (1995), de Banville and Chanaron (1999) for the French case, Arrighetti (1999) and Conti and Menghinello (1998) for the Italian case. However, outsourcing yields other advantages, in particular in terms of product and process innovation. For instance, Clark and Fujimoto (1991) or Michie and Sheehan (1999) show that R&D and product innovation are higher in disintegrated firms.[2]

Concerning the organisation of production and market structure, such changes mean that the relevant unit of analysis becomes the relationships among firms rather than the single firm. In this paper we focus on the processes of outsourcing among firms that usually assume the form of subcontracting relationships.

---

1 See Acs and Audretsch (1990), (1993), Baldwin (1998) Carree and Thurik (1998), Doi and Cowling (1998), Henley (1994), Loweman and Sengenberger (1991), Traù (1997).

2 Heshmati (2003) offers an updated survey of the literature on the relation between productivity growth and outsourcing.

Specifically, outsourcing involves turning over the functions that fall outside firm's core competencies to another firm whose core competencies are the functions being outsourced. In this way a specific governance form is created, which typically includes the exchange of proprietary information between the user and the supplier.

This paper derives theoretical insights on such information exchanges by comparing some country cases. The aim is to show that the more a supplier is given autonomy of decision and, for this purpose, access to proprietary information, the higher the performance of the network (constituted by the user and the supplier(s)) in terms of innovation. The literature has amply shown the static efficiency advantages of outsourcing; in this paper, our aim therefore is to outline dynamic efficiency, more precisely learning, leading to innovation.

We focus on Japan, France and Italy. Japan has been chosen because it is a paradigm of an industrial system based on vertical networks, Italy for the historical predominance of small firms' localised systems, and France for being the European country that experiences the largest decrease in vertical integration in the 1990s.[3] We review some empirical evidence related to two different types of supplier networks, namely networks characterised by the presence of large firms and more or less dependent suppliers (Section 2) and localised networks of small firms (Section 3). Sections 4 and 5 provide a theoretical framework for interpreting the empirical evidence. In particular, we outline the dynamic efficiency advantages (innovation) of supply relationships where the supplier is involved in decision-making and product development. Section 4 outlines some definitions, while section 5 examines the activity of information management involved in the production process in order to show these dynamic efficiency advantages. Specifically, the more the relationships among suppliers and users are characterised by two way communication, decentralised information processing, and accordingly balanced contractual power, the more the incentives to innovate autonomously and to improve firms' efficiency. Finally, Section 6 sets out some concluding remarks.

---

[3] According to Arrighetti (1999), who considers the UK, Germany, France and Italy, the largest decrease in vertical integration has occurred in France (-6,2%), more than the Italian case (-5,6%). Generally the degree of disintegration in France ends up quite similar to the Italian one, but very different from the other two countries. The rate of growth of outsourcing in France is also similar to the Italian rate and different from the English and German rates.

2. Outsourcing Processes of Large Firms

Following the diffusion of the flexible production system, which combines economies of scale and scope by pushing product differentiation to the last stages of the production process, unlike the Fordist system which exploited economies of scale only,[4] large firms have progressively disintegrated vertically and established particular relationships with suppliers. Such relationships vary across countries and industries, but some regularity can be identified, into different models of subcontracting by large firms.

The Japanese model of subcontracting has traditionally been seen as based on an asymmetry of bargaining power between a large downstream firm and small upstream firms[5]. The aim of subcontracting for large firms were primarily to reduce investment in fixed capital by shifting it to subcontractors, to exploit differences in wages between large and small firms (higher in the large firms), to reduce procurement costs, and often to try and shift the effects of temporary recessions to suppliers. Such imbalance of power was interpreted as a competitive pressure on suppliers: they have to reduce cost and provide the required quality otherwise they lose customers. Hence the incentive for performance was much higher than in the case where the supplier was part of a vertically integrated firm, whatever be the degree of centralisation of the firm and the autonomy of the division producing the parts.

Such relationships between large firms and their suppliers have progressively become more complex and involve more than pressure for performance. Aoki (1988) and Asanuma (1989) were the first to support this argument. In particular, Asanuma claimed that the Japanese subcontracting relationships have four main characteristics. First, relationships are long-term and duration is determined by the product life cycles. Each time a new product is launched, the large firm makes a sort of call for the best offer from suppliers. At that stage, suppliers compete. Firms however tend to keep the same suppliers; product change is therefore an occasion to renegotiate the contract. Second, the Japanese subcontracting relationship is institutionalised and hierarchically organised. Subcontractors are differentiated according to the type of product bought by the

[4] See Labory (1997), for a discussion of the flexible production system and associated strategies on product markets.

[5] See Miwa (1995), (1996), for an account of this view.

large firm. The first type consists in traded products, which are bought on the market without any intervention in design by the large firm. In this case, the subcontractors are chosen on the basis of quality, and constitute the most autonomous subcontractors. They are "general suppliers" and "ordinary subcontractors" according to Asanuma's definition. The second type is made of ordered products, which can be designed either by the supplier or the large firm itself (or jointly). In the latter case, the supplier only executes orders from the large firms according to its indications, and is very dependent on the large firm. Suppliers designing or co-designing the product enjoy more bargaining power. Both cases however constitute the first layer of the hierarchy of subcontractors: first-tier suppliers and associated companies. Third, the Japanese subcontracting relationship is contractual and characterised by specific procedures. According to Asanuma, such procedures unfold as follows. After a supplier is chosen, when the new product is still in the development phase, a basic contract is made, with broad specification (no specification of quantities to be delivered, neither of prices, etc.). The contract is made more precise as decisions on the manufacturing process are made, using complementary contracts.[6] Last, suppliers are contractually encouraged to innovate since they can enjoy the payoffs of their innovation for a certain time period (e.g., one year at Toyota).

Therefore, in Japan, the relationship between the large firm and its suppliers is characterised by the coexistence of co-operation and competition. Competition prevails not only in the suppliers' selection phase, but also after the contract has been signed. The performance of suppliers in terms of quality and costs are indeed constantly assessed and compared with other suppliers. If the supplier does not perform well, orders are reduced and, as the last resort, the supplier is changed. However, the large firm has also interest in co-operating with the supplier to avoid switching and associated costs (time to learn the specification of the product, the technology of production, time required to set up trust, etc.). Consequently, the large firm also seeks stable relationships with its suppliers, helping to resolve problems and continuously exchanging information in order to improve the system. The know-how generated by such a relationship is twofold. On the one hand, it is technical, regarding the product and production system. On the other

6 Quantities and prices start to be fixed in a very precise way especially in case of just-in-time production (see Coriat 1991).

hand, it is "relational", due to the incentives and knowledge creation generated by the coexistence of co-operation and competition.

Aoki (1995) gives other insights into this issue by conceptualising the notion of relational rents. According to Aoki, "group-specific returns" are created by the co-operative relationships between the user and the supplier. Such benefits constitute a relational rent in the sense that they are generated by the high informational efficiency of the contractual relationship developed within the network. Such efficiency allows enjoying the benefits of vertical integration in terms of co-ordination while also enjoying the advantages of markets, in that, incentives to innovate are provided.

Hence information flows in the Japanese supply network are intense and complex. Technological and market information are shared so that the co-ordination of the production process and a common language are established. However, the supplier specialises in an autonomous way and therefore has scope to develop ideas and innovate. One could characterise the advantage of such network as the result of specialisation (dealing with a particular subset of the overall information set related to the development of the product) and sharing of generic knowledge (exchange of information and collective creation of knowledge) that imply both co-ordination and innovation. A source of recent evidence on this point is given by the Reports of the Japanese SMEA (Small and Medium Enterprises Agency). According to them, in the 90s the structure of subcontracting has definitively changed in the direction of greater partnership between the various participants. Thus, Japanese subcontractors have raised their profiles by enhancing product quality and by diversifying away from one main contractor. This evolution is clearly linked to a technological up scaling of smaller firms. The criteria for the selection of subcontractors by large firms have accordingly changed. The demand for "thorough cost reduction", "greater quality and precision", or "quality assurance" double their importance when compared with the early 1980s and now rank first. Conversely, the more traditional demands for "stable quantities of products", "fixing delivery time" drop sharply in significance. This changing nature of outsourcing has lead to a more horizontal network of inter-firm relationships that goes beyond the vertical *keiretsu* structure.

In Italy, most large firms have outsourced by adjusting to subcontractors' characteristics and radically changing their internal organization. For instance, Camuffo and Volpato (2001) describe the case of the car industry, while Crestanello (1999) discusses the textile and clothing industry case. First-tier subcontractors have tended to become less numerous to take responsibility not only for the production of specific parts but for technological innovation and components design as well. In addition, outsourcing increasingly concerns production services, be they low added value and more labour-intensive services (security, cleaning and catering) or more complex services such as logistics, computer maintenance, or transportation.

In the case of the textile industry, Crestanello (1999) distinguishes two main types of suppliers according to their degree of autonomy. The first type is the dependent supplier, which just executes orders from the client firm. This kind of relationship is hierarchical, and information flows are typically one-way, from the user to the supplier. The second type is more autonomous and is involved in co-designing of products. The subcontractor in this case faces more competitive pressure, from other potential suppliers, but has more bargaining power on the price of the product.

Insights into the characteristics of these relationships in the car industry are given by the example of the carmaker Fiat. Recent works (Volpato and Stocchetti 2000, Bianchi, Enrietti and Lanzetta 2001, Camuffo and Volpato 2001) show that outsourcing is relatively common at Fiat, in both production and services. While in the 1970s and 1980s, outsourcing concerned mainly low value added production phases, since the late 1980s it involved important production phases such as the assembly of suspension units and crucial services like plant maintenance and logistics. The most evident measure of the extent of this process is given by the reduction in employment level by 38 per cent from 133,431 units in 1990 to 82,450 units in 1999 despite the maintenance of the same production level.

The downsizing of Fiat has been accompanied by the restructuring of the suppliers' relationships. Subcontractors are divided into three groups. The first-level subcontractors are those producing more complex components that are designed in close collaboration with Fiat and that are usually modules to be assembled internally by Fiat. The other two groups produce more standardised components and their activity is relatively more independent from Fiat.

The rationale for outsourcing appears to be the increase in the specialisation of activities. Subcontractors are chosen on the basis of their specific technical knowledge and not of lower labour costs.[7] First-tier suppliers carry out specific tasks that correspond to a module. In order to make the different parts complementary, Fiat has organised the production of cars by arranging the different phases in such a way that the information necessary to produce each of them can be processed autonomously..While in the past car components were designed and engineered by the car manufacturer who led the whole project and suppliers simply manufactured them, the supply chain is now decentralised according to the pattern described in Volpato and Stocchetti (2000, p. 9): First, the fundamental aspect of coordination based upon ex ante planning is that any individual operator does not need information on the whole chain of operations. Any chain operator must know only start and end date for a given activity, and must be concerned about precisely meeting its specific deadline. This implies a hierarchical management of information. But forms of simultaneous coordination on the whole of operations, aimed at compressing chain slacks require on line access to the whole sequence of operations, in order to carry out adaptations any time in which downwards demand triggers a wave of change, which involves the whole upward operation chain. In other words, this implies forms of network connections among operators. The decision-making processes related to product development involve both the car manufacturer and first-tier suppliers. According to the continuous improvement both in product and process technology, nowadays the competencies that are necessary in order to manufacture a competitive car encompass a wide range of fields of expertise. As a result, critical decisions might often take place in an inter-firm process and thus an agreement among peers could be required.

---

7 This change of perspective has important consequences for collective bargaining. Trade unions are indeed successful in extending their bargaining power to the subcontractors. For example, an agreement signed in 1998, which externalises logistics from Fiat Mirafiori's establishment to a Dutch multinational, keeps all the rights provided by the old agreement (the kind of employment contract, the benefits available in Fiat, the guarantee of job security and insurance for accident) to the new relationship.

The involvement of first-tier suppliers in the product development process implies their access to some strategic information of the large firm. The main consequence is that the supplier gains bargaining power and the relationships between the large firm and the suppliers become contractually more balanced. Given the possibility of opportunism and resulting hold-up problem, duration is substantial, related in practice to the product life cycle. Even in this case, the long duration of relationships allows enjoying some of the benefits of vertical integration, while simultaneously avoiding its drawbacks, such as the lack of incentive for performance for the component maker. It is noteworthy that Fiat incurred the problem of excessive outsourcing: some R&D functions have also been delegated to outside suppliers and it seems that this lead the large firm to lose too much control over the strategic phases of the production process; after the bad performance of the firm, Fiat has tended to re-internalise some of these functions.

In France, the relationships with suppliers have increasingly been defined as "partnership" relationships, characterised by a system of reciprocal commitments, whereby the supplier commits to delivery time, quality and price, while the contractor commits to order time, participation in investment and transfer of techniques and know-how. The transfer of techniques and know-how can take the form of the provision by the large firm of some of its machinery, or the maintenance and switching of tools, and technical co-operation (on manufacturing methods, product specifications and so on).

Until the 1970s, the dominance of the large firm over its suppliers was total: technical, industrial and commercial, and the relationships with suppliers were based on the criterion of minimum price for the specific volume. Delivery time was secondary and solved by stocks. Such Fordist inter-industrial practices (with the division of tasks, specialisation, the separation of conception and manufacturing and one-way—top to bottom—information flows) was characterised by:

- Open booking: no contract was signed and the supplier had to face fluctuations in demand with strict price controls.
- High competition: the large firm kept several potential suppliers for each part, so that only the least cost supplier was chosen.
- No autonomy on product development, only execution of orders from the large firm.

Hence the suppliers' scope and incentives to innovate were limited.

After the 1970s, new relationships have progressively been set up, following both the vertical disintegration of large firms and the imitation of the Japanese model. Besides JIT, French firms imitated some aspects of the particular contractor-supplier relationships, such as the already-mentioned pyramidal structure and both the financial participation in some subcontractors and the establishment of suppliers' clubs, with the first-tier suppliers only. In Japan, such clubs are called *kyoryokukai*. Partnership relationships have several characteristics, close to the Japanese model: trust, based in mutual commitment; technological expertise of the supplier on its product (not just execution of orders); short delivery times (JIT); and duration: procurement contracts are signed.

In terms of information flows and knowledge exchange, two phases have to be distinguished. In a first phase, broadly in the 1980s, French producers outsource to reduce costs. Hence relationships remain authoritative, the buyer making precise requirements to the supplier and the supplier having mainly execution tasks. More recently, in what can be called a second phase, broadly in the 1990s, co-operative relationships have been developed with some suppliers, involving them earlier in the component design process (Dyer 1996, de Banville and Chanaron 1999). Important changes occur: the supplier has progressively been involved in product development and innovation; profit gains and technological and economic information have been shared. Hence information flows in the partnership relationships have become two-way and differentiated, as in the Japanese model (Leclerc, Perrin and Villeval 1999). While generic information is shared and constitutes the common denominator of the network, each actor specialises in a certain part of the overall information set related to the final product. Such features regard the first tier of suppliers, because it is the only tier to be involved in co-design. Information advantages are similar to those of the Japanese case.

These three national cases points to a number of hypotheses that can be theoretically checked:

1. Large firms tend to develop horizontal networks with their first tier suppliers who are involved not only in cost reduction and time saving in production but co-design and innovation as well.
2. Moving from lower tiers to the first tier of the supplier network, information flows between the buyer and the suppliers shift from one-way information flows.
3. These processes, which lower firms' average size, seem to improve the suppliers' autonomous capacity of innovation. The next section examines the case of outsourcing among small firms.

3. Outsourcing Processes of Small Firms

Although large firm disintegration has been a major factor to the growth of the occupational share of small firms, the process of outsourcing among small firms has also been significant in France, Italy and Japan, where vertical disintegration has concerned an increasing number of firms since the 1970s.

Regarding Japan, the "White Paper on Small and Medium Enterprises in Japan" (SMEA 2001) offers interesting evidence. Like in the large firm case, supplier relationships among small firms have also moved from pure cost reduction orientation to more flexible interactions and more product development initiative.

Although there is historical evidence that the probability of working as subcontractor is negatively related to firm size in many Japanese industries in the 1970s and 1980s (Kimura 2002), the data collected for the *Survey of the structure of subcontract work in Japan,* published by SMEA since 1996, shows that in the 1990s a radical restructuring of the subcontracting relationships occurred. The percentage of small firms engaged in exclusive subcontracting contracts halved during the period 1987-1995, while dispersed and semi-dispersed contracts increased by more than twenty per cent (SMEA 2001). Such a partial opening of supply chains and the consequent development of productive structures with many apexes have lead small firms to higher specialisation. In particular, the requirements of buyers to their suppliers have significantly changed even for lower tiers. The changing nature of subcontracting relationships naturally led to network structures with more intense communication among small firms, flexibly extending beyond *keiretsu* and rearranging more horizontally the whole Japanese supply chain (Lakshmanan and Okumura, 1995).

This change of attitude takes us far from the more diffuse patterns of subcontracting relationships of the 1960s and the 1970s, when small firms mainly played the role of suppliers of low cost labour. This population of small firms, mainly composed of capacity subcontractors,[8] had a comparative advantage for the "dualistic" Japanese manufacturing industry (Koshiro, 1990) where "the abuse by large firms of their subcontractors was one of the most significant political issues" (Friedman, 1988, p. 166). The turning point can be dated from the early 1990s, during the high yen crisis, following the 1985 appreciation of the yen, (Glasmeier and Sugiura, 1991) represented an external shock causing a process of selection above all among the capacity subcontractors whose productive activity was reduced in favour of outward direct investment. At the same time, a gradual increase of specialised subcontracting was necessary to cope with the shift of the Japanese system toward production at a higher technological level. Even if this process had the net effect of reducing the employment of small Japanese firms as a whole, because the shrinking of the large population of capacity subcontractors was only partially compensated by the growth of specialised subcontractors, it contributed to improve domestic efficiency by reflecting the growing importance of technical change in relation to simple cheap-labour advantages of capacity subcontractors (Carnazza et al., 2001). Market characteristics and technological change can explain why outsourcing has become the main pattern of relationships even among small firms: specialisation has allowed them to improve their capacity to process information and build contractually more balanced, specialised and innovative partnerships with other small firms.

Finally, this process has increased the importance of industrial clusters of small firm in the Japanese industrial organisation. According to the 1996 SMEA survey, there are 537 clusters widely dispersed across Japan. Most of them are characterised by the presence of hierarchically structured relationships between manufacturers, first-tier suppliers, and second-tier suppliers. At the same time a detailed analysis

---

8 Carnazza, Innocenti and Vercelli (2001), distinguish between capacity and specialised subcontracting. Specialised subcontracting means a relationship between a contractor and a subcontractor where the former continuously relies on the latter for the supply of an input for which there is no in-house supply. Capacity-based subcontracting indicates a relationship where the contractor hands over supply to the subcontractor only in the case of temporarily high levels of demand (Carnazza et al., 2001).

by Yamawaki (2002) of a sample of 14 major cases of Japanese manufacturing clusters concludes that: "Among the advantages identified in the paper, that created by the existence of specialised suppliers in a localised industry is considered the most important element in creating agglomeration economies. A supplier's skills and capabilities complement other suppliers' skills and capabilities, which in turn complement manufacturers' skills and capabilities. Through such a network, firms develop the skills specific to a cluster." (Yamawaki 2002, p. 139).

For the Italian case, a recent study promoted by the Bank of Italy (Signorini, 2000) analyzes the processes of outsourcing among small firms in the Italian industrial districts. The main finding—confirmed by Conti and Menghinello, 1998, Corò and Grandinetti, 1999, and Innocenti, 2003)—is that the processes of outsourcing characterised by high levels of knowledge specificity and product quality only involve firms belonging to the same local system, among which vertical cooperation is arranged on the basis of long term duration, explicit ex-ante agreements and implicit renewal over time. Production characterised by low knowledge specificity and intensive use of labour is shifted to low labour costs countries. The latter type of subcontracting is however considered valuable only if close co-operation between the contractor and the subcontractor is not crucial.

The difference between these two types of subcontracting can be better pointed out by describing what changes have concerned subcontracting relationships in industrial districts since 1970. These patterns of evolution are very similar to those sketched above for the case of the outsourcing of large vs. small firms. A significant part of these relationships among small firms turned from one-way to two-way information flows. Two major factors explain this change. First, the increased technological level of production induces small firms to increase their specialisation. This implies the creation of more stable agreements, the multiplication of the tiers of subcontractors and more balanced contractual powers between suppliers and buyers. At the same time, capacity-based subcontracting, which was largely used in the past as excess capacity to be exploited during temporary phases of demand expansion, becomes less attractive. Second, the final markets in which Italian industrial districts are specialised have become increasingly fragmented. The production of these local systems is largely concentrated on the high quality segments of three macro-sectors: the so-called "fashion system" (textiles, leather, clothes, shoes, glasses); the goods for the house (wood, furniture, ceramics, accessories); the machinery produced for the previous two macro-sectors. These production systems have acquired the characteristics of niche markets, where customer needs are deeply diversified and the product life cycle has shortened. Rather than price, firms' market strategies are increasingly dependent on design innovation, product differentiation, customisation, after-sales services and brand loyalty. These requirements appear to be only satisfied by intensifying the process of outsourcing and asking suppliers to co-develop products or parts.

Concerning French small firms, a number of empirical studies surveyed in Aniello and Le Galés (2001) interpret the recent restructuring process of French manufacturing as a transformation of the industrial organisation towards clusters similar to the Italian industrial districts. This process is in fact a local rooting of production by the setting up of supplier networks between small firms, whose origin can be traced back to the evolution of the relationships between large and small firms described in the previous section: the shift towards more involvement of suppliers in co-design and productive innovation has also been followed by small firms and their suppliers (Courlet and Pecqueur 1991, Ganne 1992).

A specific case is the region of Mediterranean France, where a virtuous process of development has been triggered by a network of small and medium enterprises, which were historically prevalent in this region (Hansen 1990). The processes of vertical disintegration have caused the emergence of specialised areas where inter-small firms' linkages allow to exploit external economies through the expansion of the regional network as a whole.

In general there is a growing strand of literature on the French industry in which the development of trust between large and small firms and the creation of partnerships between contractors and subcontractors are assessed as the main factor enhancing productivity (Linhart 1991, Lorenz 1992, Lorenz 1993, Gorgeu and Mathieu 1993). These contributions support the view that small firms increase generally their autonomous capacity of innovation and consequently of making profits by specializing in narrower production phases and by outsourcing the pruned processes to other small firms. According to these authors this evolution has improved the French industry's international competitiveness.

Overall, this outline of the outsourcing process of small firms supports similar hypotheses to those outlined in the previous section:

1. The advantages of being small mainly result from the opportunity to specialise in narrower phases of the productive chain.
2. In the 1990s, small firms prefer to outsource any activity other than their *core* activity because externalization increases the probability of innovation.
3. Although communication costs may be higher in local systems of small firms than in hierarchically dominated organisations, horizontal competition permits to maintain efficiency. Independent small firms tend to base their competitiveness on the dominance of a niche market, where it is essential to maintain a monopolistic position. Therefore, small firms are particularly keen on keeping their strategic information and not leaking it to potential competitors. They not only actively cooperate vertically with other small suppliers and users but they also compete horizontally by protecting their own specificity.

Hence during the 1990s the trend in outsourcing has been to increasingly involve suppliers in decision-making, suppliers not being merely executors of orders but having a say in both the production organisation of their product and product development. Such rising involvement only concerns however a limited number of suppliers, those of the first tiers. Hence between the firm and its first tier of supplier a more balanced network is established, in that the relationship is less hierarchical and authoritative. This generates not only static efficiency effects (cost reduction) but also dynamic efficiency effects (innovation) that have not been extensively discussed and demonstrated in both the empirical and theoretical literature. Therefore, we provide in the next sections a theoretical framework for understanding these latter effects.

4. The Network as an Information Conveyor

The first step in defining the theoretical framework is to provide some definitions. In the first place, we assume that knowledge is, to some degree, always tacit, while information is the only part of knowledge that can be transferred. Knowledge can be considered as an infinite set — mainly because it is the outcome of a mental process — that includes information as a closed set (Fransman 1994). While information can be communicated, knowledge cannot ever be communicated perfectly. In other words, information is knowledge made explicit, which can be communicated to others. The process of knowledge creation can be described as a sequence where the subject collects information, that is explicit knowledge communicated by others, and combines it with the previously possessed knowledge, which is both explicit and tacit. The outcome is new knowledge that is only partially communicated to others.

We also assume a specific meaning of hierarchy. Hierarchy has been defined as a system where "only a few individuals (or only one individual) can undertake projects, while others provide support in decision-making", as opposed to a polyarchy, i.e., a system in which "there are several decision makers who can undertake projects (or ideas) independently of one another" (Sah and Stiglitz 1986, p. 716). This definition helps to compare the integrated firm, i.e. a self-contained hierarchical system, with the decentralised network, which is a polyarchy where several independent decision makers autonomously undertake productive projects. By the same token, if the integrated firm is the place where all residual rights of control accrue to the owner, then the decentralised network can be seen as a system in which multiple owners possess rights of control on separate competencies.

The choice of an organisational pattern can thus be represented as the selection of a point on the line joining the extreme cases of the fully hierarchical firm, which can be defined as an ideal organization collecting all the productive units under only one hierarchy, and the "monadic" network, which is a network in which each producer is an autonomous decision-maker. Outsourcing, which corresponds to the decentralization of competencies, represents a movement along the direction going from the fully hierarchical firm to the totally decentralised network. In this setting all the intermediate types of organizations have to deal with the same problem—co-ordinate in the presence of specialisation. Taking the above definition of information and knowledge, this activity amounts to internally diffuse the information necessary to make complementary the specialist knowledge possessed by the various decision-makers. Co-ordination has to be obtained while minimising knowledge transfers because "Communication, like decision-making, is always imperfect. No individual ever fully communicates perfectly what he knows to another" (Sah and Stiglitz 1986, p. 717). In this way the process of information management becomes a key variable to explain performance differentials across different organizational structures.

According to this interpretation, the network would assume the role of information conveyor, which diffuses information among firms possessing separate pieces of knowledge. The choice of the most efficient organisation and the boundary of the firm would depend on the degree of decentralisation that is optimal when it makes each firm able to collect and process all the information pertinent to the specialist knowledge it owns. Specifically, separate firms could efficiently conduct two adjacent production phases if a single firm can process all the information concerning each phase without the knowledge employed in the other production phase. By specialising in the processing of a narrower set of information, each firm can establish a full correspondence between the information it processes and the information that is pertinent to the knowledge they utilise.

5. A Phase Model of Outsourcing

The empirical literature summarised in sections 2 and 3 shows that small and large firms share similar patterns in the diffusion of the processes of outsourcing in France, Italy and Japan. In both cases outsourcing is associated with the intensification of competition mainly based on non-price factors. Regardless of their size, firms have developed horizontal networks with their main suppliers, first tier suppliers being involved not only in cost reduction and time saving in production but also in information processing and knowledge creation. They have implemented a two-phase outsourcing strategy. First, outsourcing aimed at cost reduction was limited to second tier suppliers involved in structured tasks such as scheduling and logistics or in activities characterised by low knowledge specificity. Second, first tier suppliers have been involved in product development, and thus have started to create their own strategic knowledge. As a result information flows that were one-way flows, wherein the buyer gives orders to the supplier and the latter executes, have transformed into two-way communication. This has occurred since design and specifically innovation is a complex task, which requires a high level of specialisation (accumulation of specific knowledge) together with intense communication (between modules specialising in specific kinds of knowledge).

This evolution can be interpreted on the basis of the definitions given in Section 4 and hinges on two issues. The first concerns information management, that is, the process through which productive units collect, process and transmit information with the purpose of creating knowledge. The second issue is that of making the different pieces of knowledge created through the managing of information complementary.

Table 1: The Management of Information

Phases	Main Problems	Decisions	Costs
		Choice of senders	Selection costs
1. Collection of information	Inability to absorb information Information overload	Criteria for information collection	Collection costs
2. Processing of information	Partition of decision-making and implementation Delay between decision and implementation	Matching decision with implementation Timing of implementation	Matching Costs Communication costs
3. Transmission of information	Tacit knowledge Information appropriability	Modalities of transmission Choice of receivers	Transmission costs Appropriability costs

The management of information can be viewed as comprising three phases, each defined by problems, decisions to be taken and sources of costs (see Table 1).

The first phase is information collection. The subject who collects information has to choose the senders from whom he receives information and the criteria for collecting information. Both decisions imply costs—respectively selection and collection costs—that can be lowered by specialisation: a subject specialising in this phase progressively invests to build a receiving channel (Demsetz, 1991) which is used again for new information collection. Narrowing the scope of information collection not only reduces the cost of information collection but also reduces the variety of information collected. This weakens the absorptive capacity of the firm (Cohen and Levinthal, 1990), resulting in narrowing of its knowledge base.

The second phase is information processing. The information collected in the first phase is complemented by the knowledge previously possessed by the decision maker. Costs are given by matching the decision with the subjects who implement it (matching costs) and by the time elapsing between the information processing and the implementation of the decision (communication costs). Both costs are influenced by specialisation. In particular, the efficiency of this phase depends on the net effect of the reduction of matching costs due to the decrease in the number of decisions implemented by the processing subject and of the increase in communication costs necessary for connecting the act of decision-making and of implementation (Bolton and Dewatripont, 1994). De Canio and Watkins (1998) show that an increase in the capabilities of processing allows a flattening of the organisations mainly by decreasing matching costs.

The third phase is information transmission in which modalities of transmission are chosen and receivers are selected. The sources of costs are both transmission costs, which depend on the sender's skill of conveying tacit knowledge through information, and appropriability costs, which are determined by the capacity of the receiver to exploit information to create knowledge.

By applying this classification, we define the decentralisation of information as the increase in the share of information processed by the same subject who collects it. In the firm, the decentralisation of information increases when the task of coping with emergent events of a specified activity is transferred hierarchically downwards (Aoki 1986). This implies that the upper layers don't need to process information related to that specific activity and that all the information collected by the lower layer is processed directly by the collector. Similarly, the decentralisation of information in the network is given by the increase of the share of information processed by the same firm, which collects it. We can define a network as fully hierarchical if it includes a single firm processing all the information, including that collected by the other members of the network. In contrast, the same firm that collects it in a fully decentralised network processes each piece of information. In the intermediate cases, information will be partially transmitted by the collecting firm to another firm for processing it. Independent decision-making is the outcome of decentralised information processing, the difference to be emphasised is not that between the firm and the network but that between a decentralised organisation—that is, a polyarchy where autonomous decision makers undertake projects independently—and a hierarchical organisation, where decisions are taken by the centre "overseeing" the whole production process.

In the case of a network, the effects of the degree of information decentralisation can be examined by means of the classification given in Table 1.

Phase 1: Collection of Information

The receiver chooses the senders and the criteria for collecting information. In the fully hierarchical network, where only one firm processes information, these choices are made by the firms which collect information and not by the firm which processes it. This splitting between collecting and processing causes an increase in costs. The decentralisation of information reduces these costs by increasing the quantity of information processed by the same firm that collects it. The ability of collecting information is consequently improved and the risks of information overload falls. Both selection and collection costs decrease. If the relationship between supplier and user becomes long term the efficiency of this phase is further improved. As senders are the same and the same criteria are used and improved over time, scale economies in the collection of information can be fully exploited.

Phase 2: Processing of Information

The processing of information makes collected information complementary to previously possessed knowledge. In the case of fully hierarchical networks, exclusively the firm which takes decisions processes information. The decision maker must give orders instead of information to the lower layers of the hierarchy because tacit knowledge must be excluded from the content of the orders. Otherwise the decision maker would lose the control of production. This centralised mode of functioning is the source of matching costs, namely to match the orders with the executing firm, and of communication costs, to diffuse orders among the firms of the network. In the decentralised network, reducing the number of firms that execute orders decreases matching and communication costs and increases the number at those who process the information collected.

Phase 3: Transmission of Information

In the fully hierarchical network transmission, costs increase in relation to the number of layers composing the hierarchy. The difficulties of conveying tacit knowledge by means of information increases with the distance between layers. The other source of cost, information appropriability, depends on the specificity of information. The more generic is the information transmitted by firms, the higher is the risk of being imitated. The decentralisation of information replaces the transmission of orders with the exchange of inputs between supplier and user. Tacit knowledge is incorporated into the inputs. Real communication is limited to the vertical communication between supplier and user. The proximity of their productive phases enhances their ability to communicate and lowers transmission costs. Appropriability costs are also reduced because information becomes more specific. Being production modularised, each module relies on its own exclusive knowledge and this prevents other productive units from appropriating the specific knowledge of the specialised unit.

This representation of information management can also give insights into how decentralised information is made complementary across the network by improving the communication of tacit knowledge. If collaboration is limited to adjacent productive phases linked by long-term relationships and a continuous and frequent exchange of information, not only information but also tacit knowledge is progressively shared, allowing efficient complementarities between the two productive phases. Specifically, we can describe the establishment of relationships between suppliers and users as a sequence of three phases, which differ according to the state of the prominent information:

a) *The information is disseminated.* The user decides to outsource the production of a new input and addresses a request to a population of potential suppliers. Some suppliers study the feasibility of the product specifying the range of possible investments.

b) *The information is shared.* The user accepts one (or more) proposal on the basis of the outline of the product characteristics. The user and the supplier co-project the prototype of the input and make the investments.

c) *The information is modularised.* The supplier produces the input and autonomously decides any change to the process that can derive from local shocks and unforeseen contingencies (errors, imperfections, adaptations to its own productive process). The user inserts the input in their product, autonomously introducing the adaptations that come from unforeseen contingencies relative to its production process.

Signals of problems which can be derived from the market are solved in the decentralised mode by means of providing information relevant to each specific module.

This sequence creates and makes common to the user and the supplier a shared body of knowledge in the information sharing phase, in which the problem of complementarities between the adjacent stages are solved. After that, the process of information modularisation allows the firms' contractual power to be balanced since it prevents weakening the incentives for introducing innovations. If the firm collects, processes and transmits information and is also the residual claimant to the rents from innovation because it is protected from being expropriated of its specific knowledge, it will have strong incentives for improving its performance by creating new knowledge and consequently by innovating. It is specifically the increase in the amount of information processed by the collecting firm—which we have defined as the decentralisation of information—which creates better incentives for knowledge creation.

6. Concluding Remarks

The decentralisation of information, by delegating the processing of information to autonomous suppliers rather than keeping propriety or maintaining control over the whole productive chain of the network, make the production process complementary not through hierarchical arrangements but through a shared body of knowledge created in the phase of information sharing. Information decentralisation provides the suppliers with higher incentives to develop specialised knowledge related to the particular stage of the production process they are dealing with because their contractual power is protected and enhanced by the modularisation of information.

Our phase model emphasises as to how the governance form of the production network is a key variable to create efficient suppliers' networks. In particular, the balanced distribution of contractual power along the productive chain is a signal of the high degree of information decentralisation.

This theoretical interpretation can also explain why large and small firms share similar patterns of relationships in the processes of outsourcing. For both types of firms information decentralisation leads to an increase in knowledge creation by the subcontractors. Information decentralisation also implies that incentives are enforced because users cannot easily replace suppliers and the contractual power is more equally distributed. In this way the pattern of governance traditionally characterizing relationships in local systems of small firms, especially in most Italian industrial districts, has been progressively extended to networks previously led by a large firm. This convergence has a number of implications for industrial policies. In particular, the financial support to the creation of medium and large firms in local systems of small firms, or the establishment of large plants in industrially underdeveloped regions may not be that advantageous in as far as they establish or maintain control over the present or the future network and take measures to monitor and to direct the activities of the suppliers, thereby reducing their innovative potential. Likewise the provision of business services or public support to consortiums and associations of firms are bound to fail if they are harmful to the contractual equilibrium. Policies aimed at establishing new local systems of production should take this point into consideration. For example, financial support to a large firm to enter into clusters of small firms is often seen positively because small firms gain access to wider markets and to financial resources. Our analysis points to the risk that the difference in bargaining powers of the different actors may result in a distortion in information management, and a loss of capacity to create knowledge. The capacity of the whole network to create knowledge and develop innovation may therefore be weakened.

In addition, the issue of what happens to the second and lower tier suppliers should also be addressed. We have shown that first tier suppliers can be involved in knowledge creation with the user and this increases the innovation performance of the network. However, we have not discussed what happens to lower tier suppliers: being excluded from this knowledge creation process, are they worse off? Are there possibilities of moving to first tiers lowered? Such questions are left for future research.

(Alessandro Innocenti, University of Siena. He can be reached at innocenti@unisi.it Sandrine Labory, Faculty of Economics, University of Ferrara. He can be reached at Sandrine.Labory@unife.it).

References

Abraham K G, Taylor S K (1996), 'Firms' Use of Outside Contractcrs: Theory and Evidence', *Journal of Labour Economics,* 14, 394-424.

Acs Z J, Audretsch D B (1990), 'Innovation and SmallFirms', Cambridge, Mit Press.

Acs Z J, Audretsch D B (eds.) (1993), Small Firms and Entrepreneurships: an East-West Perspective, Cambridge, Cambridge University Press.

Aniello V, Le Galès P (2001), 'Between Large Firms and Marginal Local Economies: The Making of Systems of Local Governance in France', in C Crouch, P Le Galés, C Trigilia, H. Voelzkow (eds.), *Local Production Systems in Europe – Rise or Demise?,* Oxford, Oxford University Press, 220-243.

Aoki M (1986), 'Horizontal Versus Vertical Information Structures of the Firm', *American Economic Review,* 76, 971-983.

Aoki M (1988), 'Information, Incentives and Bargaining Structures in the Japanese Economy', Cambridge and New York, Cambridge University Press.

Aoki M (1995), 'Decentralized Information Processing and Hierarchical Monitoring: The Case of Japan', in B H Koo, D H Perkins (eds.), *Social Capability and Long-Term Economic Growth,* London, St. Martin Press, 159-180.

Arrighetti A (1999), 'Integrazione verticale in Italia e in Europa: tendenze e ipotesi interpretative', in F. Traù (ed.), *La questione dimensionale nell'industria italiana,* Bologna, Il Mulino, 113-147.

Asanuma B (1989), 'Manufacturer-supplier relations in Japan and the concept of relation-specific skill', *Journal of the Japanese and International Economies,* 3, 1-30.

Baldwin, J R (1998), 'Were Small Producers the Engine of Growth in the Canadian Manufacturing Sector in the 1980s', *Small Business Economics,* 10, 349-364.

Bensaou M (1999), 'Collaboration Support Technologies in Interorganisational Relationships: An Empirical Exploration in Buyer-Supplier Joint Design Activities', INSEAD Working Paper 99/78 TM/ABA.

Bianchi R, Enrietti A, Lanzetti R (2001), 'The Car Technological District in Piedmont: Definition, Dynamics, Policy', *International Journal of Automotive Technology and Management,* 1, 23-36.

Bolton P, Dewatripont M (1994), 'The Firm as a Communication Network', *Quarterly Journal of Economics,* 99, 809-39.

Camuffo A, Volpato G (2001), 'From Lean to Modular Manufacturing? The Case of FIAT 178 World Car', IMVP Working Papers, MIT's Centre for Technology, Policy and Industrial Development.

Carnazza P, Innocenti A, Vercelli A (2001), 'Small Firms and Manufacturing Employment', in A. Boltho, A Vercelli, H Yoshikawa (eds.), *Comparing Economic Systems. Italy and Japan,* Houndmills, Palgrave, 158-76.

Carree M A, Thurik A R (1998), 'Small Firms and Economic Growth in Europe', *American Economic Journal,* 26, 137-146.

Chandler A (1962), 'Strategy and Structure', Cambridge Mass, MIT Press.

Clark K B, Fujimoto T (1991), 'Product Development Performance', Boston, Harvard Business School Press.

Cohen W, Levinthal D (1990), 'Absorptive Capacity: A New Perspective on Learning and Innovation', *Administrative Science Quarterly,* 35, 103-134.

Conti G, Menghinello S (1998), 'Modelli di impresa e di industria nei contesti di competizione globale: l'internazionalizzazione produttiva nei sistemi locali del made in Italy', *L'industria,* 19, 315-347.

Coriat B (1991), *Penser à l'Envers. Travailet Organisation dans laFirmJaponaise,* Paris, C Bourgois.

Coriat B (1995), 'Variety, Routines and Networks: The Metamorphosis of the Fordist Firm', *Industrial and Corporate Change,* 4, 205-227.

Corò G, Grandinetti R (1999), 'Strategie di delocalizzazione e processi evolutivi nei distretti industriali italiani', *L'industria,* 20, 897-924.

Courlet C, Pecquer B (1991). 'Local Industrial Systems and Externalities: An Essay in Typology', *Entrepreneurship and Regional Development,* 3, 305-315.

Crestanello P (1999), L'industria veneta dell'abbigliamento. Internazionalizzazioneproduttiva e imprese di subfornitura, Milano, Franco Angeli.

Cusumano M, Takeishi A (1991), 'Supplier Relations and Management: A Survey of Japanese Transplant and US Plants', *Strategic Management Journal,* 12, 563-588.

de Banville E, Chanaron, J-J (1999), 'Inter-firm Relationships and Industrial Models', in Y Lung, J J Chanaron, T Fujimoto, D Raff (eds.), *Coping with Variety,* , Aldershot, Ashgate, 364-392.

DeCanio S, Watkins W (1998), 'Information Processing and Organisational Structure', *Journal of Economic Behaviour and Organisation,* 36, 275-294.

Demsetz H (1991), 'The Theory of the Firm Revisited', in O E Williamson, S G Winter (eds.), *The Nature of the Firm,* Oxford, Oxford University Press.

Doi N, Cowling M (1998), 'The Evolution of Firm Size and Employment Share Distribution in Japanese and UK Manufacturing: A Study of Small Business Presence', *Small Business Economics,* 10, 283-292.

Dyer J (1996), 'How Chrysler Created an American Keiretsu', *Harvard Business Review,* 56, 32-46. ENSR (various years), *The European Observatory for SMEs, Reports,* Brussels, ENSR.

Fransman M (1994), 'Information, Knowledge, Vision and Theories of the Firm', *Industrial and Corporate Change,* 3, 713-738.

Friedman D (1988), The Misunderstood Miracle. Industrial Development and Political Change in Japan, Ithaca, Cornell University Press.

Ganne B (1992), 'Place et évolution des systèmes industriels locaux en France. Economie politique d'une transformation', in G Benko, A Lipietz (eds.), *Les régions quigagnent. Districts et réseaux: les nouveauxparadigmes de lagéographie économique,* Paris, Presses Universitaires, 315-345.

Glasmeier A, Sugiura N (1991), 'Japan's Manufacturing System: Small Business, Subcontracting and Regional Complex Formation', *International Journal of Urban and Regional Research,* 23, 23-40.

Gorgeu A, Mathieu R (1993), 'Dix ans de relations de sous-traitance dans l'industrie française', *Travail,* 28,23.

Hansen N (1990), 'Innovative Regional Milieux, Small Firms, and Regional Development: Evidence from Mediterranean France', *The Annals of Regional Science,* 24, 107-23.

Helper S (1991), 'Strategy and Irreversibility in Supplier Relations: The Case of the US Automobile Industry', *Business History Review,* 65, 781-824.

Hesmati A (2003), 'Productivity Growth, Efficiency and Outsourcing in Manufacturing and Service Industry', *Journal of Economic Surveys,* 17, 79-112.

Innocenti A (2003), 'Production Outsourcing in Italian Manufacturing Industry', in M Di Matteo, P Piacentini (eds.), *The Italian Economy at the Dawn of the 21st Century,* , Aldershot, Ashgate, 212-235.

Kimura F (2002), 'Subcontracting and the Performance of Small and Medium Firms in Japan', *Small Business Economics,* 18, 163-175.

Koshiro K (1990), 'The Re-emergence of Small Enterprises: Japan', in W Sengenberger, G W Loveman, M J Piore (eds.), *The Re-emergence of Small Enterprises: Industrial Restructuring in Industrialised Countries,* Geneva, International Labour Organisation, 172-222.

Labory S (1997), *Firm Structure and Market Structure in Imperfectly Competitive Markets,* Ph D Thesis, European University Institute.

Lakshmanan T R, Okumura M (1995), 'The Nature and Evolution of Knowledge Networks in Japanese Manufacturing', *Papers in Regional Science,* 74, 63-86.

Lecler Y, Perrin J , Villeval M-C, (1999), 'Concurrent Engineering and Institutional Learning. A Comparison of French and Japanese Component Suppliers', in Y Lung, JJ Chanaron, T Fujimoto, D Raff (eds.), *Coping with Variety,* Aldershot, Ashgate, 314-334.

Linhart D (1991), 'Le torticolis de l'autruche. L'éternelle modernisation des entreprises françaises', Paris, Le Seuil.

Lorenz E H (1992) 'Trust and the Flexible Firm: International Comparisons', *Industrial Relations,* 31, 455^72.

Lorenz E H (1993) 'Flexible Production Systems and the Social Construction of Trust', *Politics & Society,* 21, 307-327.

Loveman G, Sengenberger, W (1991), 'The Re-Emergence of Small Scale Production: An International Comparison', *Small Business Economics,* 3, 1-37.

Michie J, Sheehan M (1999), 'HRM Practices, R&D Expenditure and Innovative Investment: Evidence from the UK's 1990 Workplace Industrial Relations Survey', *Industrial and Corporate Change,* 8, 211-233.

Miwa Y (1995), 'Five Misconceptions about the Japanese Economy', *Economic Notes,* 24, 1-13.

Miwa Y (1996), 'Firms and Industrial Organization in Japan', New York, New York University Press.

OECD (1996) 'Size Distribution of Output and Employment: A Data Set for Manufacturing Industries in Five OECD Countries', Economics Department Working Paper, n. 166.

Sah R K, Stiglitz J (1986), 'The Architecture of Economic Systems: Hierarchies and Polyarchies', *The American Economic Review,* 76, 716-727.

Signorini L F (ed.) (2000), *Lo sviluppo locale. Un'indagine della Banca d'Italia sui distretti industriali,,* Corigliano Calabro, Meridiana Libri.

SMEA and MITI (various years), *White Paper on Small and Medium Enterprises in Japan,* Tokyo, MITI.

Thoburn J T, Takashima M (1992), 'Industrial Subcontracting in the UK and Japan', Avebury, Aldershot.

Traù F (1997), 'Recent Trends in the Size Structure of Italian Manufacturing Firms', *Small mics,* 9, 273-285.

Volpato G, Stocchetti A (2000), 'Managing Information Flows in Supplier-Customer relationships: Issues, Methods and Emerging Problems', IMVP Working Papers, MIT's Centre for Technology, Policy and Industrial Development.

Yamawaki H (2002), 'The Evolution and Structure of Industrial Clusters in Japan', *Small Business Economics,* 18, 121-140.

14

Getting Ready for the Deluge
Outsourcing in Philippines

Richard Mills

The Philippine outsourcing sector has been steadily picking up momentum over the past few years. As of this time, it seems to have reached a tipping point. Direct employment seems to have surpassed 100,000 people and hiring growth is maintaining very high levels. Most estimates put growth rates for Business Process Outsourcing (BPO) at 40% to 50% annually, while many of the contact center organizations are blistering ahead at rates approaching 100%. While this is clearly not sustainable in the long term, it is thrilling while it lasts and this should be over the next 1.5 to 2 years. When one considers the dramatically slowing growth in India and other more mature offshore outsource destinations, the situation in Philippines is positive to say the least.

Given that the BPO sector is easily the most significant economic opportunity for Philippines at the current time, it is important that all business leaders keep up-to-date with progress. In this chapter, I will describe what real decision makers in the BPO sector are doing and saying about

Philippines. Since India is still what most people think of when the topic of outsourcing is discussed, the information will often be discussed in relation to that country.

Sykes is a large US-based contact center and IT support organization with operations in both India and Philippines. The company said earlier in the year that it would shift much of its Indian capacity to the Philippines, where it already has more than 7,000 employees.

The official company announcement from Dan Hernandez, Sykes' vice president for global strategies was, "We moved calls to other facilities in Asia to get a higher rate of return." However, knowledgeable observers in the region said that the rate of return differential must have been substantial for a company of Sykes' size and prominence to forgo India after already spending millions to put capacity in place. While there has been no formal company announcement, it seems that future growth in Asia for Sykes, will be in Philippines.

GXS (formerly known as GE Information Systems) is a large IT organization with locations throughout the world. The company has had a presence in India for years but made the decision to direct all functions with a strong customer component to Philippines because of "better economics and results." Company analysis also indicated that costs were increasing disproportionately in India. Victor Lee, who oversees professional and customer service operation in the region for GXS, is also quoted as saying that "having product development in India and professional and customer services in Philippines reduces risks."

Many in the Business Processing Outsourcing (BPO) sector will remember when Dell made a significant announcement in 2004 that they were withdrawing 1000 jobs from India back to the US because of quality problems. What is less well known is that during that same period, Dell increased the number of jobs in Philippines by over 1000.

In 2005, the company announced that it was expanding its commitment to Philippines by setting up a number of captive centers and will also keep most of its current third-party relationships as well. Dell selected Philippines for its new customer contact centers because of the "strong language and communication skills of its high-quality workforce." On the Dell website, they also stated the following: "English-savvy population, about 100 similar facilities in place and 650,000 students, the Philippines is fast becoming the contact center location of choice in Southeast Asia."

More outspoken than most, Rick McGonegal is clear that India won't be part of his company's plans for the foreseeable future. He is the Managing Director of RCG Information Technology, another good-size IT provider. The company already has a strong offshore presence in the Philippines and has assessed the Asia-Pacific region for future expansion. India, he feels, is already too crowded, with numerous companies all scrambling to hire from each other. The result is destructively high staff turnover rates, mounting salary costs and poorer English communications skills compared with that available in the Philippines. He also cited overstretched infrastructure in India as a further reason RCG wouldn't consider this destination at present. According to McGonegal, his company has its "radar set on Vietnam and China", should its current best option of the Philippines give way.

ICT Group Inc., another large contact center organization says it "has bypassed India altogether." The company opened its second call center in Manila and is about to open its third. John Brennan, chairman and chief executive of ICT, is quoted as saying in the Wall Street Journal "Philippines has several advantages over India." According to him, wages are higher in Manila than in New Delhi, Bombay or Bangalore but there is less staff turnover in the Philippines because of a relative shortage of higher-paying software development and other business-processing jobs. "Call center work is something people naturally want to migrate out of, and there are more opportunities to do that in India," he says.

ClientLogic has a similar story. The company, which is among the top 5 in its industry, is quoted by CNN as saying that "Philippine call centers have higher average staff tenure and better customer satisfaction ratings than India." Within the BPO industry, it is known that the company is experiencing stronger growth in Philippines.

Industry estimates for Convergys, another large BPO organization, are that it will employ 8000 people in Philippines by the second quarter of 2006. This is up from roughly 6000 as we approach the end of 2005. This is surprising ,if one considers that Convergys announced recently that it is undergoing a global restructuring plan affecting most areas of the company – although apparently not the Philippine operation.

Another industry story that got out recently was about developments at IBM. The company is said to have a large deal with Sprint. After more than a year of frustration in Bangalore, they pulled all voice operations out of India sending a loud message to the world that India is not a preferred destination these days.

Perhaps the most significant acquisition in the BPO sector this year was the purchase of Ambergris Solutions, arguably the leading home-grown contact center organization in Philippines. The purchaser was Telus International, the IT division of Telus Corporation, the second largest telco company in Canada. In a presentation to the Canadian Chamber, company CEO Eng Boon Lau described the exhaustive Asia-wide research his people undertook. The Philippine option was deemed as overwhelmingly superior to those of other countries, including India. An aggressive growth strategy is now in place that should make Ambergris one of the key players in the Asia Pacific region.

Even the Consulting Firms are Catching On

Many of the large research consulting firms are reporting this shift. Gartner Group, perhaps the most respected of the IT industry, recently released a report that predicted India would lose "significant market share" to countries like Philippines because it "does not have a long-term plan for improving infrastructure and increasing the supply of quality employees for the BPO industry."

XMG Global, another consulting firm, predicted that "Philippines will surpass India by 2008 in contact centers." This is a remarkable statement considering the fact that India is roughly 10 times the size of Philippines in total population.

It is a similar story for the major business journals. Many articles are reportly on the growing problems in India and viability of next step destination, countries like Philippines. Forbes (India: Good Help is Hard to Find), *BusinessWeek* (India's IT Challenge), Rediff (India: Desperately Seeking Talent) are a few examples. A simple internet search will uncover dozens of more similar headlines.

Long Live the King

Despite all of the negative statements about India, we should also understand that no one is predicting the demise of India as an outsourcing destination. The country became the "King of Outsourcing" because it was the one that proved to the world that the offshore outsourcing model works. India will continue driving the industry forward because of its huge size and remarkable competence of its senior managers.

If India does experience slower growth in the near term, it is only because of its tremendous success over the past few years. Current alleged constraints are not indicative of weakness but of India's great success. Rising salary costs may be a big deal to business bigwigs who have to somehow budget for them but it is reasonable to assume that for individual workers, who see their paychecks rise by 30% from a well timed job change, "rising costs" probably don't warrant the same degree of concern.

If Philippines is a better option today, it is only because it has been less successful at developing and attracting quality outsourcing employers in the past. The pioneering accomplishments made by India have now opened the door for Philippines to receive its share of the blessings. And as for India, we can be sure they will soon be back stronger than ever.

Philippines is this Year's Fashion

The prevailing sentiment among business leaders is that Philippines is a superior choice overall for the following reasons. First and most importantly, quality people are more available in Philippines. Filipinos are said to speak better English, have a better customer service mind-set and are more culturally attuned with the west. While India's first-rate educational institutions are said to produce better technical people, Philippines' more well-rounded liberal arts education programs are more appropriate for the larger opportunities in back-office processes.

Infrastructure requirements for BPO organizations are relatively straightforward. The most important of these are reliable and cost effective telecommunications, office space and electricity. These are mainly available in Philippines with some growing constraints in office space.

Business leaders report infrastructure deficiencies in telecommunications, office space and electricity in India that are becoming more extreme as the industry continues to grow. Even simple matters like roads are constraining growth in some Indian cities because workers have difficulty getting to work.

Expatriates also report a much improved lifestyle in Philippines as compared to India. Lastly, issues like security, government support and general business environment are said to be somewhat better in Philippines although these differences do not seem to be significant.

If Philippines is So Great, Why has it Lagged?

It is certainly true that Philippines has been slow to attract awareness of itself as an accepted, let alone preferred, destination for offshore outsourcing. The country had the same opportunity India had during the Year 2000 craze years ago, but sat around the sidelines and watched as India created dozens of world-class outsourcing organizations. During the same period Philippines created almost none. Even today, the penetration of the outsourcing sector in Philippines is said to be 2 to 3 years behind India.

It is hard to understand why this is. According to most business leaders, Filipinos speak better English, have a better customer service mind-set and the cultural gap is less. India is reported to have better technical universities but Philippines is said to be better in liberal arts (more appropriate for back-office processing). Philippines is also broadly reported to have better infrastructure and expatriate life style.

So why has India outpaced Philippines to such a degree?

It is an issue that no one seems to have a definitive answer. Some of the reasons I hear are:

1. **Better Marketing:** India has NASSCOM, a one-stop association for the entire Indian outsourcing industry that has done a fabulous job of promoting India to the world. The association represents roughly 95% of Indian industry and is a global force in promoting India to the global community and professionalizing the sector at home. Philippines, despite

being a much smaller country, has between 6 and 8 various outsourcing associations (the actual number keeps changing), all supposedly promoting Philippines. Too many of these associations are fractious in nature and seem to be constantly battling within themselves and against others who try to unify them. The result is that none are large enough or competent enough to effectively market the Philippines to global organizations. They seem to spend their limited energies promoting Philippine outsourcing to other Filipinos. Happily, a single industry association is emerging in Philippines and support for it is growing. More about this later.

2. **Better Senior Managers and Entrepreneurs:** It was reported during the dot-com boom times that close to 40% of Silicon Valley start-ups were founded by Indians. (A joke at that time was that all it took to start a dot-com was 4 Indian engineers and an American guy to sell.) Indians are clearly an entrepreneurial people who know what it takes to build world-class businesses. Filipinos, like most other people in the world, don't seem to have that same need for the recognition that building successful businesses entails.

3. **Bad Security Perception of Philippines:** Until recently, there was a real threat that India would go to nuclear war with Pakistan over the Kashmir region. Such a war would be in addition to the 2 previous horrific wars these countries have already fought in just the past few decades. They still lob a few missiles at one another even today. But for some reason, India was better about keeping this sort of information from American BPO decision makers' ears. Philippines, by comparison, has a few bungling bandits located far to the south, engaging in various flavours of hooliganism. Laughably, these bozos have somehow been labeled "Muslim insurgents" and gained international notoriety for themselves. Despite the obvious differences in situations, most people in the west have the impression that Philippines is more dangerous than India. The vagaries of public relations management seems to be something Filipinos have been poor at mastering.

I am sure there are other reasons but these might be a start. The question for the future is whether Philippines will succeed as an outsourcing destination as the worldwide BPO sector continues to undergo tremendous upheaval.

The Worldwide Industry Trends Affecting Philippines

Until just a year or so ago, Business Process Outsourcing was a simple industry to understand. The sector consisted, for the most part, of a few large American companies sending call center work and some IT processes offshore.

No longer is that the case. The next phase of this fascinating sector is much more complicated since so many things are happening all at once.

First of all, outsourcing is expanding beyond just call centers and IT into almost every conceivable business process. The current new batch of outsourcing locators are involving themselves in a myriad of activities. Some of these include: accounting, HR, financial analysis, design engineering, animation, medical services, legal services, insurance processes, banking processes, map-making, publishing content creation, research, and so on.

Given that answering telephone inquiries and software programming are microscopic parts of most company's businesses, they are significant. Some business leaders I have spoken to have used the phrase "tipping point" to describe the current life-cycle stage of services outsourcing. One fellow I spoke to thought the phrase "business process outsourcing" wasn't descriptive enough to express the vast diversity of the current environment. He felt a better phrase was something along the lines of "everything-anyone-can-possibly-imagine-as-being-outsourced outsourcing."

Second, it is no longer just large American companies (and some notable UK firms) who are aggressively sending work offshore. Now every rich country in the world is moving rapidly to join the movement. We are already seeing action from countries as diverse as Japan, France, Australia, Denmark and Singapore.

As a specific example we could look at little Canada. Until a year ago, there were very few Canadian interests in the Philippines BPO sector. Today, Canadian companies have taken controlling interest in ClientLogic (one of the largest BPO's in the world with a strong Philippine focus), Telus acquired Ambergris (arguably the most successful homegrown BPO in Philippines, Nucomm (a quality mid-sized Canadian call center outfit) set up operations and Thomson Financial (the large global information provider) continued growing. Announcements of other major investments are imminent although still confidential at the time of this writing.

Third, the movement is no longer just for the largest global companies. We are now seeing the early stages of involvement by mid-sized and small companies – even individual entrepreneurs are getting involved. Here are a few examples of smaller companies that you may not have heard about yet but soon will – YellowAsp creates layout designs for printed circuit boards, XMG Global IT Research and Advisory Inc., prepares high-end IT research, Forssman Pacific creates construction design drawings, Key-In Data Solutions does claims processing, Primesoft develops advanced Web applications, VinciWorks designs online training programs, and Pulse DesignTech offers electronics design services. The list goes on and on.

Fourth and most significantly for Philippines, the sector is becoming vastly more competitive. Most developing countries throughout the world have seen the success of India and want to participate. The result has been a frantic stampede of new destinations to compete for the same BPO jobs as Philippines. And, most of these 30 or so countries have lower costs than Philippines. Unless Philippines aggressively begin to improve its promotional activities and increase the value of its services, we risk finding ourselves bypassed.

Lastly, the early leaders of outsourcing like India are being pushed by extreme competitive pressure to quickly move up the value chain to more sophisticated processes. Remarkably sophisticated work is now starting to appear. As one example, Deutsche Bank has recently set up an operation that will perform financial analysis work for the company's CFO's located throughout the world. The company is hiring very senior financial professionals for these functions.

The Biggest Opportunity of Our Lives

Current growth rates in the BPO sector seem to be stronger than in other boom times. During the dot-com boom times, growth rates in employment were often quoted as 20% to 25% per year. People achieving these impressive rates were considered successful by industry standards. Today in Philippines, people with 20% to 25% growth are at risk of being called losers. Most BPO organizations, even the largest ones, have been growing by 40% to 50% per year. Many of the call centers are growing at rates approaching 100%.

Another point to keep in mind is that a lot of dot-com company hiring was based around dreams and funny ideas, and paid for with venture capital money rather than being funded from company revenues. In the current environment in Philippines, hiring is almost exclusively the result of client instructions that are ready to pay real money for new employees.

In the current worldwide business environment, one would be hard-pressed to find such hiring growth in any other business sector. As we begin 2006, there are approximately 100,000 people employed in the BPO industry in Philippines. Estimates are that the sector will provide work for 500,000 people over the next 4 years.

Boom times like this typically happen only once per decade and they almost always move on to different sectors. The 1990s, for instance, was important for IT and telecommunications. The 1980s was real estate and high finance (in North America).

The point is this: For those involved in the BPO sector, we are living through a period that will probably not happen again in our lifetimes. We need to make sure we harvest as much as we can while the opportunity exists. This opportunity will pass quickly if we don't reap and probably never return.

Philippines: World-Class Destination, Third-Class Marketing

One of the most important initiatives that is underway that will help us to achieve our great potential is through the association called Business Process Outsourcing Philippines (BPO/P). Philippines is developing a single strong voice for promoting and professionalizing the Philippine BPO sector which is in the model of India's NASSCOM. The Indian association is always cited as a strong reason for that country's great success as the pioneer and by far the most successful services outsourcing country in the world.

Another example is the Philippine mining sector. Because of the strong and competent leadership of the Philippine Chamber of Mines by Philip Romualdez, this industry is now back on its feet and ready to be a major job provider for this country.

The Business Processing Association of Philippines (BPA/P) has recently been put with place with strong leadership under Mitch Locsin (Executive Director) and Dan Reyes (President). A strong BPA/A will allow Philippines to promote itself in a proactive manner, rather than just reacting to bad publicity after the fact. It will also help along the process of professionalizing the industry by encouraging world-class standards of performance.

These are the goals but progress is still being hindered by the fractious nature of various industry associations – some of whom are loath to join efforts with BPA/P because they fear the loss of personal prestige. This, of course, is ridiculous and their lack of commitment to joint efforts is shameful and needs to be rectified.

This is one of the major constraints to Philippines developing itself into a world leader in Business Process Outsourcing. The product is good. We just need to market it a little better. If this can be done, there is a possibility that the Philippines can rise up and finally take its rightful place among the tigers of Asia. Let's see how we do.

(Richard Mills is considered a leading expert on Asia-Pacific outsourcing by ComputerWorld magazine. Richard has been appointed an "Expert Panelist" on offshore outsourcing by CIO Magazine and the Offshore Outsourcing. Richard has also been called "the local guru on outsourcing" by Dr. Michael Clancy, President of the Economist Business Forum and the "Asia-Pacific expert" by Call Center Magazine. Richard Mills can be reached at info@chalre.com).

15

The Changing Face of China
China as an Offshore Destination for IT and Business Process Outsourcing

China's popularity as an ITO and BPO destination is mostly reserved for the companies serving the Asia-Pacific Markets. Chinese based ITO and BPO providers are working to improve their capabilities by focusing on the West. This article highlights the findings in A T Kearney's more recent study of the ITO and BPO markets served by China and also details A T Kearney's perspective on how China is faring in its efforts to become a preferred offshore destination for ITOs and BPOs. China's large domestic market and potential for economic growth makes it a strategic offshore location for multinational companies planning to serve new markets in the future. China's ITO business is expected to grow at 44 percent annually, potentially becoming a US$2.5 billion industry by 2008.

Source: http://www.atkearney.com/shared_res/pdf/ChinaOffshore_S.pdf

Introduction

A vast and growing country, China is increasingly becoming a partner to companies big and small. The country beckons and businesses listen, wondering how, or if, they will manage to capitalize on the combination of growth, political stability, investment, developing capitalism and fresh technology. This is the changing face of China.

China is the sixth-largest economy in the world with a GDP of US$1.4 trillion. Its real gross domestic product has expanded at an average of 9 percent a year for the past 25 years. And every week, more than US$1 billion of foreign direct investment flows into the country.

Long known as the world's factory, China is now becoming an attractive location for IT offshoring (ITO) and Business Process Offshoring (BPO) *(see Figure 1).* These markets are expected to grow as the Chinese government continues to entice foreign companies with tax and tariff incentives, subsidies, and administrative convenience—all in an effort to attract more multinational companies to the country.

China's popularity as an ITO and BPO destination is mostly reserved for companies serving their Asia-Pacific markets. This is due to geographic proximity and China's language and cultural affinity with nations in Asia Pacific. Increasingly, however, China is becoming a destination in multinationals' larger global offshore strategies. Many firms are considering the country as an option to serve China's growing domestic market.

Similarly, Chinese-based ITO and BPO providers are working to improve their capabilities with an eye towards the West. The goal is to move beyond providing services to companies in Asia Pacific and begin capturing business from multinationals in the United States and Europe.

The questions for both the multinationals and China-based providers: How is China competing today? How will it compete in the global offshoring arena in the future?

This paper highlights findings in A T Kearney's most recent study of the ITO and BPO markets served by China *(see Box: About the Study).* We discuss China's strengths and weaknesses, and dispel some long-held misperceptions. Throughout the paper, we offer A.T. Kearney's perspective on how China is faring in its efforts to become a preferred offshore destination for IT and business process offshoring.

Fast Emerging Challenger

China-based ITO and BPO providers are strongest in the Asia-Pacific market due to its geographic proximity and China's language and cultural affinity to nearby nations. For example, due to a large concentration of people in China who speak Japanese, offshore clients are predominantly from Japan. In fact, more than 60 percent of China's offshore software development revenue is from companies based in Japan. Dell Computer and CSK Corp are opening Japanese-language call centers in the north-eastern city of Dalian. And according to Dalian Hi-Think Computer Technology, China's largest software exporter, more than 70 percent of revenues are from Japanese clients.

"The Japanese feel comfortable dealing with the Chinese," explains an executive with a leading Chinese ITO company. "It's easy for us to gain consensus and build trust with our Japanese clients."

In 2003, China's ITO market was roughly US$0.4 billion, with almost all activities centered around lower-end services, such as IT activities that involve modular programming (developing a smaller component of a larger application), and testing. Most of the offshoring work performed in China today is for the financial services and high tech industries. According to Gartner Group, China's ITO business is expected to grow at 44 percent annually, potentially becoming a US$2.5 billion industry by 2008.

The number of BPO service providers establishing a presence in China is also on the rise. Most of the current BPO activities in China include back-office processes, such as call centers, finance and accounting, payables and some research and development. In 2003, China's BPO market was US$0.2 billion. Over the next five years, industry insiders expect China to increase its BPO market by 20 to 30 percent annually.

Figure 1: China is Among the World's Most Attractive Offshore Locations

A T Kearney's Offshore Location Attractiveness Index (2004)

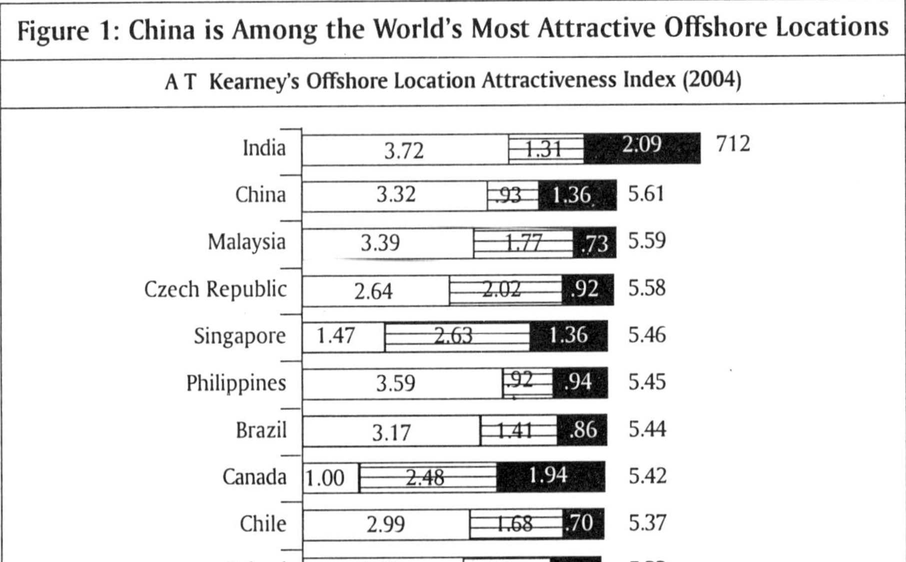

A T Kearney's Client Survey of Business Process Offshore Locations (2003)[4]

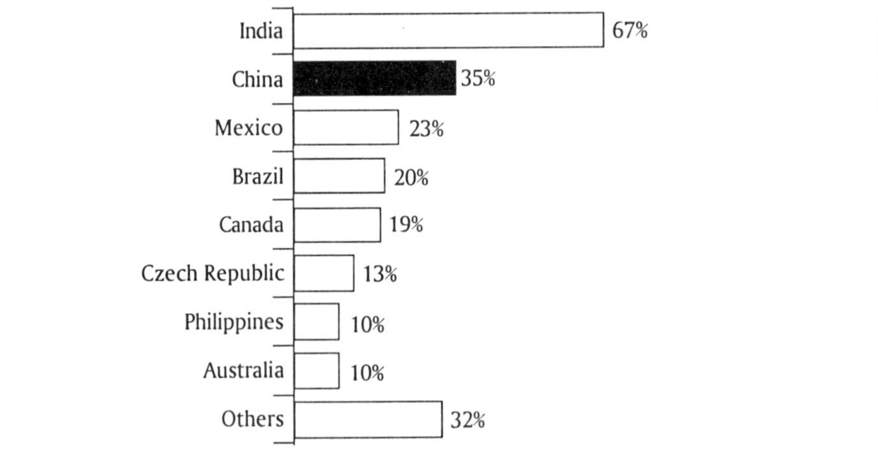

Notes: 1. Based on costs of compensation, infrastructure, and tax and regulatory requirements.

2. Based on country environment (includes economic and political aspects), infrastructure, cultural adaptability and IP security.

3. Based on business process experience and skills, labor force availability, education, language and attrition rates.

4. Includes responses from executives at 115 companies, respondents allowed to choose from more than one country.

Sources: Industry interviews and A T Kearney analysis.

China is Becoming World-Class Player

Reasons for sending IT and business processes offshore remain the same whether the destination is China, India or anywhere else. Offshoring can result in significant savings in operational and labor costs *(see Figure 2).* An entry level IT programmer based in Beijing or Shanghai, for example, makes roughly US$7,000 per year. This is comparable to what entry-level programmers in India earn (US$6,000), but is significantly less than the average salary of US$48,000 earned by an entry level programmer in the United States.

In addition, a major factor contributing to the attractiveness of India and China—and to a lesser extent Russia, Brazil and the Philippines—is the sheer breadth and depth of the skill base in terms of education levels *(see Box: India Stays Ahead of the Pack).* In recent years, the Chinese government has moved aggressively to improve technical education, both to serve the booming economy and to make the country less reliant on foreigners. The result: In 2004, China's universities will crank out 2.8 million graduates, 300,000 of whom are engineers—almost 10 times the number in Germany.[1] India, by comparison, graduates some 3.1 million students from its colleges every year, whereas the United States turns out 1.3 million college graduates a year.

Figure 2: China Helps Multinationals Achieve Key Corporate Objectives

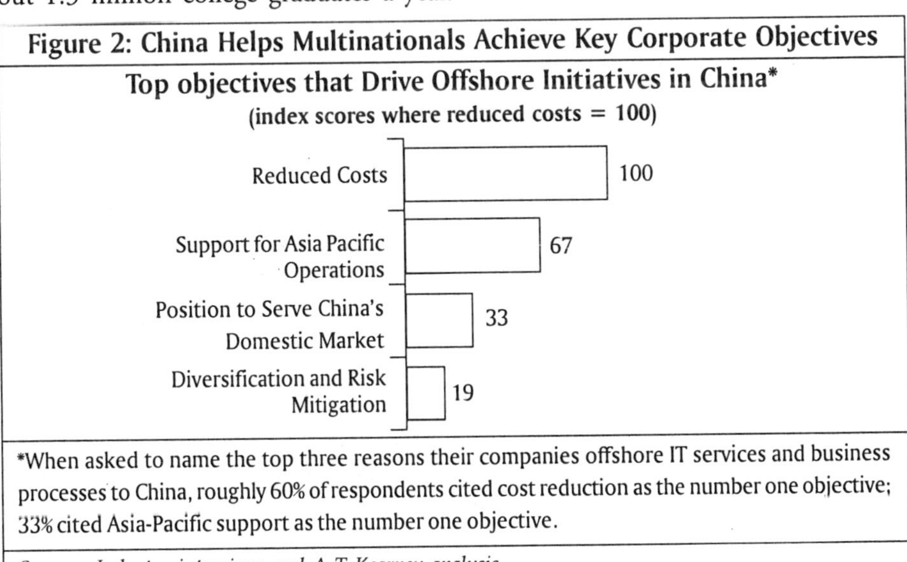

*When asked to name the top three reasons their companies offshore IT services and business processes to China, roughly 60% of respondents cited cost reduction as the number one objective; 33% cited Asia-Pacific support as the number one objective.

Sources: Industry interviews and A T Kearney analysis.

1 *The Wall Street Journal,* 15 July 2004.

China's large domestic market and potential for economic growth also make it a strategic offshore location for multinational companies planning to serve new markets in the future. Companies with offshore centers in China, for example, anticipate using these centers later as a foothold for serving a domestic outsourcing industry *(see Figures 3 and 4)*. In fact, when GE Capital International Services (GECIS) initially entered China, its main goal was to support customers in its Japanese and Korean markets. GECIS' China operations, based in Dalian, is a remote processing operation that handles back-office functions for 20 different GE businesses. Because the China market was growing so fast, GECIS now supports Greater China's domestic outsourcing market as well. "China is unique in that China itself could become a big business process outsourcing market," explains Pavan Dhamija, business development and transitions leader, GECIS. "We hope to use the BPO facilities in China to support not only Japan and Korea, but also China itself, and eventually other Asia-Pacific regions."

Cisco Systems just announced an expansion plan that takes direct aim at serving China's booming economy. In a recent news conference, John Chambers, Cisco's chief executive, told reporters that China was well on the way to become the world's technology hub as he revealed plans for building his company's first research

About the Study

In 2004, A T Kearney performed a global research study to obtain a better understanding of how China competes today—and will compete tomorrow—as an offshore destination.

The study is based on interviews with approximately 50 senior-level executives from companies in North America, Europe and Asia. These executives are directly involved in their companies' strategic decision-making processes. Participants were asked about their current business strategies and priorities related to offshoring, as well as those on the horizon. Participants were also asked to discuss what they consider off-shoring challenges and how they plan to handle them.

The analysis was designed to obtain an outside-in view, eliciting the perspectives of executives at western companies who are looking at China as an offshore destination, and executives at companies that provide ITO and BPO services.·Companies represented in the study include: Chinese ITO and BPO providers; multinationals in the United States, Japan and India that provide ITO and BPO services, software firms in China, and multinational firms in the United States and Europe that are ITO and BPO customers.

Representatives of the Chinese gov-ernment provided additional infor-mation. A T Kearney performed secondary research to establish the size and capabilities of ITO and BPO providers in China, and to identify trends in the offshoring arena.

Figure 3: China is Attractive to Multinationals that Plan to Serve New Markets in the Future

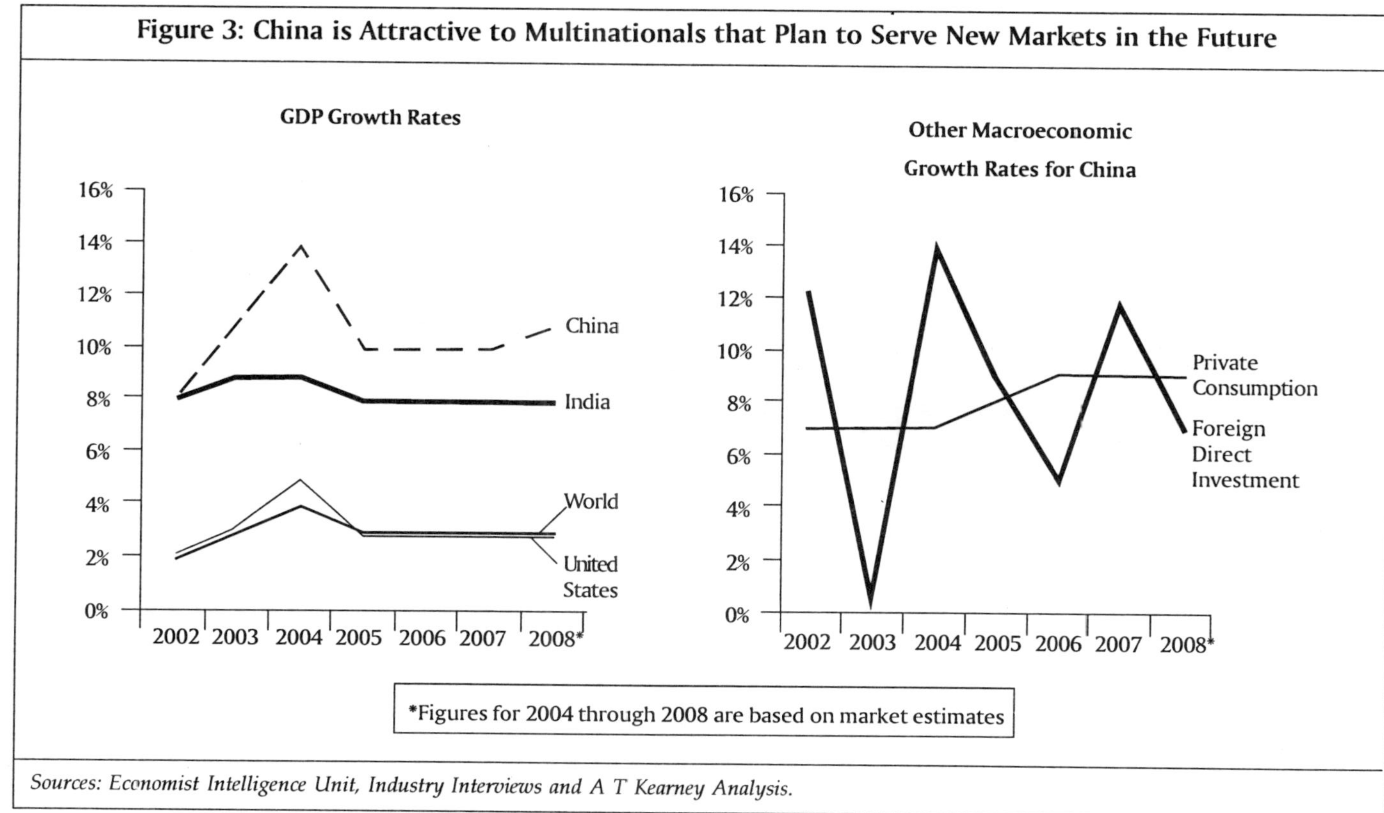

Sources: Economist Intelligence Unit, Industry Interviews and A T Kearney Analysis.

Figure 4: Companies will Use their Offshore Centers in China to Serve China's Domestic Market

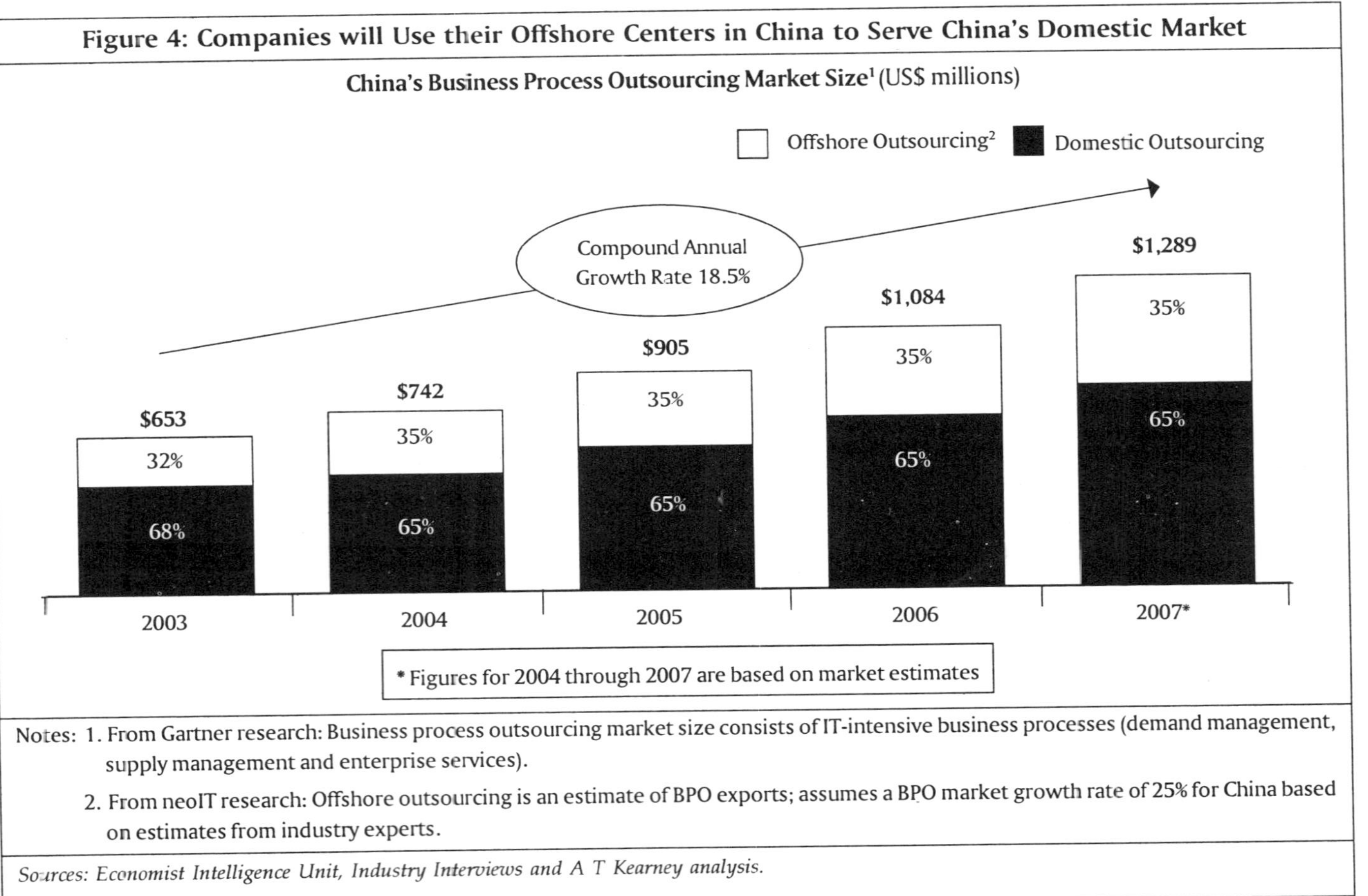

Notes: 1. From Gartner research: Business process outsourcing market size consists of IT-intensive business processes (demand management, supply management and enterprise services).

2. From neoIT research: Offshore outsourcing is an estimate of BPO exports; assumes a BPO market growth rate of 25% for China based on estimates from industry experts.

Sources: Economist Intelligence Unit, Industry Interviews and A T Kearney analysis.

center in the country. Chambers said that over the next decade, half of Cisco's top 12 business partners, and half of its main competitors, would come from China. "China will become the IT center of the world."[2]

Other firms are also moving business processes into China. Aircraft maker Airbus recently announced plans to set up an engineering facility in China to strengthen its R&D strategy. France Télécom just opened its first wholly owned R&D facility in China to pave the way to future expansion in the world's biggest telecom market. "This allows us to become one of the first foreign telecom operators to set up an R&D center in China," said Pascal Viginier, executive vice president of France Télécom Group, in an interview with *China Daily.*

At the end of the day, the best lessons in our study findings may be those learned from watching the offshore leaders – companies that adopt multi-country strategies, moving operations to multiple locations as a way to diversify risks and tap into the broadest possible pool of global talent. Even Indian outsourcers consider China as a prime offshore destination. Tata Consultancy Services (TCS), an Indian software solutions firm, unveiled its China operations in mid-2002, citing, among several reasons, the ability to focus on providing disaster-recovery, risk-mitigation and offshore services for its clients in Japan. TCS is also among the growing number of companies that plan to leverage China for both their domestic growth opportunities and to meet the growing IT needs of global companies. As Indian firms adopt increasingly broader global business strategies, China is becoming an integral part of their growth plans.

India Stays Ahead of the Pack

In addition to India's much-discussed cost leadership, it also takes a commanding lead in the people category thanks to two metrics – It offers the deepest experience in business process outsourcing combined with a large labor forced second only to that of China.

The strength of India's people is no accident. Every year the educational system graduates two million proficient English speakers with strong technical and quantitative skills. India's top engineering schools, led by the Indian Institute of Technology, are renowned worldwide. But India also benefits from its experience – it has been a large-scale off shoring destination for more than a decade. Indian service providers have worked up from coding to business process management

Contd...

[2] *News.com,* Cisco Sees China as Center of World Tech Market, 2 November 2004.

Contd...

and high-level analytics and consulting. The labor force is familiar not only with the job content, but also with the work ethic and quality and productivity expectations of major global clients.

The offshore juggernaut represents one of India's fastest growing markets. NASSCOM, the National Association of Software and Services Companies of India, has predicted that India's IT software and services export market will reach US$60 billion by 2008. Although we expect India to remain the largest offshore market, China and other countries are mounting a challenge to Indian supremacy.

Where is India vulnerable? Although its people have made India the offshoring leader, it ranks below the top 10 in terms of business environment. Infrastructure weaknesses and concerns over economic stability pull India down. In addition, while India has become increasingly integrated into the global economy in recent years, the general population is not widely exposed to other cultures, sometimes making cultural adaptation a challenge. Yet, India's environment score still out-ranks that of most other low-cost Asian locations. Government efforts to improve infrastructure and maintain economic and political stability seem likely to reinforce India's emegence as a global player.

Excerpt from "Making Offshore Decisions: A T Kearney's 2004 Offshore Location Attractiveness Index." www.atkearney.com.

Shattering Western Mantras

Before enticing new companies to their homeland, China-based providers are working with the government to change many damaging misperceptions, beginning with pointing out how the country has stepped-up its infrastructure and technology improvements.

China's infrastructure is much stronger than what people think. Because manufacturers have established production facilities in China for the past 20 years or so, the government has made significant investments in roads and rail systems. Highway and rail construction are being accelerated under the current five-year plan to adequately support the growing merchandise shipments being sent to second- and third-tier cities. Next on the agenda is connecting inland second- and third-tier cities to coastal areas and ports.

By the same token, China's software parks guarantee an uninterrupted power supply, with most equipped with backup power generators. Also, these parks and high tech corridors provide a single point of contact, which cuts down on red tape, bureaucracy and approval time, and encourages an industrial cluster effect.

"Shanghai (Pudong) is hands down better than India," asserts one survey respondent in comparing China's infrastructure with India's.

China's telecommunications system is improving as well. For years, government restrictions, especially those related to telemarketing, have hindered investment in China. Foreign investment in telecom services was limited to 50 percent of a company's total investment, and any foreign company that provided value-add telecom services had to first register with the government. The red tape and bureaucracy in establishing a call center, for example, was enormous. The good news is that in 2005, the government may lift all geographic restrictions on all value-add telecom services.[3]

Additionally, the bandwidth of China's international internet broadband connection is expanding. It is now 43 gigabits per second (gbps)—120 times the bandwidth of China had just four years ago, with international connection points in Beijing, Shanghai and Shenzhen.

Making the China Connection

While China and its leading companies continue their work to shake off the perception of weakness in the areas of infrastructure and telecommunications, our study reveals three areas that deserve further attention and improvement:

1. Protecting Intellectual Property—Is it Really an Issue?

The question of IP piracy is an important one for many western companies. Our answer for companies pursuing lower-level IT offshoring initiatives in China is that IP piracy should not be a major factor. In many ways, piracy has been managed quite successfully.

"It's known to everyone in the industry that incidents of IP problems with a client would cause significant damage to a vendor's reputation and future business," as one executive in our survey explains. "Therefore, most vendors implement internal systems to ensure IP protection."

3 Value-added telecom services are defined as e-mail, voice mail, online information storage and research, EDI, online data processing and transaction processing, value-add fax, ISP, ICP and video conferencing.

Also, protecting intellectual property is high on the Chinese government's agenda. With lost sales from counterfeiting, the government is moving quickly to ensure that property rights are respected. For example, China's IP legislative framework conforms with TRIPS (Trade-Related Aspects of Intellectual Property Rights), which is the WTO's standard for IP laws. China's constitution also provides guiding principles for IP legislation. Civil law specifically states that IP is a major civil rights issue, and infringement on trademarks, patents and copyrights is a criminal offense.

The Chinese government and local industries realize the importance of IP protection to continued economic growth. And, indeed, there are indications that China is cracking down on the counterfeiters. In September 2004, China vowed strong official action against intellectual property rights violations, including a targeted crackdown and tougher antipiracy penalties. Particular areas of focus include trademark, copyright and patent-law violations in 15 provinces and municipalities, including Beijing and Shanghai, said Vice Minister of Commerce Zhang Zhigang.[4]

For companies considering entering China, tackling the piracy problem will hinge on selecting the right business strategy *(see Box: Choosing an Offshore Business Model).* For some of our clients, we recommend entering China using a captive business model (setting up a company's own facilities in the offshore location) for IP-sensitive activities and performing regular IP audits. We also recommend building high-tech firewalls between a company's China operations and other facilities that house data-sensitive materials. Some companies go into China via a joint venture or outsource to a local provider. Of course, doing so requires due diligence on the offshore providers' internal IP protection policies and systems, and defining strict guidelines for the selected vendor.

2. Improving Language Proficiency and Education

The single biggest opportunity for China in its effort to build up its ITO and BPO services market is to increase its English-language proficiency. Although China graduates numerous English-language proficient students each year, many have solid writing and reading skills, but are still not fluent English speakers.

4 *The Wall Street Journal,* 7 September, 2004.

The reason, according to our findings, is that there are not enough opportunities to talk with native speakers. "How can we increase our language proficiency if we fail to practice?" laments one executive.

Still, companies are looking beyond China's linguistic learning curve. Our findings reveal that what counts most to employers are the same qualities and experience that have always mattered in more mature (or maturing) talent markets. These include workers with value-added functional skills, a track record of achievement and an ability to execute the job successfully. Among local professionals, these qualities are becoming increasingly common.

As the Chinese improve their English-language capabilities, more US and European companies will likely consider China as an attractive offshore locale. Already, the country is increasing its emphasis on English training in schools and has more than 1,00,000 English teachers at its IT colleges. In Shanghai, some elementary school students receive maths and science instruction in English.

Education in China is by no means limited to improving language proficiency. China is rapidly increasing its number of college graduates, which provides a huge potential pool of professional talent. There are currently almost 5,00,000 IT professionals in the IT services industry. About 80,000 new IT professionals entered the industry in 2003, representing a 60 percent increase over 2002.

"Like many successful IT houses, we build into our China-based growth strategy various cooperative programs with leading universities and technology institutes," explains Cyrill Eltschinger, CEO of IT United. "That effectively shortens the time required to train a new college graduate into an independent programmer from about one year to six months."

After many years of government efforts, China is experiencing an excess of university graduates. China expected 2.8 million college graduates to hit the job market in the summer of 2004, an increase of 6,80,000 over the same period in 2003. By 2005, the number of graduates is expected to reach a record 3.4 million *(see figure 5)*. The employment rate of university graduates will exceed 70 percent, which, at the same time, means that at least 8,00,000 graduates will join the ranks of the unemployed immediately after they leave school.[5]

[5] *Business Daily* Update, 15 June 2004.

Figure 5: China will See an Increase in College Graduates

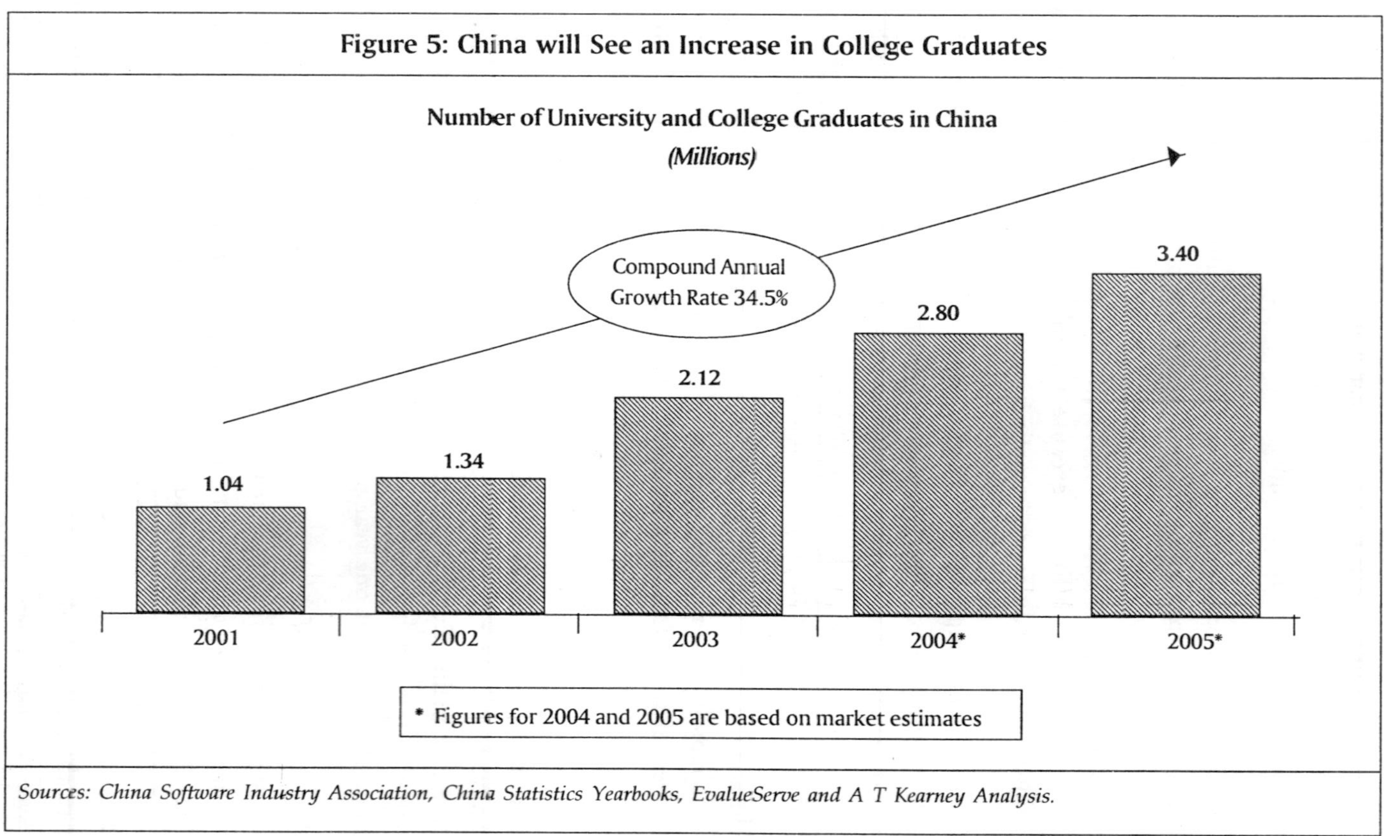

Sources: China Software Industry Association, China Statistics Yearbooks, EvalueServe and A T Kearney Analysis.

Choosing an Offshore Business Model

Business process offshoring has become a widely accepted strategy. The economics of going offshore are compelling, and a host of successful precedents have spurred a flurry of announcements by leading companies and financial institutions to relocate major parts of their operations.

Yet, due to several obstacles, only a handful of companies fully achieve the potential benefits from their offshore operations. One such hurdle is the choice of offshore business model. Making decisions about the best offshore business model—whether captive, joint venture or outsourcing— requires a rigorous evaluation, taking into account the benefits and risks of each.

Captive: For large-scale operations, captive models tend to dominate the landscape. In the 1990s, building your own offshore center was the only way to go, primarily because localITO andBPOproviders did not have significant experience, and global third-party providers, for all their steadfastness, had not yet fully developed their offshore capabilities. For functions that can achieve significant economic and non-economic benefits from offshoring, but are high risk to migrate, setting up a captive may be most appropriate.

Joint venture: A handful of companies opt for joint ventures, often in the form of BOT (build-operate-transfer) structures. This model is used by companies that want to defer risk initially, before taking the offshore plunge. They transfer responsibility for set-up and initial operations to a third-party provider, but retain an option to acquire full control at a certain point in time. In situations where benefits are low and the risks are high, companies often consider joint ventures.

Outsourcing: Smaller midmarket companies often do not have the scale to set up their own operations, so they leverage the consolidated scale of an outsourcing provider. Outsourcing is also the preferred business model for companies less willing to make up-front investments and that want to reach the breakeven point sooner; both are economic considerations that favor outsourcing. As third-party suppliers gain capabilities and scale, outsourcing initiatives will likely become more popular.

Importantly, the most experienced offshore players do not rely on a single structure across their range of business process activities. Functions that are particularly customer sensitive or require domain-specific expertise are usually performed in a captive environment, while commoditized, mostly scale-dependent processes ar dates for outsourcing.

"There are simply not enough jobs to absorb the huge number of people with bachelor's and master's degrees," explains an executive with *Foreign Policy* magazine. "Needless to say, this is a huge pool of talent that offshore service providers can tap into."

Indeed, when explaining Cisco's US$32 million investment in establishing an R&D facility to build Voice Over Internet Protocol (VOIP) technology in China, CEO John Chambers cited China's good university system and the pool of talent

Figure 6: Chinese IT Offshore Vendors are Showing Significant Improvement

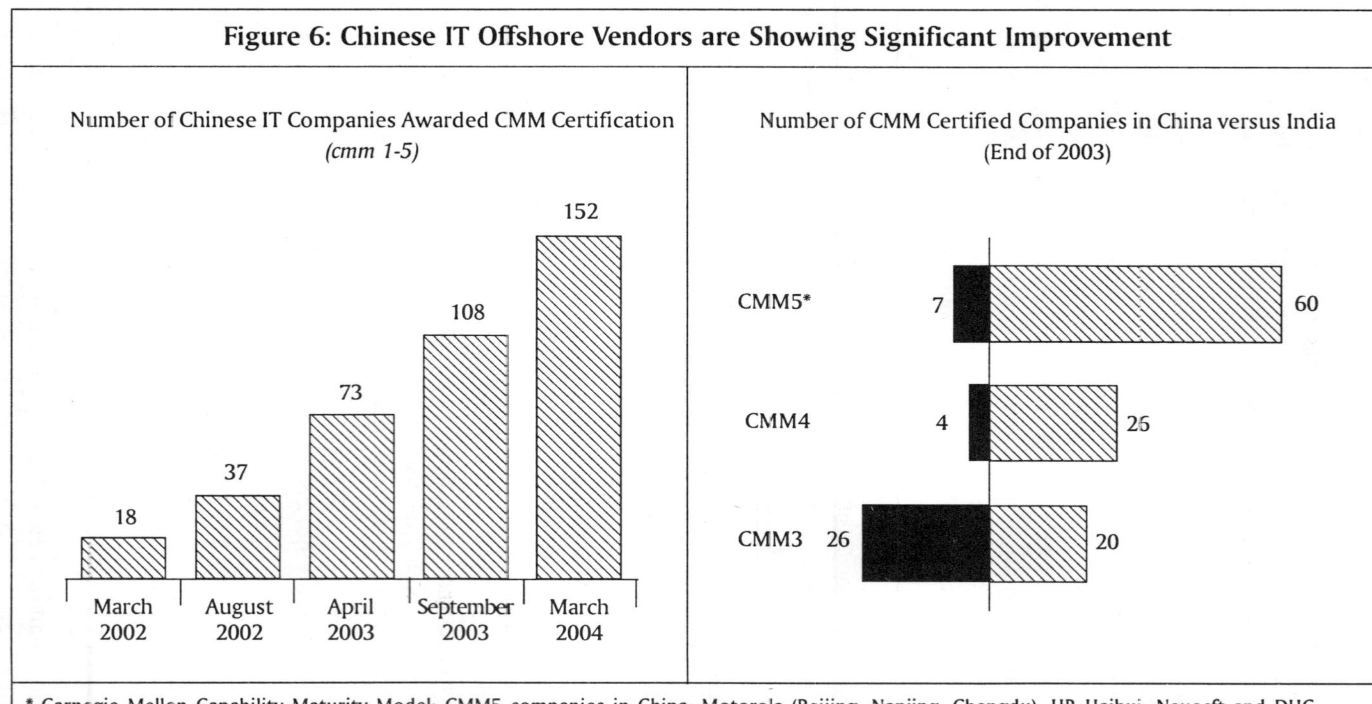

* Carnegie Mellon Capability Maturity Model; CMM5 companies in China: Motorola (Beijing, Nanjing, Chengdu), HP, Haihui, Neuosft and DHC

Source: ZDNet China and Nasscom, Software Engineering Institute and A T Kearney Analysis.

from which to recruit researchers as a key reason for moving into China. He also noted the government's business-friendly policies.

In recent years, the Chinese government has been accelerating its efforts to create a first-class high-tech labor force. China is providing coding training to workers, and cities are helping local firms cover the costs of acquiring Carnegie Mellon Capability Maturity Model (CMM) certification *(see Figure 6).* Multinationals—such as IBM and Indian firms are also working with the government to provide training.

There is still room for improvement, however. For instance, only two providers in China, Legend Beijing and Shanghai Wicresoft, have adopted COPC (Customer Operation Performance Center) standards. COPC, considered the gold standard in assessing contact center performance, has become the performance standard in more than 30 countries and has certified some 300 business locations around the world.

3. Improving Management Skills

With education levels on the rise, China-based ITO and BPO providers are in a race to improve the business management skills of key employees and increase the pool of high-caliber project managers. More than 80 percent of executives interviewed in our survey list project-management skills as a key requirement for setting up businesses in China.

Today, the challenge for China-based providers is to update the skills within their middle management ranks. Managers who have been loyal employees must learn to move beyond their traditional bureaucratic and hierarchical habits to adopt modern business management principles. Unfortunately, many are overwhelmed by a fast-changing environment and the realities of a market economy. They grew up expecting never to change jobs and only know how to do one thing.

One solution is to increase management training programs, something the multinationals—including IBM and Motorola—have been doing for some time. Motorola has a China Accelerated Management Program (CAMP) in which managers are trained in global business concepts. In addition, these larger firms are focusing on training the "softer" skills such as accountability, initiative, curiosity, business perspective, effective communications, team building and appropriate business conduct.

Also, more multinationals are interested in hiring Chinese "homegrown" professionals, motivated both by a growing market of local talent that is better able to handle such roles and by the bottom-line implications. "Although companies always tell us that they are looking for the most suitable person for a position, the cost factor inevitably has a major impact in many final hiring decisions," explains Kevin Wang, an executive with Wang & Li, a China-based human resources firm.

This was not the case a few years ago, however, when there were relatively few local professionals who could handle the job. Fast forward to today, however, and local management talent is becoming far more commonplace in China, spurred by the multinationals and their extensive training programs. For example, Motorola and IBM have almost 10,000 employees in China, including hundreds of people who have been trained to handle middle management roles and responsibilities.

Returnees to mainland China are becoming popular new hires within management ranks. Nearly 64 percent of companies in a recent study by Hewitt and Associates currently employ numerous returnees. And, according to Wang & Li, about 50 percent of director-level positions and above are filled by expatriates who return home with both high-caliber business skills and international exposure.

"Chinese returnees with extensive experience in studying and living in other countries are particularly helpful to our business dealings with western companies," explains a study participant.

According to our findings, many firms that hire returnees count on them to share their management skills and experience with their Chinese colleagues. Also, more firms are introducing mentoring programs to help younger workers move into the executive ranks. Workers are matched with experienced expatriates or former employees of multinational firms. As more workers retire and younger workers move into management positions, workers with western-style business skills will become increasingly valuable. These skills are particularly relevant to companies providing both BPO and ITO services.

Figure 7: Companies Pay More for Qualified Talent in The Major Cities

Compensation: Index of First-Year Programmers in Major ITO Destination Cities

(Beijing = 100)

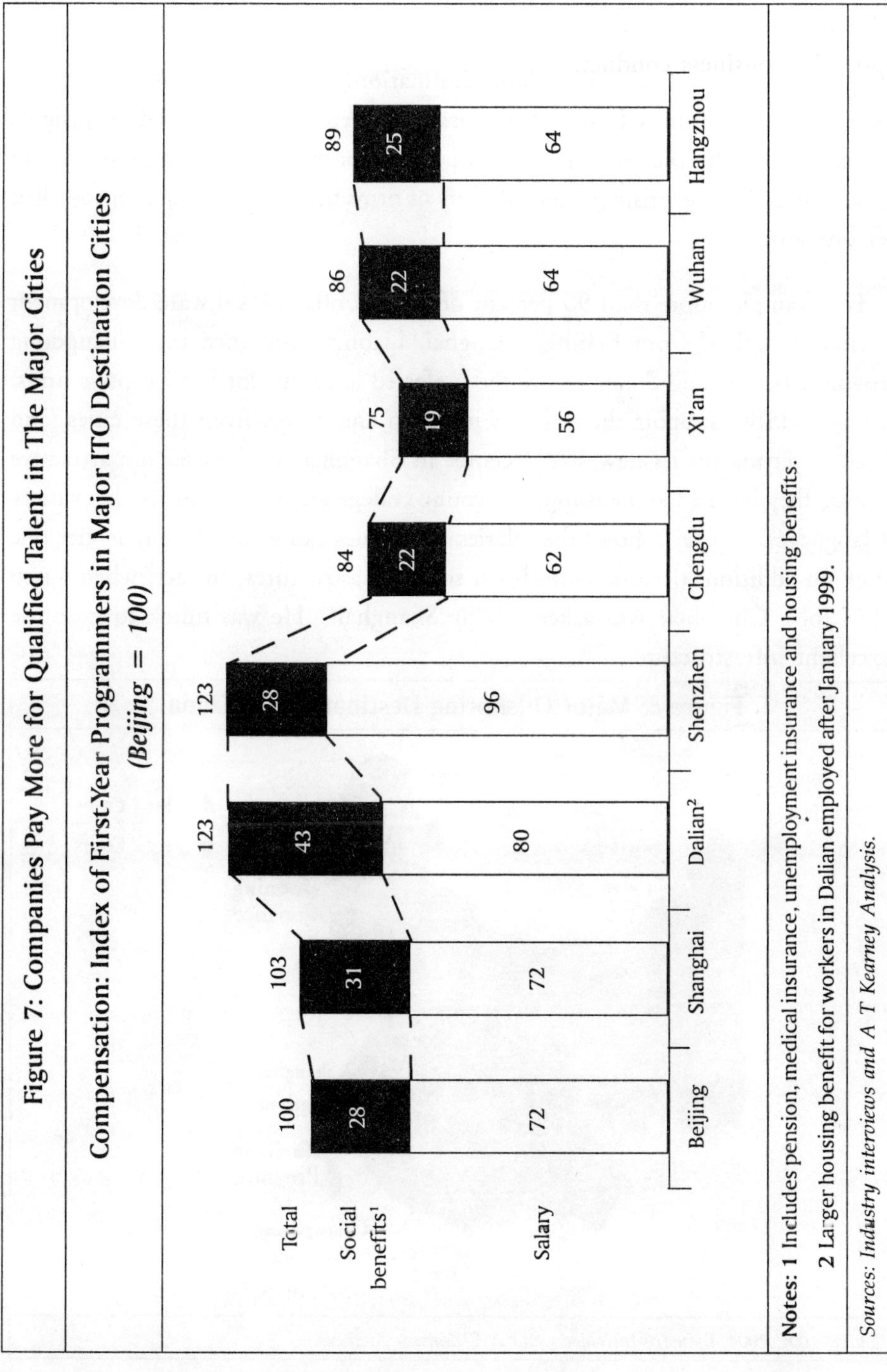

Notes: 1 Includes pension, medical insurance, unemployment insurance and housing benefits.

2 Larger housing benefit for workers in Dalian employed after January 1999.

Sources: Industry interviews and A T Kearney Analysis.

The Regions of China

After choosing China as an offshore destination, the next decision to make is where to locate within China. Companies often determine this based on insights garnered from the pioneers — firms that have both experience and success in certain cities. Not surprisingly, the majority of firms head for the major, or so-called tier-one cities.

For example, more than 90 percent of China's offshore software development revenue is derived from Beijing, Shanghai, Liaoning province and Guangdong province. Beijing and Shanghai are the preferred locations for BPO captive units. HP and HSBC support their clients in Japan and Korea from these cities, and Cisco is setting up its new R&D center in Shanghai. Both cities are attractive because they have an ample supply of young college graduates who speak a variety of languages. Figure 7 shows the salaries companies can expect to pay in tier-one cities. In addition, tier-one cities boast solid infrastructures. In fact, when Cisco CEO John Chambers was asked, "Why Shanghai?" He was quick to note the "excellent infrastructure."

Figure 8: Major Offshoring Destinations in China

Sources: IDC 2004, Industry Interviews and A T Kearney Analysis.

In recent years, several other tier-one cities have become attractive destinations within China *(see Figure 8)*. For example, Dalian is a top destination for BPO service providers serving the Asia-Pacific region. The city boasts many workers who speak Asian languages and it offers strong local government support. "Dalian is only three hours to Japan, two hours to Seoul and one hour to Beijing," says a survey participant. "The location itself is very advantageous."

Similarly, Guangzhou and Shenzhen are becoming home to most call centers serving Hong Kong customers. Shenzhen has stronger local government support and better infrastructure than Guangzhou, but both cities boast an abundance of Cantonese and Mandarin speakers.

Conclusion

China-based providers are only starting to build their presence in the global economy. As they do, the issues for multinationals are how to enter China, and how to capitalize on their own competitive advantages. Companies that have been in China since the 1990s have a solid edge over newcomers.

China presents a unique opportunity for multinational companies that wish to support their Asia-Pacific operations or grow their China presence because of its cultural, Asian languages and geographic advantages. As China continues to improve, dispelling misperceptions and improving on its drawbacks—from IP piracy, non-Chinese language deficiency and limited management skills—it will undoubtedly host more competition, from home and abroad.

(A T Kearney is a global strategic management consulting firm known for helping clients gain lasting results through a unique combination of strategic insight and collaborative working style. The firm was established in 1926 to provide management advice concerning issues on the CEO's agenda. Today, we serve the largest global clients in all major industries. A T Kearney's offices are located in major business centers in 35 countries. Email: insight@atkearney.com)

16

R&D Outsourcing: Indian Scenario

N Janardhan Rao and Ravi Babu Adusumilli

R&D has been considered as more important to an organization for sustaining the competitive advantage. Outsourcing R&D activities helps companies continue their R&D activities without having to worry about the money they will have to spend. Many companies have been striving to outsource a significant portion of their R&D activities to outside the home country in coming years. A recent McKinsey survey of global executives has ranked India as a more attractive destination for R&D investments than China. Already there are 150 MNCs such as IBM, Texas Instruments, Google, GE, Electrolux, DaimlerChrysler and Hyundai, who have opened their R&D laboratories in India. In the pharma industry, rising costs in developed nations, expiring patents, low R&D costs in countries such as India and China, and market competition are forcing MNCs to outsource R&D and manufacturing activities.

The world has seen the globalization of services and manufacturing activities so far. But new trends are evolving sending critical value chain activities such as R&D (Research and Development) which is gaining ground across geographies specifically to India. India has a miniscule share in the outsourcing market of \$800 bn; this indicates that there is a lot of scope for work to be outsourced to India from across sectors and service lines in the years to come. Western nations started outsourcing as strategic tool to cut costs. The first wave of outsourcing was driven by cheap factor costs in developing nations. China grabbed the opportunity in labor-intensive industries such as textiles and toys. However, India has missed the opportunity for many reasons like regulations, government policies and protectionism measures. The second wave of outsourcing included services such as business functions or processes. This time India took full advantage, thanks to its vast pool of English speaking population. The latest wave has R&D activities being outsourced. Traditionally, R&D has been considered as critical to an organization for sustaining the competitive advantage. R&D budgets of companies have been falling down in recent years as a result of eroding profit margins. Premier products generally produce high margins during the growth stage of their lifecycle, but the profits decline when they reach the maturity stage. So, companies have to invest heavily in R&D activities to bring new products quickly to the market. And outsourcing has been their solution. Outsourcing R&D activities helps companies continue their R&D activities without having to worry too much about the money they will have to spend. Vic Kulkarni, President, CEO and Co-founder of Sequence Design, Inc., USA says, "The benefits for Western companies are enormous as big as global companies want it to be, given the high degree of education and skill consistently demonstrated by Indian engineers and managers." Many companies have been ambitious enough to outsource a significant portion of their R&D activities to outside the home country in coming years. Falling costs of telecommunications is helping foreign companies move research activities to India in sectors such as automotive, electronics, IT, biotechnology and pharma.

Testing the Waters

Global companies are testing the waters in developing nations by setting up small facilities. They are not yet ready to outsource cutting-edge research activities. Outsourced R&D work right now is mostly restricted to improving the existing products. But, there are some companies that have slowly began sending critical research activities to development centers outside their home country after realizing the benefits. Though India has missed the opportunity during the first wave of outsourcing, today it is ahead of China in attracting investments in R&D facilities in country. A recent McKinsey survey of global executives has placed India as a more attractive destination for R&D investments than China. Already 150 MNCs such as IBM, Texas Instruments, Google, GE, Electrolux, DaimlerChrysler and Hyundai have opened their R&D laboratories in India. Recently, Boeing has began working with HCL to co-develop software for the navigation system and landing gear to the cockpit controls for its upcoming 7E7 Dreamliner jet. Indian pharma majors such as Ranbaxy, Dr. Reddy's Laboratories and Sun Pharma have been attracting the attention of foreign companies for collaborative and contract manufacturing in drug discovery and clinical research. The Indian telecom market has been growing; in fact it has become the second largest after China. Global telecom majors such as Nokia, Qualcomm, Alcatel, LG and Motorola have forayed into R&D activities in India. India and China are producing lakhs of engineers every year to meet the demand from the industry. The advantage for India comes from its English speaking graduates. However, China has made the teaching of English language mandatory in primary schools to overcome such barriers. In Intellectual Property Rights (IPR) protection too, India has the advantage over the China in attracting research organizations. According to Kulkarni, "China is seen more as a technology customer for advanced tools and hardware than as an innovator. India is just the opposite; it is India's time to extend their leadership in this decade to widen the gap, so they will retain this perception."

Many companies are looking to exploit the advantages that India offers them by outsourcing their research activities to the country. Business models adopted by the companies vary across the industries and depends on their business requirements. As Kulkarni says, Indian companies can adopt new business models with the development of offshore outsourced R&D models, such as:

- BOT – Build, Operate and Transfer model by firms in India where they build an operation.
- Joint Ventures – 'Skin in the game' of investment and ownership from both sides.
- Royalty agreements in outsourcing originally created IP (especially when universities start creating new patents through joint development with a company).

A Big Opportunity

Having a huge pool of English-speaking technical graduates and being a low-cost destination, India has a huge opportunity in the IT, pharma, biotechnology, electronics and automobiles sectors. Countries that can combine lower cost manufacturing with adequate regulatory protection of intellectual property are well-positioned to attract large MNCs in R&D activities.

In the pharma industry, rising costs in developed nations, expiring patents, low R&D costs in countries such as India and China and market competition are forcing MNCs to outsource R&D and manufacturing activities. Cost savings of up to 30-50% is possible in India. A pool of trained chemists, excellent track record of innovation and US Food and Drug Administration (US FDA) approved manufacturing facilities enable local players to offer significant benefits in the drug development process. Contract research opportunities are growing in areas such as clinical research, custom synthesis, Active Pharma Ingredient (API) sourcing and contract manufacturing. In collaborative R&D pre-clinical testing and clinical trails are increasing rapidly. Large generic houses in the US are increasingly sourcing their future generic API from independent manufacturers. Ranbaxy, Eli Lilly and Lupin, Cyanamid have pioneered contract manufacturing deals in the country. The global pharma market, which includes API, research, formulations and manufacturing is estimated to be $48 bn.

The biotechnology industry holds a $9 bn market potential by 2010 across various industry segments in India. Having a huge knowledge pool, successful pharmaceutical industry and rich biodiversity, the industry is expected to grow at 25-30% per annum from the present level of $400 mn. R&D outsourcing in biotechnology has great opportunity for Indian biotech players to perform contract research activities for global biotech majors. Currently, global spending on R&D outsourcing is approximately $7 bn and is expected to grow by 30% per annum for the next 5 years. Having a large number of R&D labs in the public sector conducting research in specific areas of biotechnology coupled with the private companies in Bangalore is an advantage for India. Global majors such as IBM Life Sciences, Incite Genomics, Affymetrix and Antex Biologics have shown interest in partnering with Indian companies. India has investment opportunities in areas of vaccines, bioactive therapeutic proteins, genetically modified seeds, bio-informatics and clinical trails which cost just 10% of what it would in developed markets.

India is increasingly becoming the base for Completely Built Units (CBUs) as well as outsourcing components for global majors. Traditionally, global auto majors have been manufacturing components in India to leverage the low-costs, now they want vendors to provide the design of modules. Most Indian entities of global auto majors have set up R&D facilities to research on materials, designs and new product development. With increasing FDI in the automobile sector, Indian companies are upgrading their quality levels to international standards. Companies like Ford, General Motors, DaimlerChrysler, Toyota, Honda, Nissan, BMW, Bosch, and Johnson controls now have engineering designs in India or are outsourcing the work to third party vendors. India has opportunities in the areas of Computer Aided Design/Computer Aided Manufacturing (CAD/CAM) services, full-fledged manufacturing engineering, modeling and analytics and embedded systems used in automobiles.

After facing one of the worst recession and subsequent changes in industry structure and value chain, global semiconductor companies are increasingly turning to outsourcing design and fabrication capabilities in order to survive. India may not be the mass producer of chips, but it has the strength to design them. Some front line companies, which are having their center for excellence here are Texas Instruments, Motorola, Alliance Semi Conductor, Intel, ST Electronics and AMD. In the electronics sector, chip design mania is being witnessed in India with over 10,000 engineers at companies like Intel, TI, Cisco, ST, Analog Devices and Infineon designing chips for specific applications. "In the past, lack of knowledge about end customers' needs was the main inhibitor for Indian designers, which is not the case anymore," says Kulkarni. VLSI design is clearly a great opportunity both in terms of chip design as well as R&D for creating the Electronic Design Automation (EDA) software. This globalization trend is now shifting focus from low-cost to algorithm or software development hi-tech projects like RTL code generation for the chip's micro-architecture, block-level verification and physical design.

The lifecycle of software products are getting shorter with changing consumer preferences, new products and new technology. Product development in the IT industry is gaining ground as global IT majors are transferring work to Indian firms for faster development. Products such as consumer software products, ERP, SCM, CAD/CAM are being outsourced to India. This is a more profitable area than IT services. In the US alone $20 bn are spent on developing products. But, it requires domain expertise and software architecture experience. A recent study by Frost & Sullivan has predicted that the R&D outsourcing market in India is set to grow from $1.3 bn in 2003 to over $8 bn by 2008.

The Way Forward

To be ahead of competition from nations like China, Thailand, Taiwan, which were known for the replicating the products by mass production, India has to focus on true 'R' as opposed to 'D' to become a world-class software R&D nation. "India as a nation has not delivered on its promise of developing its creative skills. Despite our knowledge and command of the English language we haven't been able to develop any next-generation IT-related product from concept to creation to its branding and global productization yet? For example, the next killer applications like Excel or the next Napster or the next Google and so on?" says Kulkarni.

Promote close relations between universities, research organizations and the software industry. The government's role here is to provide the necessary infrastructure facilities to new start research and development facilities by creating clusters for sectors and providing tax incentives to R&D spending for all potential sectors. There must be easy access to capital funding following the path of Venture Capitalists (VCs) in the Silicon Valley for funding innovative research areas. Keeping salaries at the affordable level is another important factor, otherwise escalating costs will force MNCs to look elsewhere. The English language as an advantage will probably disappear in the next couple of years as other nations like China, Armenia, Russia and even Egypt have shown a tremendous initiative to overcome this hurdle. India must encourage its engineers to think independently and must get over being known as just "English-speaking good programmers" so that it gets its fair share of the R&D globalization pie.

(N Janardhan Rao, Deputy Editor at the Icfai University Press, Hyderabad. He can be reached at janardhanrao@icfaipress.org and

Ravi Babu Adusumilli, Research Associate at the Icfai University Press, Hyderabad. He can be reached at ravi@icfaipress.org).

17

BPO in Sri Lanka – Prospects, Problems and Challenges

T Venkat Ram Raj

Formerly known as Ceylon, the land of gems is attracting the attention of the BPO world. The father of BPO in Sri Lanka, Kris Canekeratne along with other BPO gurus in India and with the support of the local government is working hard to build a strong BPO base in Sri Lanka. Learning from the success story of India, the policy makers and other stakeholders are aiming at making Sri Lanka a very attractive BPO destination. The article provides insights into the prospects, problems and challenges of Sri Lankan BPO sector and offers a few suggestions to select stakeholders how to design a better future for the sunrise sector.

BPO is one of the crucial sectors fueling the growth of Sri Lanka in the present decade.

– Mangala Moonesinghe,
High Commissioner of Sri Lanka to India[1].

1 The High Commissioner has addressed the Faculty and Scholars of The Icfai Business School, Hyderabad, on August 20, 2005.

Mayukha, meaning first rays of the sun touched the land of gems[2]. Just then an executive who logged out of his work has raised his head, looked at the sun and returned to his home with a lot of hope on the sunrise sector. Recall the words of an eminent writer and novelist[3], "He who works when the whole world sleeps and rests, will undoubtedly succeed". Who is he? He is an English speaking graduate and a computer literate. He is young, energetic and enthusiastic. He is a Sri Lankan.

If a work can be performed with equal efficiency in two parts of the world, there is a chance of two events occurring. The first is, the work force will move to a place where it gets more wages and the second is, the work will move to a place where it is done cheaper. Throughout the previous decade we could witness the first event occurring and henceforth we will witness the second one occurring.

BPO is an act of contracting a specific business task to a third-party service provider. It has been a phenomenon, which can be highly beneficial for many reasons, including concentration on core activities and partnering with outside experts, which can help in accelerating growth. Operational costs are also reduced as outsourcing provides access to the external provider's lower cost structure. Some of the common drawbacks of the BPO could be selecting a wrong vendor, poor contract construction and high costs of exit. There could be certain infrastructural and operational problems, which can be country specific like under developed power generation capacity and poor communication systems.

Evolution of BPO in Sri Lanka

After being battered with civil war for two decades, the violence in Sri Lanka has come down to some extent with the signing of Cease Fire Agreement (CFA) between LTTE and the government. Though Tsunami disaster added further hardships, with the assistance received from the international community, the people are hopeful of a new era. The Government of Sri Lanka is focusing on the expansion of the service sector for nation's development as it contributes nearly 50% to the GDP[4]. Due to its strategic location in the Indian Ocean, Sri Lanka has a competitive advantage in offering various services to the rest of the world

---

2 *http://www.members.tripod.com/infctr/*

3 Yandamuri Veerendranath is a famous critic and novelist in Telugu.

4 "Confronting the Outsourcing/Offshoring Challenges", Jayasri Priyalal, Hemantha Weerakoon, June 29-30, 2005.

over her neighbors. Sri Lanka, like India and others, is also keen on offering offshoring facilities to North America and Europe. Being still in its nascent stage[5], BPO in Sri Lanka, is preparing itself to face heavy competition from an experienced and larger BPO base in India.

As a pioneering BPO company in Sri Lanka, HSBC indicated that it would be offering about 3000 jobs to Sri Lankan Youth in its BPO center. At the inception of its BPO unit in March 2004, the MD Lorne Bally said that the corporation would pump Rs.2.5 bn as an initial investment providing employment to 600 personnel. Office Tiger, Virtusa, Timex, WNS and CBN Sat are some of the international organizations that have set up BPOs in Sri Lanka, according to the Board of Investments in Sri Lanka. The Sri Lankan Government has been actively encouraging the spread of computer literacy to fuel the growth of BPO sector. Further, the government has established Information and Communication Technology Agency of Sri Lanka (ICTA) as a successor institution to Council for Information Technology (CINTEC) through enacting the ICT Act No. 27 of 2003. To facilitate the successful implementation of National Policy on Information and Communication Technology and Action Plan, the government has come up with the e-Sri Lanka program.

e-Sri Lanka

The e-Sri Lanka program is aimed at ensuring more effective, citizen-centered, and business-friendly governance through re-engineering Government Programs, empowering rural sector along with the disabled, women, and youth through increased and affordable access to information and communication tools, developing leadership and ICT skills in people, creating employment in the IT/ ITES industry and enhancing competitiveness of all stakeholders.

Sri Lanka presently offers offshore development services for countries like USA, Ireland, UK and Australia. It is expected that Sri Lanka can achieve $1 bn in ICT related exports by 2012. And to achieve this, it needs a right mix of industry, academia and a proper policy environment conducive to ICT growth. Sri Lanka's strategy is not only to compete on price but also on quality and value-addition to the users.

---

[5] BPO industry in Sri Lanka started in 2004.

Since its inception in 2003, ICT agency has been persuading[6] IT/ITES companies worldwide to off shore their business processes to Lanka[7]. The Sri Lankan government is confident of its uniqueness in terms of location and skill-set. Sri Lanka is constantly putting its efforts to achieve a reputation of a niche player in the fastest growing BPO sector. The ICT Agency of Sri Lanka has recently made presentations in Japan promoting Sri Lanka as a destination for outsourcing. The event was organized by Jetro and the Software Exporter's Association[8] (SEA) of Sri Lanka with the main objective of branding Sri Lanka as the best outsourcing destination in Asia. ICTA has been participating in several business linkage tours, the latest one being in Singapore in October 2005, with the belief that such tours can contribute significantly towards strengthening the local IT/ITES sector. Its efforts didn't go in vain, as some of the internationally known names like WPA, HSBC, Astron, Hellocorp, Office Tiger, WNS Global Services, etc., have set up operations in Sri Lanka. Sri Lankan BPOs are presently offering a wide range of services to their offshoring clients, which include front and back-office services, voice and non-voice based services, etc. Virtusa, HSBC and Timex are not only the well-known companies in India but also in Sri Lanka.

Around 8,000 people in Sri Lanka hold a college degree and a large man power base of around 20,000 hold various IT diplomas and certificates, making them prospective BPO employees[9]. Virtusa is the largest IT firm in Sri Lanka and is sure of employing around 20% of the IT graduates that the country produces in the current year. In the year 2004, BPO industry pioneer in India, Raman Roy ventured with Sri Lanka's largest industrial conglomerate, John Keells Holdings (JKH) to develop the BPO businesses across Asia[10]. Under the deal, Raman Roy and Associates (RRA) and JKH have agreed to invest around Rs.100 cr in the Indian and Sri Lankan BPO sectors in the next one year.

BPO in Sri Lanka: Prospects

Sri Lanka's success in the BPO sphere is based on three key pillars, Infrastructure, People and Technology. As quoted by Mangala Moonesinghe, the BPO industry

6 The Board of Investment, Sri Lanka has organized the IT Nations Pavilion in 2004 for the first time to attract the foreign investment in the IT sector.

7 *http.//www.ciol.com/content/special/blrit2004/article.asp? =63579*

8 *http://www.icta.lk/Insidepages/News&event/261105whatsnew.asp*

9 *http://knowledge.wharton.upenn.edu/100902_ss5.html*

10 *http://economictimes.indiatimes.com/articleshow/1332911.cms*

can change the face of Sri Lanka and revolutionize the predominantly agriculture and tourism-based economy. Sri Lanka's biggest advantage is being a neighbor to India, who is a key player in the BPO world. Sri Lanka looks forward to leverage on this aspect. International BPO customers want to spread their risks across multiple destinations instead of depending on one nation like India or China and this can be the main reason behind the prosperity of BPO industry in Sri Lanka. The following estimates will spotlight the future of BPO in Sri Lanka.

- Sri Lanka can achieve $1 bn in total ICT related export services by 2012.
- KPO revenues in Sri Lanka are estimated to touch around $2 bn by 2010.
- Sri Lanka hopes to generate employment for 3,00,000 people over the next 10 years[11], out of which more than 30,000 jobs are going to be generated by the IT/ITES sector[12].
- The policy makers in Sri Lanka are considering BPO as the next BIG THING after tea, apparel and tourism[13].
- According to Kris Canekeratne, father of BPO[14] in Sri Lanka, since the days of unrest are over with a cease fire between the government and the Tigers, the BPO sector would see brighter days.
- BPO revenues can sky-rocket to $1 bn in a $20 bn Sri Lankan economy in near future[15]. And the story goes on... the glory goes on....

Moreover, globally, as the KPO revenues are expected to rise to $25 bn by 2010, Sri Lanka can utilize its low cost and educated talent pool and can target this big money. As it is not very easy to develop the labor pool for KPOs, Sri Lanka can focus more on cultivating the creative workforce necessary to handle higher end knowledge processes. This will not only create more value-added jobs but also help the employees to enjoy higher salary levels. Global outsourcing market[16] is huge and by catering to just 4% of it, India could generate revenues

---

11 *http://was4.hewitt.com/hewitt/ap/resource/rptspubs/hewittquart/HQ_12/articles/globe_source_asia.html*

12 Posted on BBC NEWS online UK edition, July 13, 2004.

13 *http://www.wnsgs.com/wns/pdf/build_billion_dollar_bpo.pdf*

14 *http://knowledge.wharton.upenn.edu/100902_ss5.html*

15 *http://www.wnsgs.com/wns/pdf/build_billion_dollar_bpo.pdf*

16 The current outsourcing industry is worth about US$121-135 bn.

of $5.2 bn and create 400,000 direct jobs and about one million indirect jobs. This statistic gives an idea about the magnitude of business that Sri Lanka can actually generate in the BPO space. Sri Lanka can take Indian BPO sector as bench mark and can learn the tricks of the trade. To put it mildly, the prospects for the Sri Lankan BPO sector seems bright provided it can overcome some inherent problems and hurdles.

BPO in Sri Lanka: The Problems

Having seen the prospects for the BPO sector in Sri Lanka, let us briefly outline some of the urgent priorities for Sri Lanka. Global connectivity, robust and reliable telecommunications infrastructure are the backbone of the BPO industry. There is only one fibre optic cable connecting Sri Lanka to the rest of the world and if that goes down, one cannot run any business because in the BPO game, even a two second stoppage may prove dearer and hence, is not acceptable. So there is a definite and urgent requirement for updated telecom infrastructure in Sri Lanka.

Another major area of concern is the education system in Sri Lanka which creates educated non-employable people. This has to be addressed immediately and the whole education system should be revamped to generate people with an entrepreneurial attitude rather than job seekers. Comparatively limited number of universities across Sri Lanka offer inadequate number of specialized courses and produce a low number of graduates. The Sri Lankan universities not only churn out a very less number of professionals and graduates but also with low caliber.

Due to the internal disturbances for decades, Sri Lanka is seen as highly susceptible to political uncertainties, civil wars and terrorism, making the foreign investors a bit circumspect. Thus building a credible and bankable image in the eyes of investors at large is both a problem and a challenge to the government and people of Sri Lanka. The regulatory authorities need to bring several changes in the socio-cultural set up to suit the BPO industry. Reforms relating to allowing women to work at night have to be conceived. Issues pertaining to data security, data transfer and working on national holidays need to be sorted out.

The telecommunications costs in the island are relatively high. The cost of a 3-minute fixed line phone call in Sri Lanka is almost double the cost in India. Mobile costs too are significantly higher than those in India. Also the Sri Lankan businesses pay very high electric costs because of the government's policy to cross-subsidize residential customers[17]. Unreliable power supply increases costs to acquire and operate expensive generators often inhibiting firms from investing productively in their core businesses.[18]

Size does matter. Sri Lanka does not have a very large pool of skilled labor compared to China and India[19]. Sri Lanka's population is less than 19 million and hence the country's labor force figures to only 7 million.

BPO in Sri Lanka: Challenges

The challenges faced by Sri Lanka in BPO sector can be categorized into three types viz., Supply side challenges, Demand side challenges and Environmental challenges.

Supply Side Challenges

- The challenge is to raise the standards and quality of the curriculums offered by various private and state-owned institutions.
- To adequately supply skilled and competent people to work particularly in ICT.
- Another challenge is to develop the BPO sector with a very less work force. It is 7 million[20] out of a population of 19.2 million.
- Job aspirants in the BPO sector do not posses adequate IT and English Language skills to work in foreign Call centers. Hence the challenge is to imbibe such skill set in the Sri Lankan Youth.
- Inadequate infrastructure in terms of power supply, roads and modes of transportation is another challenge.

Demand Side Challenges

- Anti-outsourcing bills and backlash in the western countries.

---

17 World Bank, Sri Lanka: Improving the Rural and Urban Investment Climate, 2005, p.20.

18 Ibid., p.19.

19 *CIA World Factbook,* March 2005. (*www.nationmaster.com*)

20 According to Central Bank of Sri Lanka reports (2004).

- Due to increased outsourcing by western countries, the demand is going up day-by-day and to meet this is a biggest challenge before a small country like Sri Lanka.

Environmental Side Challenges

- The biggest challenge is to promote Sri Lanka as an investor-friendly country especially when it is suffering from terrorism and civil war.
- To provide a congenial and techno-savvy environment backed by vibrant democracy.

Competitive Position of Sri Lanka as a BPO Destination

The initial investment needed to set up a development center is lower in Sri Lanka compared to India[21]. Also the salary levels in the island are modest and with higher employee retention rates. According to Raman Roy, Sri Lanka is equally talented in the terms of intellectual and trained manpower compared to India, which makes it an ideal destination for offshore BPO business[22]. Though Sri Lanka is not well developed, it can provide quality infrastructure. Sri Lanka has 95% paved roads[23]. Sri Lanka boasts itself of possessing the cheapest labor and lowest office rental costs.

Comparative Office Rental Rates in 2003

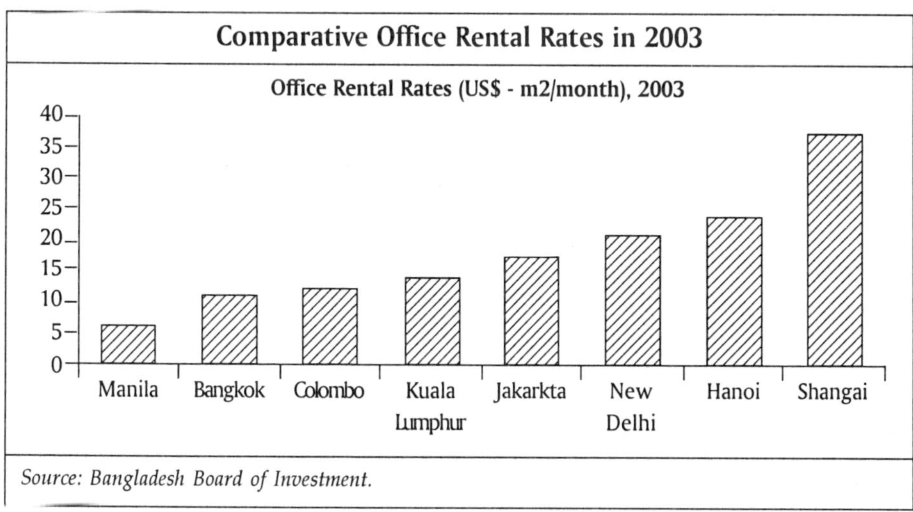

Source: Bangladesh Board of Investment.

21 *The Economic Times*. March 28, 2006, Virtusa banks on scalability here.

22 *The Economic Times*, December 15, 2005, Raman roy takes BPO Ship to Lanka.

23 *http://www.wnsgs.com/wns/pdf/build_billion_dollar_bpo.pdf*

Office rents in Colombo are low compared to other major Asian cities. The average monthly cost per square meter is very low – about $11.60 in Colombo[24], whereas in New Delhi it is comparatively costlier[25]. Office space in Shanghai costs nearly three times as much compared to Colombo. The graph[26] provides a comparative structure of office rental rates at Colombo vis-à-vis other major BPO destinations in the world.

Sri Lanka's main strengths as a potential offshoring destination lie in the relatively low wage and cost structure. Even highly skilled and well-qualified workers are paid low salaries relative to other Asian countries. Despite its small size, the country turns out a significant number of technically qualified individuals especially in IT, accounting and business management[25].

Table: Competitive Position of Sri Lanka

BPO	Sri Lanka	Bangladesh	Pakistan	Philippines	Ireland
Government Support	High	High	High	High	High
Labor Pool	High	Medium	Low	Medium	Low
Infrastructure	Low	Low	Medium	High	High
Educational System	Medium	Low	Low	High	High
Cost Advantage	High	High	High	Medium	Medium
Time/Distance Advantage	High	High	Medium	Medium	Low
English Proficiency	Medium	Low	Low	High	High

It is clear from the Table that Sri Lanka has an edge over some of its competitors in the areas of government support, labor pool, cost advantage and the relative 12 hour time/distance advantage. The areas of improvement include, building infrastructure, improvising the education system and enhancing the English speaking skills among the potential employees of the BPO sector.

Suggestions to BPOs

If the BPOs want to work more effectively and take full advantage of the emerging opportunities in island nation, they need to fulfill the following necessities.

---

24 In New Delhi it ranges between $15.45 and $26.15.

25 *http://siteresources.worldbank.org/INTEDEVELOPMENT/Resources/Offshoring-in-Sri-Lanka.doc*

26 *http://siteresources.worldbank.org/INTEDEVELOPMENT/Resources/Offshoring-in-Sri-Lanka.doc*

- To exploit the emerging opportunities and meet the challenges ahead, the BPOs in the island country should offer high end and a more comprehensive range of services[27] by integrating vertically. The BPOs will have to move up the value chain by offering KPO services, because by 2010 Sri Lanka may become a costly place to outsource aiming at cost savings. The companies should offer high-end services where the prices can be charged higher (from low value added services like data entry, telecalling, transcription, tax forms preparation, maintaining HR data bases, etc., the vendors should move towards high value-added services like fraud detection, credit evaluation, CRM and R&D outsourcing).
- The BPO firms in Sri Lanka should set up bases in Africa, Latin America and other low cost countries to be competitive cost-wise – to fill the cultural gaps and to develop the linguistic capabilities. For Spanish language capabilities, bases in Philippines and Mexico can be set up. For French language capabilities, Madagascar, Algeria, Morocco, Senegal and Mauritaina can be the base and for serving German clients, centers can be set up in Namibia.
- Build and maintain good relations with clients. Over half of all outsourcing clients renegotiate a contract and in 25% of these cases the service provider lost the contract. Around 20-25% of all outsourcing relationships fail within first two-years and 50% within five years[28]. Hence, it is suggested that the BPO firms need to take steps to maintain good relations with their clients. The BPO companies, to reduce the potential misunderstanding with their clients, instead of writing the tightly worded, legally perfect and definable contracts, should rather develop enduring relationships.
- Take the client's approval for taking crucial business decisions, particularly selling a part of/whole of your business to outsiders. Probably it is only in BPO sector that the companies need somebody else's (an outsider's or customer's) permission to take their crucial business decisions. This is because any decision that a BPO firm takes equally affects its clients and their businesses.

---

27 *http://www.rediff.com/money/2005/jan/27bpo.htm*

28 *The Economic Times*, October 5, 2004.

Suggestions to Government

The Sri Lankan government should play the constructive role[29] in building a bright future for the BPO sector. Following are the suggestions for a better governance and support the sector.

- **A law to ensure data security:** The foremost task before the government is to pass a law to ensure data security. The opponents of offshoring are making it an issue all over the world because many incidents are occurring due to mishandling the data.
- **Build infrastructure:** The government's immediate priority should be to build appropriate infrastructure to aid the growth of the BPO sector by establishing a) hard infrastructure like roads, ports, power, telecom facilities, etc., and b) soft infrastructure like encouraging policies.
- **Provide friendly environment:** As the island nation is known for its internal conflicts, it mandatory for the government to create a friendly political and social climate.
- **Encourage non-residents:** The government can also consider encouraging the Sri Lankans settled elsewhere in the world to mobilize the investments in the island by providing tax incentives and other measures.

Conclusion

Sri Lanka has made a small but promising start in the BPO arena. In the late 1990s and early 2000s we saw India improving its economy. Now, it is the turn of the emerald island; which looks like a small dot near the southern most tip of India. The country, which has been over the years torn by civil wars, terrorism and political instability is rising up like a phoenix from the ashes. The country needs to develop itself economically and politically. For this there is a huge need for jobs, which can fulfill the dreams of the educated unemployed youth and BPO can be the answer to their woes.

(Prof. T Venkat Ram Raj, Faculty Member, The Icfai Business School, Hyderabad. He can be reached at tvramraj@ibsindia.org)

18

Joburg, The African BPO Hub Executive Summary

South Africa has an indigenous call center community of more than 410 sites—which is bigger than that of India, Scotland, Wales, Ireland, the Philippines, Italy or Spain. Gauteng and Joburg are moving powerfully into the call and contact center industry, which the government has targeted as a priority. Already 60% of contact center operations for South Africa are in Joburg. A report by McKinsey and Company in 2004 into South Africa's call center industry noted that South Africa has a strong customer service culture, and that South Africans were seen as helpful and non-transactional.

Johannesburg is a compelling destination for call centres and South Africa has a strong Business Process Outsourcing and Offshoring (BPO&O) industry. This is due in no small part to the country's remarkable history and the quality of its economy, business leaders and, above all, its can-do citizens. South Africa is world renowned for the calibre of its people.

Former president Nelson Mandela is internationally revered; the country produced four Nobel Peace Prize winners in less than three decades – Mandela, Chief Albert Luthuli, Archbishop Desmond Tutu and former president Frederick

Source: http://www.callcentres.co.za/Documents © www.callcentres.co.za. Reprinted with permission.

Wde Klerk. It has produced Nobel laureates in medicine, science and literature, including writers JM Coetzee and Nadine Gordimer.

SA's negotiated peace after almost half a century of violent repression under apartheid has served as a model for ending conflicts from Sri Lanka to Northern Ireland.

And it has spawned some of the world's most important corporations. De Beers manages the international diamond trade. Anglo American, Anglo Gold and BH Billiton are the world's most important gold producers – South Africa has produced 40% of the world's gold and most of the world's platinum.

South Africa is the world's 30th largest economy according to the World Bank, ranked above Greece and Thailand, but below Finland, Indonesia and Norway.

It was voted the 24th most competitive country in the world by the Economist Intelligence Unit in 2001, in a survey that placed India at 29 and Germany at 28. And that was before South Africa's economy showed the rapid gains of 2004 and 2005, pushing growth to its highest levels in 60 years.

Johannesburg, the best known city in South Africa and capital of the Gauteng, the smallest but most prosperous province of South Africa. Gauteng accounts for 11% of African Gross Domestic Product and 34% of South Africa's GDP.

Gauteng and Joburg are moving powerfully into the call and contact centre industry, which government has targeted as a priority. Already, 60% of contact centre operations for South Africa are in Joburg. The contact centre industry has grown at average of 8% a year since 2002 and is poised for explosive new growth.

A grade rentals in Joburg are 40% to 70% cheaper than in London, New York or other G7 capital cities. The average cost of electricity in the city is US$0.038, cheaper than in New York ($0.14) or London ($0.20). It has the finest telecommunications network in Africa, which is almost entirely digitalised.

Nine million people – 18% of all South Africans – live in and around Johannesburg. The province is home to 51% of all value-added financial and business services operating in South Africa. The human development index for Gauteng is 0.70, which is higher than the 0.59 national average.

Plans are under way to train 40,000 call centre agents a year as more international outsourcers choose Johannesburg for its low-cost, hi-tech office space; competitively priced and reliable telecommunications infrastructure; near zero risk of natural disasters; highly skilled employees with pleasing English accents; and a high diversity of native speakers of foreign languages, ranging from Hebrew to German, French, Italian, Spanish and even Mandarin.

Investors have access to willing and capable advisers in the Gauteng Economic Development Agency or Contact in Gauteng (the industry body to promote BPO and contact centre work in Gauteng), assisting with their queries, their visits and setting up business in the province.

A report by international management consultancy McKinsey & Company estimates that between 65,000 and 1,00,000 new jobs (15,000-25,000 direct, and 45,000-75,000 indirect) could be created in the call centre industry by 2008, and $90m-$175m could be attracted in cumulative foreign direct investment, resulting in a GDP contribution of between 0.3-0.5%.

South Africa has an indigenous call centre community of more than 410 sites – which is bigger than that of India, Scotland, Wales, Ireland, the Philippines, Italy or Spain. Some sites have up to 1,800 seats, and one operator controls 15 locales.

South Africa's attractiveness as a call centre destination is based on a number of factors:

- SA is 30% to 40% cheaper than the UK or USA.
- It occupies a favourable time zone position for Europe and the United States.
- South African operators are good at handling complex, non-scripted calls. At present one British financial services company is achieving a 40% saving in their South Africa-based call centres.
- About 70% of South Africa's business process outsourcing operations service UK clients, with most located in Joburg.
- South Africa delivers distinctive quality of service with 89% to 95% first call resolution compared to 66% in India. Operations such as Budget

Insurance have established that about 98% of the agents achieve UK KPIs and the operation also saves 40% on costs. (McKinsey, 2004)

- Joburg is a cosmopolitan, sophisticated city, which is among the cheapest and most beautiful residential areas in the world.
- The South African business culture closely mirrors those of the United Kingdom, Europe and the USA.
- SA offers state-of-the-art technology and telecommunications.
- Telecoms are almost 100% digital, reliable and competitively priced.
- Telkom, the main landline telephone supplier, has the world's biggest underground cable network, with 3,43,000 km of fibre optic cables.
- ISDN and ADSL lines are common in homes and businesses. Wireless networks are rapidly being spread out across the country.
- South Africa has the world's fastest growing rate of mobile telephony.
- Literacy in South Africa is 30% higher than in India.
- "Attrition is ridiculously low," Mitial recorded in a 2002 study of the SA call centre industry.
- 15% of agents have university degrees.
- In a global survey, South Africa's call centres were found to have the highest rate, at 92%, of automated management information systems.
- McKinsey (2004) found that South Africa had a large scalabe telecom infrastructure with many experienced players, "flexible operations (call-centre virtual model), good technical know-how and capability."
- South Africa is economically and politically stable.
- South Africa is the gateway to Africa and has the finest infrastructure on the continent.
- Financial services are centred in Joburg and in 2004 accounted for 18.5% of GDP.

- Omega Research Services notes that 83% of investors say South Africa's strong financial services sector and best practices corporate governance regime are important strengths.
- Omega also notes that 69% of investors say fiscal policy in the management of public finance and personal income tax in South Africa is excellent.
- In 2003, South Africa's automotive sector was ranked 20th in the world and produced 84% of African automotive output.
- SA has a customer-focused service culture.
- South African tax on total distributed profits is 38.5%; lower than India's 43%.

A report by McKinsey and Company in 2004 into South Africa's call centre industry noted that South Africa has a strong customer service culture, and that SAs were seen as "helpful and non-transactional." It found that organisations like Nedbank and Swisscard found payment services efficient and a strong credit culture and a suitable infrastructure with appropriate technological platforms enhanced payment services through contact centres. McKinsey noted that SA was a "leader in smart card technology e.g., Aplitec."

In terms of collections, McKinsey found that South African call centres have "good conversion/recovery rates and sophisticated collections systems" with a "sufficient pool of financial talent to perform book valuations."

McKinsey found that in insurance SA had product sophistication and similar life products to the UK, staff shared common qualifications to their peers in the UK or USA, especially actuarial skills and the insurance industry was non-unionised with an educated workforce that had good product knowledge and market understanding. The actuarial services/risk underwriting environment had the largest fellow base outside the UK. It found that "large SA asset managers have a growing profile in US/UK (e.g., Investec, Old Mutual)."

McKinsey said South Africa's three competitive pillars were a:

- "Solid Foundation: meets gating criteria on cost (30% to 40% less), international connectivity superior to – Indian centres, attractive social environment/lifestyle, strong business infrastructure, economic and political stability."

- "Commitment to cost improvement: Commitment to cost competitiveness in the medium to long term through e.g., telecom deregulation, accessing lower cost labour pool and economic incentives."
- "Structural elements of distinctiveness: Emerging distinctive ness on quality, based on a combination of structural advantages: industry expertise/ sophistication in financial services and insurance, strong culture and language familiarity, vibrant domestic industry and high end specialist services in core industries."

The Economist Intelligence Unit, in its November 2004 country forecast of South Africa, observed: "President Thabo Mbeki has fully consolidated his power base within the ruling African National Congress and is expected to face little or no opposition from within party ranks... Economic policy... will continue to focus on increasing economic growth and investment to create employment. The rand remains strong... The ratio of budget deficit/GDP is estimated to rise from 3.2% in 2004/05 to 3.5% in 2005/06, and then fall to 3.2% in 2006/07."

The gross national income of South Africa is a fifth greater than Egypt's, which is the second largest economy in Africa. Gauteng is classified as Africa's fourth largest economy (after South Africa, Egypt and Algeria).

The financial services industry accounts for 18.5% of GDP. Manufacturing has a contribution of 16.4%, while the wholesale and retail sector accounts for 13.9%.

There is a large pool of highly educated employees, with an average literacy rate of 86%, and government has placed a strong emphasis on skills upgrading with tax breaks to enterprises that train staff.

South African Reserve Bank governor Tito Mboweni says the South African banking sector is among the most sophisticated in the world, "with a moderate level of private-sector indebtedness and a respectable and first-rate regulatory and legal framework". McKinsey agreed with the governor and noted that technological platforms were "excellent", financial services were well regulated and complied with international regulations.

South Africa's banks are regulated in accordance with the principles of the Basel Committee on Banking Supervision. Customers have online, real-time, nationwide access to bank accounts 24 hours a day, every day of the year.

There are 38 registered banks in South Africa, including 15 South African-controlled banks, six non-resident controlled banks (subsidiaries), 15 local branches of international banks, and two mutual banks. In addition, 44 international banks have authorised representative offices in South Africa.

Johannesburg is the location for 78% of corporate head offices and the financial services organisations. The rentals in the central business district are among the lowest of any similar major city in the world, with access to state-of-the-art technology, communications and security. A range of international research studies have shown that Joburg is one of the cheapest international cities to live in. Homes tend to be spacious and luxurious, often with beautiful gardens; Joburg has the highest ratio of swimming pools per household in the world, and many homes in plush suburbs also have tennis courts. There has been a strong trend toward complex living in recent years, with a plethora of high-security complexes, often with golf courses, convenient lock-up-and-go townhouses or cluster homes with communal sporting and leisure facilities.

Foreigners find the city friendly and easy to access from all international destinations. It has splendid dry, warm weather, beautiful homes and a child-friendly environment, with good schools and the best shopping centres in the world. Joburg also has a wide range of sophisticated recreational and entertainment options.

But it is a city that works hard. Johannesburg is the largest and most significant local economy in South Africa, responsible for 17% of national production and 13% of employment.

The city has a 2030 planning vision, its aim is that Johannesburg "will be a world-class city with service deliverables and efficiencies which meet world's best practices. Its economy and labour force will specialise in the service sector and will be strongly outward orientated such that the city economy operates on a global scale."

Its highways are already better than those in Germany and many parts of the USA, Eskom, the electricity utility that has its home in Johannesburg, generates 80% of African power. 60% of South Africa's research and development takes place in Joburg. The trees within its gardens and parks make it the largest urban forest in the world. The Johannesburg Securities Exchange is one of the top 10 performers in the world. More than 70% of the South African film and television industry is based in Joburg. Film production in SA is 40% cheaper than in the USA and a fifth less expensive than Australia.

The Gautrain, a high-speed train to Pretoria and the Johannesburg International Airport, is due to be completed in 2010. There are plans to make Ellis Park an international sports precinct, with the approach of the 2010 Soccer World Cup hosted in South Africa.

Those who live in Joburg, or Jozi, swear that no place on earth has better weather, and is quite as friendly, as dynamic or as filled with opportunity.

INDEX